Modern Materialism: Readings on Mind-Body Identity

Modern Materialism: Readings on Mind-Body Identity

edited by John O'Connor
Case Western Reserve University

Under the general editorship of Robert J. Fogelin
Yale University

Harcourt, Brace & World, Inc.
New York Chicago San Francisco Atlanta

Library of Congress Catalog Card Number: 79-87233

Printed in the United States of America

Preface

A central concern of contemporary Western philosophy has been the question "What is a human being?" Until recently, many of the most important writings on this topic were produced in Great Britain under the influence of the analytic philosophers Ludwig Wittgenstein, Gilbert Ryle, John Austin, and P. F. Strawson. Since the late 1950's, the center of the discussion, and of analytic philosophy, has shifted to the United States and Australia. With this change has come a change in philosophical emphasis. The British philosophers were wary of adopting a world view and took little interest in the natural sciences. American and Australian analytic philosophers show the opposite inclinations; they generally hold that an adequate philosophy must attempt to give a unified account of the world and of human beings, they believe that such an account must be based upon the findings and, to an extent, the methodology of science, and they are producing significant works in the philosophy of science and related areas. Despite these differences, the question "What is a human being?" continues to be a principal focus of their thinking.

The papers in this volume are almost all by philosophers who teach in the United States or Australia; the one exception, the paper by U. T. Place, is written in much the same spirit as the others. The papers present the most thorough and substantive discussions of the cluster of views known as physicalism and mind-body identity. While these views are in the broad tradition of materialism that goes back at least to Democritus, they are sophisticated in ways that older views were not, thanks to new developments in science, computer technology, the philosophy of science, the philosophy of mind, and the philosophy of language.

The significant writings about physicalism and mind-body identity are still few enough in number so that most of them could be included here. Short "discussion notes" were omitted to make room for more comprehensive discussions. The general order of the papers is chronological; when one paper comments at length about another, however, the two appear side by side.

For their help in the preparation of this volume, I wish to thank Robert J. Fogelin, Richard M. Rorty, David K. Lewis, Catriona Shafer, and Ladye Montgomery, who prepared the bibliography.

John O'Connor

Contents

Modern Materialism: Readings on Mind-Body Identity

Introduction

Many different views have been held about what a human being is. One influential view is that a human being is a composite of a body and something else called a mind, soul, or spirit. Another important view is that man is a complicated physical mechanism. There are, of course, many different forms which these two views may take.

Some philosophers believe that the question "What is a human being?" has a single ultimate answer—*the* correct answer. Instead of merely attempting to decide what human beings happen to be like, they are interested in what one might call the nature or essence of human beings. Questions of essence, while probably primarily a philosopher's concern, are certainly not unknown in the everyday world. The usual way questions of this sort are expressed is in the form "But what is it *really?*" Sometimes what a thing really is can be a matter of dispute and can even have embarrassing consequences. For example, suppose that an out-of-town relative sends you a peculiar glass object as a wedding present and fails to mention what it is. Writing a thank-you note can be quite a task. Is it the kind of thing one uses every day, or is it designed for special occasions? What room does it belong in? Of all the things one can do with it (and maybe one cannot do anything with it very well), which is the correct one? In other words, while it could be used in several ways, what is it really? Or, in philosopher's jargon, what is its essence? This particular question may well be trivial; thanking one's relative for an ash tray when the object is really a candy dish will probably not have important consequences, unless the relative is very wealthy.

Philosophical questions about man's essence are more serious than questions about glass dishes: the answers one accepts are bound to influence one's view of himself and his fellow men. For example, of the philosophers who have felt that man has an essence, many have said that his essence is rationality. For these thinkers, any animal or machine found to be rational must be considered a human being, even if it lacks certain other features ordinarily associated with human beings. Further, any being found not to be rational might not need to be treated like a human being. Similar consequences follow from the belief held by many other thinkers that man's essence is freedom.

In recent times philosophers have become much less sure of the advisability of talking about essences and have turned to finding out what features the things that we call human beings have. Some contemporary philosophers believe that if man actually is both the rational animal (though experiments with certain other forms of animal life have led to questions about how one should characterize rationality) and also the pouchless featherless biped, then either description will be perfectly adequate to characterize him. Of course, no philosopher would deny that some true descriptions of man are more interesting and fruitful than others, and, therefore, when a contemporary philosopher asks "What is a human being?" he presumably is concerned with the question "What important descriptions are true of human beings?" where "important" is explained in terms of what is significant for man's understanding of himself and his place in the world.

MAN AND NATURE

Perhaps the most basic way of classifying views about human beings is according to their answers to the question "Is man like or unlike the rest of the things in the world?" As it stands, this question is not precise enough to be answered in a simple manner. Some examples will make clearer what complexities are involved.

Many philosophers who reflect upon man in relation to the rest of nature are struck by the fact that human beings seem quite different from rocks, water, trees, and stars and even dogs, apes, and koalas. They notice that none of these seem capable of the complex and intricate patterns of rational behavior human beings engage in. When these philosophers "look inside themselves" they discover a realm of conscious activity that seems very different from what goes on in the rest of nature. These observations cause them to think that there must be some feature of human beings that is different in kind from the features of the rest of the things in the world. They do not believe that the human brain is merely a very complicated mechanism; even the most complicated mechanism, they think, would not be capable of reproducing what is distinctive about human behavior. The conclusion that some of these philosophers draw is that men have minds or souls—that is, some distinctive component that is the seat of consciousness and rational activity and is shared only by other human beings (and perhaps God and angels). Other philosophers, struck by the same phenomena, do not go so far as to say that there is some entity in a man called a mind or a soul, but they say instead that man has certain "mental" properties different in kind from anything found in the rest of nature. That is, it is men and not minds that think, but thinking is an activity that is very different from any physical process.

The idea that man is very different from the rest of the things in the world forms part of many theories. Dissimilar as these theories may be in other respects, they all must try to explain how the mental (conscious, rational, emotional) side of human beings relates to the physical side (including the body and its behavior and the brain). Some typical explanations of the relationship between the two sides of human beings are (1) that they interact causally, (2) that they are totally independent and God makes sure that happenings on the physical side (for example, being stuck with a pin) are correlated with happenings on the mental side (feeling pain), and (3) that the two sides are independent but were "programmed" by God to appear to relate to each other in the way they seem to. Intensive discussion of these alternatives has disclosed difficulties in each of them; philosophers who feel that man is different in kind (not merely in degree) from the rest of nature have yet to formulate a truly satisfactory theory.

Other philosophers who reflect upon man and nature have drawn a completely different conclusion. They have been struck by the fact that human beings are quite like the rest of nature. They hold that man has developed through a process of evolution from simpler forms of life and believe that human behavior, while complex, is not different in kind from that of certain insects. These men remind us that science is more and more able to explain so-called mental phenomena on the basis of physical laws, as is shown by recent work in the chemical basis of schizophrenia, for example. They also note that computers seem to be more and more capable of approximating what men call rationality. On this basis, they conclude that an adequate account of human beings can be given in terms of the sciences that seem to be capable of producing adequate accounts of the rest of nature. They agree that man is a very complex and interesting mechanism but see no need to say any more than that. The history of philosophy contains many different views sharing the belief that man, while in some ways different in degree from the rest of nature, is not different in kind from it. (A current theory of this sort in the materialist tradition will be examined in detail below.)

A similar division of views about man can be made in terms of the methods the philosophers specify for studying him. If man is very unlike the rest of the natural world, then one would naturally assume that the methods used to discover its features would probably turn out to be inappropriate when applied to man. On the other hand, if man is like the rest of nature, then one would expect to find that the same methods that produce knowledge and understanding about the rest of the world would stand a good chance of success when applied to man. This poses a "relativity" problem: one will presumably choose a method of investigating what a human being is at least in part according to whether one thinks that man is similar to the rest of nature. However, the method is supposed to answer the question of whether man is similar to the rest of nature. Hence, a sort of "chicken-egg" situation arises. What probably goes on in many cases is this: a philosopher is impressed by man's being like or unlike the rest of nature. (This may result from previous argumentation in another area of inquiry.) He then adopts a method that he feels will be appropriate to use, given his initial impression. He attempts to indicate the results this method will yield, and to show that there is nothing inherently defective about either the answer or the method. If this enterprise is successful, the philosopher has a strong candidate for an adequate account of human beings. Of course, in practice a complete program of this kind has rarely been attempted by philosophers. Contemporary philosophers realize that a vast amount of research, both scientific and conceptual, would be needed to achieve a comprehensive view of man. Therefore, a large part of their effort is aimed at showing that a particular account based upon a particular methodology is or is not inherently defective. That is, they are interested in discovering whether a view of a given sort and a method of a given sort at least show promise of being able to give an adequate answer to the question "What is a human being?"

PHYSICALISM

A traditional view concerning human beings that has become the object of intensive current discussion holds (1) that man is like nature in that both consist of the same materials—those materials studied by natural science, in particular physics—and (2) that an account of human beings expressed in terms of a scientific theory is a complete and adequate account. In the past this view was called materialism; in its modern form, it has become known to philosophers as *physicalism.* This is perhaps a better name for it, since "materialism" suggests that everything is made up of matter and contemporary physics has shown that there is a lot more to the world than matter; indeed, the line between matter and force is anything but sharp. The word "physicalism," on the other hand, seems more flexible; it merely suggests that man, whatever he is, can be described adequately with the terms and concepts employed by the science of physics. (Of course, should physics someday begin to explain phenomena in terms of immaterial, immortal souls, then the term "physicalism" would no longer serve as an appropriate label for the modern form of materialism. However, it would be difficult to find a contemporary physicist or philosopher who envisages such a development.)

The term "physicalism" also suggests the method of inquiry that the theory favors. The physicalist believes that the methods of natural science, in particular physics, can be counted upon to give a comprehensive description of a human being. The physicalists do not deny that a man can learn something about himself by, for example, reading a novel or going to a movie. Well he might. All that the physicalists need say is that what the man learns about by these endeavors is a complicated physical mechanism.

Some physicalists claim that scientific methodology should be used to justify the choice of a philosophical theory (in addition to the choice of a scientific theory). They argue that since physicalism is a simpler and more economical theory concerning human beings than other philosophical accounts—including, for example, the view that man is a composite of body and soul—it should be selected as a philosophical theory. However, one need not accept this argument to be a physicalist. The reading by Quine discusses this.

It is easier to explain why philosophers have felt attracted to or repelled by physicalism than it is to describe all the forms the view takes or to evaluate them. Physicalism places man squarely within the universe, and therefore it seems like a highly plausible account to philosophers who believe that there are great similarities between human beings and the rest of the things in the universe. Physicalism also uses a single set of terms to characterize both human beings and the rest of nature; many philosophers believe that this is necessary if we are to achieve the simplest and most comprehensive account of nature. They hope that one set of physical laws will someday be available that will give a complete account of the universe. Physicalism also has the virtue of "putting man in his place," hopefully without reducing him to such insignificance that he feels himself to be without value. It therefore seems attractive to philosophers who feel that Western religions have elevated human beings to too high a status in the universe, especially in view of modern astronomical and cosmological theories that claim that human beings live on a little ball whirling around one of billions of stars (a rather mediocre star at that) in a galaxy that is only one among billions of galaxies. Finally, the contention of physicalism that man is no more than a complicated physical mechanism appeals to philosophers who are impressed by the apparent success of science in describing and explaining phenomena of nature (including human behavior and even so-called mental phenomena) in physical terms, and who feel that it is reasonable to grant that someday all features of human beings will be explained in physical terms.

The features of physicalism that make it at least initially unacceptable to many philosophers are also easy to discover. Some find it very hard to think of themselves as physical objects, even very complicated physical objects. While almost all philosophers grant that they *have* bodies, many are unwilling to say that they *are* their bodies. (See Nagel's paper for a discussion of this point.) Perhaps the main reason for this unwillingness is their belief that nothing physical is capable of mental activity, of being conscious, of having thoughts, feelings, and emotions, of "seeing" after-images, and so on. A complicated physical mechanism is no different in principle from a simple mechanism, and a simple mechanism is not—indeed could not be—conscious.

Program

A proponent of physicalism has two main tasks. First of all, he must indicate what form a physicalist account of human beings might take. Of course, no philosopher would claim to be able to work out in detail an account of human beings in physical terms. This will take a long time, even if one assumes that it can be done at all. Further, it will be a task primarily for the neurophysiologist, chemist, engineer, physicist, and other scientists. Still, a philosopher has to be able to muster enough evidence to show that a physicalist account is even worth considering. This task, however, while extremely interesting, is not the chief focus of the authors whose papers are collected in this book. (Some of the papers, for example those by Kim and Brandt with Kim, do consider a related question: given that physicalism has some initial plausibility, does it have any more evidential support than some alternative theories of mind. That is, granted that it is plausible, is it any more plausible than, for example, a theory according to which a human being is a composite of mental and physical components that interact causally?)

The authors represented here are primarily concerned with the second task of the physicalist, which is to demonstrate that there is no difficulty in principle in the adoption of physicalism. That is, they are concerned to show that physicalism offers at least a possible account of human beings. As noted above, the chief objection to physicalism is that it offers no way of accounting for the mental life of human beings. Minds are not physical, it is argued, and consciousness is not a physical property. Since human beings have minds and are conscious, physicalism is bound to be an inadequate view. Given the seriousness of this charge, it is not surprising that philosophers who are sympathetic to physicalism spend much of their time and effort attempting to show that the charge is not true. To achieve this end, they propose various views concerning the mental aspects of human beings, the physical aspects of human beings, and the relation between the two. (See Brandt and Kim for a detailed discussion of these matters.)

The "Mental"

There are several positions philosophers of physicalist sympathies might take with respect to "mental" phenomena. Three chief positions will be mentioned. (It should be noticed that even though the physicalist may grant that human beings have what is called a "mental" life, he will go on to argue that this mental life can be described and accounted for in physical terms.)

1. According to one theory, "thought," "sensation," "emotion," "after-image," "itch," and other mental terms all stand for entities. That is, thoughts, sensations, emotions, after-images, and itches are things; when we report seeing, for example, an orange after-image, we are reporting the presence of an actual thing that is orange. This theory is rarely defended by physicalists, since, as will be discussed below, it is very difficult to find anything in the physical realm that will serve as, for example, the orange of the after-image.

2. At the other extreme is the view that there are no such things as thoughts, sensations, after-images, emotions, or itches. According to this theory, so-called mentalistic statements are to be analyzed into disposition statements about the subject of the experience. Thus, if we say of a person that he feels guilty (where "feeling guilty" is apparently a mental rather than a physical term), we are really just saying that he will try to make amends for what he has done, will apologize to anyone he has harmed by the action he feels guilty about, will resolve never to do the thing again, etc. (Whether such analyses can ever be spelled out once and for all, and whether a failure to spell them out is important, will not be considered here.) Philosophers who adopt this theory argue that any so-called mental term can be eliminated in context through such an analysis and, therefore, it follows that these terms do not refer to anything at all. To have a mental life according to this theory is just to be disposed to behave in certain ways in certain circumstances. This philosophical movement, while often unwilling to have itself called physicalistic, is an ally of the phys-

icalist position insofar as it attempts to describe the mental life of man in terms of bodily dispositions. (Some proponents of this view, which is often called "logical behaviorism," maintain that the view is not physicalistic since it is concerned with dispositions to *act* and not merely to behave. Whether or not this distinction is genuinely viable is outside the scope of this book.) Philosophers who call themselves physicalists in a more narrow sense are often sympathetic to attempts to eliminate a range of mental entities through dispositional analyses. However, they feel that, while such analyses might be successful for some mental concepts, they will not work across the board. For example, if one feels a very slight twinge of pain in his little finger, it is not clear that this means the person has any disposition to act in any particular way. Again, if one sees an orange after-image, one feels at a loss to construct an analysis in terms of dispositions. Perhaps a person might not feel like behaving in any way at all. Another reason why some physicalists feel unhappy with such dispositional analyses arises from the so-called first-person case. If I say of Smith that he has a great pain in his hand, there might be some plausibility in saying that I am merely attributing to Smith a particular disposition, for example, to move away from the source of heat that he is touching. However, if I say of myself that I am in great pain, it seems highly implausible to say that I am merely attributing to myself some disposition to behave in certain ways. Presumably I am reporting an experience. Hence, a full-scale dispositional analysis is not satisfying to some physicalists on the ground that it leaves out experiences. (The article by Place and the first selection by Smart discuss this.)

3. Most physicalists attempt to work out a theory of the mental that avoids the extremes of talking physicalistically, on the one hand, about mental entities and their properties (like after-images and their colors), and denying, on the other hand, that there are any such things as experiences at all. A typical theory of this type might take the following form: The terms that are amenable to dispositional analysis in context are so analyzed. The mental terms not amenable are treated in such a way that a person who uses them is said to be speaking of experiences that human beings have but not of "mental" entities that human beings experience. There are no such things as pains in the world, but there are experiences we call "being-in-pain." (The physicalist might then go on to say that the experience of being-in-pain is really a physical process.) Such a view may seem more plausible if we

consider one or two analogous cases. We sometimes say "He did it for her sake." It is sometimes assumed that for this sentence to be true the word "sake" must stand for something. Then it might seem that, since he did it for her sake, there is something in the world that is a sake (and it belonged to her). Yet most people would reject this inference. We do not commit ourselves to the existence of things called "sakes" just because we use the phrase "for her sake." Again, in German one says of a hungry person that he has hunger ("*Er hat Hunger*"). Yet no one would claim that this means there is something called "hunger" and he has it. In a similar way, physicalists can argue that it does not follow that, just because we say "He has a pain," there is something that is a pain and he has it. Rather, we might say "He pains" and avoid the suggestion that pains are entities in the world. According to this sort of analysis, then, men are sometimes in pain but there are no pains. Somewhat similar analyses can be presented concerning other mental terms such as "after-image." (Smart's first article does this.) If such analyses are successful, then it would seem that mental entities might be dispensed with while experiences (of having after-images, pains, and the like) can be retained. The physicalist can then go on to give some physical account of these experiences. (If such a program can be carried out, then a problem for the physicalist mentioned above—accounting for the orange of the after-image—is apparently avoided, since if there are no such things as after-images then of course there are no colors of after-images.)

One objection to this sort of analysis is that it falsifies the facts: we have direct experience of pains and after-images, so it is fanciful to deny that there are such things. (Cornman's article considers this.) Several different replies might be made by the physicalist, among them the following: while it is true that we do have experience, how we should describe it is determined by pragmatic considerations based upon our needs and interests. Since as philosophers we are interested in giving the simplest, most comprehensive, organized account of the world, this aim should determine the way we describe experience. Since we can describe it in terms of physical processes and leave nothing out (in terms of explanatory power), we need not have such things as sensations in our universe of discourse. That it, we can choose how to describe our experience and, since there is no good reason to describe it as viewing or sensing objects on some sort of inner screen, and since there is a good reason (simplicity of theory, given out knowledge of physiology) to describe it as having physical processes occur, we should choose to describe it in physical terms. (See Quine's article for this sort of argument.)

Whether this reply is successful is still an open question. (The readings by Rorty and Cornman discuss it further.) In general physicalists defend some account of the mental that is close to the third theory discussed above. They go on to argue that the mental life, so characterized, can be described in physical terms. This leads to a consideration of what sort of phenomena these philosophers have in mind when they talk about the physical side of man.

The Physical

A variety of views concerning the physical aspect of human beings are held by physicalists. These are the major ones.

1. For physicalist philosophers who hold that all mental terms can be eliminated through analyses in context in terms of dispositions to behave in certain ways, the only physical component of human beings that is important for accounting for the mental life of humans is the body described in behavioral terms. Since, however, most physicalists find that dispositional analyses have a limited scope, these philosophers supplement their account of the physical in ways mentioned in theory 3 below. (As noted before, some philosophers who accept an across-the-board dispositional analysis of mental terms deny that they are physicalists.)

2. Another possible view is that the brain and central nervous system are the only important physical components of human beings. However, since many physicalists are perfectly willing to accept dispositional analyses of certain mental terms, and since these analyses make mention of the body from a behavioral point of view, an account of the physical limited to the neurophysiological is not commonly defended.

3. The view held by most contemporary physicalists is that the physical aspect of man that is relevant to an account of his mental life consists of both his body (considered in macroscopic behavioral terms) and his brain and central nervous system. These philosophers believe that if some mental terms can be analyzed in terms of dispositions to behave in certain ways and others can be understood as referring to experiences that are really physical processes, then the physicalist position is in very fine shape. Whether these two accounts of

the physical can be ultimately reduced to one simple unified account is a question the phyicalist would like to answer affirmatively, but more work will be needed before we arrive at the answer.

4. A recent suggestion (as in the articles by Putnam) is that perhaps neither a dispositional analysis nor a physiological account (perhaps mentioning physical and chemical laws) will serve the purposes of the physicalist. Rather, if any sort of physicalist account is to be successful, it must couch the laws it makes use of in terms of the functional organization of the mechanism, or the person. Part of the ground for this claim is that it is possible for two different mechanisms (a person and a robot, perhaps) to be psychologically very similar and yet be made of different materials and have somewhat different dispositions to behave. Hence, no physio-chemical description and no dispositional analysis will fit both mechanisms. What might work is some account of the mechanisms and their components in terms of the functional roles played by the components. Whether such an extension of the physical would be so extreme that the term "physicalism" would lose its meaning in an important sense is an open question that presumably will remain open until examples of such an account are produced.

Once a physicalist has adopted some views about the mental and physical aspects of human beings, he is ready to face the difficult problem of giving some account of the mental in terms of the physical. Contemporary physicalists have tended to favor some form of the account known as the *identity theory*—that is, the theory that holds that the mental life of human beings is identical with some part of the physical side of human beings.

THE IDENTITY THEORY

The identity theory says that there is a mind-body identity—that is, that the mental life of human beings, whatever it consists in (experienced mental entities, dispositions to behave in certain ways, experiences), is actually identical with certain physical features and processes of human beings. Before discussing the various forms of the identity theory, some remarks about the sort of identity and the status of the identity will be presented.

1. Some true identity statements have traditionally been called "necessary." Examples are: "2 plus 2 is identical with 4," "A bachelor

is identical with an unmarried man," "7 is identical with the smallest prime greater than 5." These identity statements express what have been called necessary truths. Other true identity statements are contingent. Examples are: "Lyndon Johnson is identical with the President of the United States in 1968," "Wilt Chamberlain is identical with the highest scorer in professional basketball history (as of 1969)," "9 is the number of known planets." These statements are true, as some philosophers have said, not by virtue of meaning but by virtue of certain facts. Contemporary physicalists who espouse some form of the identity theory agree that, for things named by mental terms that are not amenable to dispositional analysis, the identity that holds between the mental and the physical is a contingent identity. (In other words, if a philosopher maintains, for example, that the experience of having an after-image is identical with some physical process, the statement expressing the identity is held to be contingently true.) Thus, contemporary physicalists do not claim that when a person says he is having an experience of an after-image he *means* that a certain physical process is going on. He may not even know there are such physical processes. What is claimed is that in fact he happens to be referring to a physical process. (Place's article and the first article by Smart take this up.)

2. Even though physicalists seem to agree about the contingent status of the identity statements they propose, there is some disagreement about whether the identity is arrived at through a process of discovery or a process of decision. That is, some philosophers say that it is a fact that can be discovered about experiences that they are identical with certain brain processes, for example. Others claim that there is no conceivable discovery that could show that things such as experiences and brain processes are identical, as opposed to being merely constantly correlated. According to these philosophers we must do the identifying ourselves if there is to be an identity. (The articles by Kim and Brandt and Kim discuss this point.)

3. Traditionally it has been felt that two things are identical if and only if they share all their nonmodal properties. This is sometimes called strict identity. However, some philosophers have felt that the sort of identities that scientists claim exist between microscopic and macroscopic events, processes, or entities are actually weaker than strict identities. They observe that while there is a sense in which a table is identical with a cluster of electrons, certain features of the

table seem not to be shared by the cluster of electrons. The table may be standing still, for example, but the cluster of electrons is constantly in motion. This has led some philosophers to say that the sort of identity that might suffice for a physicalist is some sort of theoretical identity, an identity based upon a scientific theory. (See Nagel's article for consideration of this.) Whether an identity can be defined this loosely and yet actually remain an identity is a moot question. Some philosophers feel that anything short of strict identity would be merely a correlation of two things, and this would not be sufficient for an identity theorist. (See Sellars' article for a discussion of this.)

4. Finally, some physicalists question whether the identities that the identity theorist should hope to discover are general or particular. A general identity holds that every entity, event, or process of a kind A is identical with an entity, event, or process of kind B. For example, every creature with a heart is identical with a creature with a kidney. A particular identity, on the other hand, holds that this individual entity, event, or process is identical with that individual one but makes no claim about all things of a certain kind A being identical with things of kind B. Given the apparent difficulty of finding (at least at the present time) general identity statements linking the mental and the physical, it is tempting for a physicalist to limit his claim to particular identities. However, a large part of the evidence for the identity theory seems to consist in whatever explanations of mental phenomena scientists can make using physical laws. These laws are general statements, and therefore the principles that link the physical and the mental would presumably also be general statements. Indeed, if there are no general links, there would seem to be little reason to accept the physical theory as an account of the mental. The physicalist who restricts his claim to particular identities has, therefore, the following problem: the evidence he needs to give plausibility to his view is in terms of general statements. Therefore, it would seem that if general statements linking the physical and the mental cannot be found, not only is there reason to doubt the correctness of an identity theory claiming that there are general identities; there is in effect no evidence for the claim that there are particular identities. Whether an identity theory that mixed general and particular identity statements could be developed is another question. (See Nagel's article on the subject.)

What Is Identical to What

Different versions of the identity theory hold different things to be identical. However, most contemporary physicalists concentrate on accounting in terms of identity for the relation between the mental life and the neurophysiological side of human beings, and therefore the following discussion will limit itself to identity theories aimed at this task. Only versions involving strict identity will be considered. Some of the most important views are these:

1. For a physicalist who accepts the existence of mental entities (pains, other sensations, after-images), each mental entity would be held to be identical with some entity in the brain or central nervous system. Thus a pain of a certain sort might be taken to be identical with some occurrence in the nervous system. As has been pointed out before, a serious drawback to this theory is that a number of so-called mental entities apparently have properties that cannot be found in any physical counterpart with which they might be identified—the orange after-image is orange, but no one has found anything in the brain or nervous system that is orange. This means that nothing physical of the appropriate sort could be strictly identical to the after-image, since the "mental" entity has a property that no physical entity has. (See Sellars' article for a discussion of this point.)

2. In a desire to avoid this difficulty, some have adopted the view that, while there are experiences, there are no mental entities and then have gone on to argue that what is identical is the *person* (or perhaps the body) who has the experience and the neurophysiological process. That is, a person who has a pain is identical with the person undergoing a certain neurophysiological process. (See Nagel for a consideration of such a theory.) Unfortunately, this form of the identity theory appears to be too weak to be a defense of physicalism. It could well gain the assent of any dualist (a philosopher who believes that a person consists of a soul and body related in such a way that, whenever the soul has an experience of some sort, there is a corresponding neurophysiological occurrence in the body), because the person who had the experience (in his soul) would be identical to the person who had the brain process (in his body). A physicalist needs something stronger. (Sellars takes up this argument.)

3. A third and much more widely held form of the identity theory

is that there are identities between experiences and brain processes. (Smart's first article considers this.) According to this theory, there are no mental entities, but there are experiences—for example, having an after-image. This experience is identical with some brain process. Which particular process it is may require a lot of neurophysiological investigation to discover, of course. The identity theorist does not claim merely that whenever a person has a certain after-image he is undergoing some brain process, for this view could be held by a dualist. Rather, he claims that the experience is the brain process. There is one thing and not two. In this way the identity theorist hopes to avoid the pitfalls of, on the one hand, trying to find physical properties that will serve as the properties of so-called mental entities and, on the other hand, weakening his account so much that even a dualist could accept it.

This position has been challenged in a number of ways. Some philosophers argue that brain processes cannot be strictly identical to experiences because they do not share all their properties. For example, brain processes have a definite location, but experiences are located either not at all or in terms of the person who has them. (See Malcolm and Nagel on this point.) The spatial properties of the two sorts of things are therefore different, and so no identity obtains. A physicalist might reply that if we discover identities of the sort he envisages, we will discover that experiences do in fact have definite spatial locations (in the brain) that we were previously unaware of. Or he might argue that we could, by convention, set up a system for talking about the spatial locations of experiences. (See the first paper by Smart, and the one by Kim.)

Another objection is that it is conceivable that one person undergoing a certain experience has a brain process of one sort while another undergoing the same experience has a brain process of a slightly different sort. If so, it is not clear how the identity statements should be formed, for it would be odd to say that A is identical with either B or C. (See Nagel and Putnam's second article.)

Finally, some object that according to this form of the identity theory an experience I have can be made accessible (perhaps through a surgical operation opening the skull) to others. Yet it is a characteristic of experiences that they are private—one and only one person has any particular experience. A physicalist might take several tacks here, one being to say that if the identity theory is correct, then experiences are not private in the way that some philosophers have believed they are. (See Rorty on this point.)

At the present time a number of physicalists feel that this third form of the identity theory is the most promising way of explaining the relation between the mental life of a human being and his physical makeup. Whether the theory can meet present and future objections and whether the required identity statements will be forthcoming from scientific research is something that only time and further study will decide.

The Relations of Physicalism and the Identity Theory

Although some contemporary philosophers apparently believe that every physicalist is an identity theorist and vice versa, this is not the case. True, physicalists often turn to some form of identity theory (especially the third form just discussed) in an attempt to show how a physicalistic account of mental activity is possible. Yet it is possible to be a physicalist without believing in any form of the identity theory. For example, if one holds that all human beings are complicated physical mechanisms and that whenever some bit of mental activity occurs all that is going on is a physical process, but at the same time denies that each time a person has a certain experience the same sort of physiological process is going on, one is then a physicalist without holding to the identity theory. Perhaps the neurophysiological side of human beings is so complicated that it is hopeless to try to find identity statements linking it with experience. Or perhaps the relation itself is much too complicated. (Of course, a philosopher who believed this would have to give some account of how so-called mental processes relate to physical ones.) And just as one can be a physicalist without accepting the identity theory, one can accept the identity theory and not be a physicalist. As was noted above, philosophers who believe in a nonphysical soul can accept an identity theory that holds that the person who has an experience is identical with the person who has a certain brain process.

It is clear, therefore, that only some forms of the identity theory (especially the third just discussed) are distinctively physicalistic. And even this third form may not necessarily be physicalistic. It is argued that if a "mental" experience is really identical to a brain process, then it is equally correct to say that certain physical processes are really identical to experiences. What, then, it is asked, is the point of calling such a position physicalist? Why not call it mentalist, since it grants the existence of "mental" experiences? That is, if one is a true physicalist, should he not eliminate experiences? One cannot claim that experiences are really physical without in a sense denying that they are experiences at all. (See Brandt and Kim on this point.) Perhaps the most interesting physicalist reply is that the identity theory in the hands of a physicalist is merely a way of satisfying his opponents who feel there is some peculiarly mental aspect of human beings. Once one comes to adopt the physicalist view of the world, he will not need to be told that mental processes are identical to physical ones, for he will not have much use for the concept of mental processes. He will come to take experiences as physical occurrences. (See Rorty's article for discussion of a similar point.)

Some Objections

The previous discussion has raised a number of objections to physicalism and the forms of identity theory that physicalists sometimes adopt. It will be helpful to summarize the major objections here so that we may see upon what quite different considerations they are grounded.

1. Some philosophers feel that even if physicalism has some initial plausibility it is unsatisfactory as an account of human beings because no machine is capable of the creativity and ingenuity of human beings. Recent work with computers, however, has tended to show that machines are more capable than was previously thought. (See Smart's second article and Putnam's two articles.)

2. Some philosophers object to physicalism in general and the identity theory in particular on the grounds that our ordinary concepts are incompatible with the way the physicalist would require that we speak about, for example, experiences. Physicalists in general are not very impressed with such objections. (See Malcolm for objections of this sort. Rorty and especially Feyerabend consider the objection from a physicalist point of view.)

3. Others object to the possibility of finding an account in terms of identities that will do what the physicalist wants. (See Putnam's second article and the article by Brandt and Kim.)

4. Finally, some philosophers argue that phyicalists have not presented sufficient grounds for taking the step of *identifying* the physical and the mental. (See Kim and Brandt and Kim.) Whether this

is a valid objection depends in part upon issues in the philosophy of science as related to philosophical theories: what makes one theory better than another.

CONCLUSION

This introduction has discussed the cluster of views known as physicalism and various forms of the identity theory that physicalists adopt in their attempts to account for the mental life of human beings. The essays that follow treat in detail many points considered here, some from interestingly different perspectives. They represent the most sophisticated contemporary efforts to evaluate materialism in its modern form. It is hoped that they mark the beginning of a joint philosophical and scientific enterprise that will lead to a new and deeper understanding of what human beings are.

1 *U. T. Place*

Is Consciousness a Brain Process?

U. T. Place was born on October 24, 1924, in Northallerton, Yorkshire, England. He was educated at Oxford University and is now Lecturer in Clinical Psychology in the Department of Psychiatry at the University of Leeds. His chief interests include the mind-body problem, the logic of explanations of behavior, and the conceptual and experimental analysis of mood and emotion. He has contributed articles to several important philosophical journals.

The thesis that consciousness is a process in the brain is put forward as a reasonable scientific hypothesis, not to be dismissed on logical grounds alone. The conditions under which two sets of observations are treated as observations of the same process, rather than as observations of two independent correlated processes, are discussed. It is suggested that we can identify consciousness with a given pattern of brain activity, if we can explain the subject's introspective observations by reference to the brain processes with which they are correlated. It is argued that the problem of providing a physiological explanation of introspective observations is made to seem more difficult than it really is by the "phenomenological fallacy," the mistaken idea that descriptions of the appearances of things are descriptions of the actual state of affairs in a mysterious internal environment.

FROM *The British Journal of Psychology,* XLVII (February, 1956). Reprinted by permission of the author and the editors.

INTRODUCTION

The view that there exists a separate class of events, mental events, which cannot be described in terms of the concepts employed by the physical sciences no longer commands the universal and unquestioning acceptance among philosophers and psychologists which it once did. Modern physicalism, however, unlike the materialism of the seventeenth and eighteenth centuries, is behavioristic. Consciousness on this view is either a special type of behavior, "sampling" or "running-back-and-forth" behavior as Tolman has it,[1] or a disposition to behave in a certain way, an itch for example being a temporary propensity to scratch. In the case of cognitive concepts like "knowing," "believing," "understanding," "remembering," and volitional concepts like "wanting" and "intending," there can be little doubt, I think, that an analysis in terms of dispositions to behave is fundamentally sound.[2] On the other hand, there would seem to be an intractable residue of concepts clustering around the notions of consciousness, experience, sensation, and mental imagery, where some sort of inner process story is unavoidable.[3] It is possible, of course, that a satisfactory behavioristic account of this conceptual residuum will ultimately be found. For our present purposes, however, I shall assume that this cannot be done and that statements about pains and twinges, about how things look, sound, and feel, about things dreamed of or pictured in the mind's eye, are statements referring to events and processes which are in some sense private or internal to the individual of whom they are predicated. The question I wish to raise is whether in making this assumption we are inevitably committed to a dualist position in which sensations and mental images form a separate category of processes over and above the physical and physiological processes with which they are known to be correlated. I shall argue that an acceptance of inner processes does not entail dualism and that the thesis that consciousness is a process in the brain cannot be dismissed on logical grounds.

[1] E. C. Tolman, *Purposive Behavior in Animals and Men* (Berkeley: University of California Press, 1932).
[2] L. Wittgenstein, *Philosophical Investigations* (Oxford: Blackwell, 1953); G. Ryle, *The Concept of Mind* (London: Hutchinson's University Library, 1949).
[3] U. T. Place, "The Concept of Heed," *British Journal of Psychology*, XLV (1954), pp. 243–55.

THE "IS" OF DEFINITION AND THE "IS" OF COMPOSITION

I want to stress from the outset that in defending the thesis that consciousness is a process in the brain, I am not trying to argue that when we describe our dreams, fantasies, and sensations we are talking about processes in our brains. That is, I am not claiming that statements about sensations and mental images are reducible to or analyzable into statements about brain processes, in the way in which "cognition statements" are analyzable into statements about behavior. To say that statements about consciousness are statements about brain processes is manifestly false. This is shown (a) by the fact that you can describe your sensations and mental imagery without knowing anything about your brain processes or even that such things exist, (b) by the fact that statements about one's consciousness and statements about one's brain processes are verified in entirely different ways, and (c) by the fact that there is nothing self-contradictory about the statement "X has a pain but there is nothing going on in his brain." What I do want to assert, however, is that the statement "Consciousness is a process in the brain," although not necessarily true, is not necessarily false. "Consciousness is a process in the brain," on my view is neither self-contradictory nor self-evident; it is a reasonable scientific hypothesis, in the way that the statement "Lightning is a motion of electric charges" is a reasonable scientific hypothesis.

The all but universally accepted view that an assertion of identity between consciousness and brain processes can be ruled out on logical grounds alone, derives, I suspect, from a failure to distinguish between what we may call the "is" of definition and the "is" of composition. The distinction I have in mind here is the difference between the function of the word "is" in statements like "A square is an equilateral rectangle," "Red is a color," "To understand an instruction is to be able to act appropriately under the appropriate circumstances," and its function in statements like "His table is an old packing case," "Her hat is a bundle of straw tied together with string," "A cloud is a mass of water droplets or other particles in suspension." These two types of "is" statements have one thing in common. In both cases it makes sense to add the qualification "and nothing else." In this they differ from those statements in which the "is" is an "is" of predication; the statements "Toby is 80 years old and nothing else," "Her hat is red and nothing else" or "Giraffes are tall and nothing else," for example, are nonsense. This logical feature may be described by saying that in both cases both the grammatical subject and the grammatical predicate are expressions which provide an adequate characterization of the state of affairs to which they both refer.

In another respect, however, the two groups of statements are strikingly different. Statements like "A square is an equilateral rectangle" are necessary statements which are true by definition. Statements like "His table is an old packing case," on the other hand, are contingent statements which have to be verified by observation. In the case of statements like "A square is an equilateral rectangle" or "Red is a color," there is a relationship between the meaning of the expression forming the grammatical predicate and the meaning of the expression forming the grammatical subject, such that whenever the subject expression is applicable the predicate must also be applicable. If you can describe something as red then you must also be able to describe it as colored. In the case of statements like "His table is an old packing case," on the other hand, there is no such relationship between the meanings of the expressions "his table" and "old packing case"; it merely so happens that in this case both expressions are applicable to and at the same time provide an adequate characterization of the same object. Those who contend that the statement "Consciousness is a brain process" is logically untenable base their claim, I suspect, on the mistaken assumption that if the meanings of two statements or expressions are quite unconnected, they cannot both provide an adequate characterization of the same object or state of affairs: if something is a state of consciousness, it cannot be a brain process, since there is nothing self-contradictory in supposing that someone feels a pain when there is nothing happening inside his skull. By the same token we might be led to conclude that a table cannot be an old packing case, since there is nothing self-contradictory in supposing that someone has a table, but is not in possession of an old packing case.

THE LOGICAL INDEPENDENCE OF EXPRESSIONS AND THE ONTOLOGICAL INDEPENDENCE OF ENTITIES

There is, of course, an important difference between the table/packing case case and the consciousness/brain process case in that the statement "His table is an old packing case" is a particular proposition which refers only to one particular case, whereas the statement "Consciousness is a process in the brain" is a general or universal proposition applying to all states of consciousness whatever. It is fairly clear, I think, that if we lived in a world in which all tables without exception were packing cases, the concepts of "table" and "packing case" in our language would not have their present logically independent status. In such a world a table would be a species of packing case in much the same way that red is a species of color. It seems to be a rule of language that whenever a given variety of object or state of affairs has two characteristics or sets of characteristics, one of which is unique to the variety of object or state of affairs in question, the expression used to refer to the characteristic or set of characteristics which defines the variety of object or state of affairs in question will always entail the expression used to refer to the other characteristic or set of characteristics. If this rule admitted of no exception it would follow that any expression which is logically independent of another expression which uniquely characterizes a given variety of object or state of affairs, must refer to a characteristic or set of characteristics which is not normally or necessarily associated with the object or state of affairs in question. It is because this rule applies almost universally, I suggest, that we are normally justified in arguing from the logical independence of two expressions to the ontological independence of the states of affairs to which they refer. This would explain both the undoubted force of the argument that consciousness and brain processes must be independent entities because the expressions used to refer to them are logically independent and, in general, the curious phenomenon whereby questions about the furniture of the universe are often fought and not infrequently decided merely on a point of logic.

The argument from the logical independence of two expressions to the ontological independence of the entities to which they refer breaks down in the case of brain processes and consciousness, I believe, because this is one of a relatively small number of cases where the rule stated above does not apply. These exceptions are to be found, I suggest, in those cases where the operations which have to be performed in order to verify the presence of the two sets of characteristics inhering in the object or state of affairs in question can seldom if ever be performed simultaneously. A good example here is the case of the cloud and the mass of droplets or other particles in suspension. A cloud is a large semi-transparent mass with a fleecy texture suspended in the atmosphere whose shape is subject to continual and kaleidoscopic change. When observed at close quarters, however, it is found to consist of a mass of tiny particles, usually water droplets, in continuous motion. On the basis of this second observation we conclude that a cloud is a mass of tiny particles and nothing else. But there is no logical connection in our language between a cloud and a mass of tiny particles; there is nothing self-contradictory in talking about a cloud which is not composed of tiny particles in suspension. There is no contradiction involved in supposing that clouds consist of a dense mass of fibrous tissue; indeed, such a consistency seems to be implied by many of the functions performed by clouds in fairy stories and mythology. It is clear from this that the terms "cloud" and "mass of tiny particles in suspension" mean quite different things. Yet we do not conclude from this that there must be two things, the mass of particles in suspension and the cloud. The reason for this, I suggest, is that although the characteristics of being a cloud and being a mass of tiny particles in suspension are invariably associated, we never make the observations necessary to verify the statement "That is a cloud" and those necessary to verify the statement "This is a mass of tiny particles in suspension" at one and the same time. We can observe the micro-structure of a cloud only when we are enveloped by it, a condition which effectively prevents us from observing those characteristics which from a distance lead us to describe it as a cloud. Indeed, so disparate are these two experiences that we use different words to describe them. That which is a cloud when we observe it from a distance becomes a fog or mist when we are enveloped by it.

WHEN ARE TWO SETS OF OBSERVATIONS OBSERVATIONS OF THE SAME EVENT?

The example of the cloud and the mass of tiny particles in suspension was chosen because it is one of the few cases of a general proposition involving what I have called the "is" of composition which does not involve us in scientific technicalities. It is useful because it brings out the connection between the ordinary everyday cases of the "is" of composition like the table/packing case example and the more technical cases like "Lightning is a motion of electric charges" where the analogy with the consciousness/brain process case is most marked. The limitation of the cloud/tiny particles in suspension case is that it does not bring out sufficiently clearly the crucial problem of how the identity of the states of affairs referred to by the two expressions is established. In the cloud case the fact that something is a cloud and the fact that something is a mass of tiny particles in suspension are both verified by the normal processes of visual observation. It is arguable, moreover, that the identity of the entities referred to by the two expressions is established by the continuity between the two sets of observations as the observer moves towards or away from the cloud. In the case of brain processes and consciousness there is no such continuity between the two sets of observations involved. A closer introspective scrutiny will never reveal the passage of nerve impulses over a thousand synapses in the way that a closer scrutiny of a cloud will reveal a mass of tiny particles in suspension. The operations required to verify statements about consciousness and statements about brain processes are fundamentally different.

To find a parallel for this feature we must examine other cases where an identity is asserted between something whose occurrence is verified by the ordinary processes of observation and something whose occurrence is established by special scientific procedures. For this purpose I have chosen the case where we say that lightning is a motion of electric charges. As in the case of consciousness, however closely we scrutinize the lightning we shall never be able to observe the electric charges, and just as the operations for determining the nature of one's state of consciousness are radically different from those involved in determining the nature of one's brain processes, so the operations for determining the occurrence of lightning are radically different from those involved in determining the occurrence of a motion of electric charges. What is it, therefore, that leads us to say that the two sets of observations are observations of the same event? It cannot be merely the fact that the two sets of observations are systematically correlated such that whenever there is lightning there is always a motion of electric charges. There are innumerable cases of such correlations where we have no temptation to say that the two sets of observations are observations of the same event. There is a systematic correlation, for example, between the movement of the tides and the stages of the moon, but this does not lead us to say that records of tidal levels are records of the moon's stages or vice versa. We speak rather of a causal connection between two independent events or processes.

The answer here seems to be that we treat the two sets of observations as observations of the same event in those cases where the technical scientific observations set in the context of the appropriate body of scientific theory provide an immediate explanation of the observations made by the man in the street. Thus we conclude that lightning is nothing more than a motion of electric charges, because we know that a motion of electric charges through the atmosphere, such as occurs when lightning is reported, gives rise to the type of visual stimulation which would lead an observer to report a flash of lightning. In the moon/tide case, on the other hand, there is no such direct causal connection between the stages of the moon and the observations made by the man who measures the height of the tide. The causal connection is between the moon and the tides, not between the moon and the measurement of the tides.

THE PHYSIOLOGICAL EXPLANATION OF INTROSPECTION AND THE PHENOMENOLOGICAL FALLACY

If this account is correct, it should follow that in order to establish the identity of consciousness and certain processes in the brain, it would be necessary to show that the introspective observations reported by the subject can be accounted for in terms of processes which are known to have occurred in his brain. In the light of this suggestion it is extremely interesting to find that when a physiologist as distinct from a philosopher finds it difficult to see how consciousness could be a process in the brain, what worries him is not any supposed self-contradiction involved in such an assumption, but the apparent impossibility of accounting for the reports given by the subject of his conscious processes in terms of the known properties of the central nervous system. Sir Charles Sherrington has posed the problem as follows:

> The chain of events stretching from the sun's radiation entering the eye to, on the one hand, the contraction of the pupillary muscles, and on the other, to the electrical disturbances in the brain-cortex are all straightforward steps in a sequence of physical "causation," such as, thanks to science, are intelligible. But in the second serial chain

> there follows on, or attends, the stage of brain-cortex reaction an event or set of events quite inexplicable to us, which both as to themselves and as to the causal tie between them and what preceded them science does not help us; a set of events seemingly incommensurable with any of the events leading up to it. The self "sees" the sun; it senses a two-dimensional disc of brightness, located in the "sky," this last a field of lesser brightness, and overhead shaped as a rather flattened dome, coping the self and a hundred other visual things as well. Of hint that this is within the head there is none. Vision is saturated with this strange property called "projection," the unargued inference that what it sees is at a "distance" from the seeing "self." Enough has been said to stress that in the sequence of events a step is reached where a physical situation in the brain leads to a psychical, which however contains no hint of the brain or any other bodily part. . . . The supposition has to be, it would seem, two continuous series of events, one physicochemical, the other psychical, and at times interaction between them.[4]

Just as the physiologist is not likely to be impressed by the philosopher's contention that there is some self-contradiction involved in supposing consciousness to be a brain process, so the philosopher is unlikely to be impressed by the considerations which lead Sherrington to conclude that there are two sets of events, one physicochemical, the other psychical. Sherrington's argument for all its emotional appeal depends on a fairly simple logical mistake, which is unfortunately all too frequently made by psychologists and physiologists and not infrequently in the past by the philosophers themselves. This logical mistake, which I shall refer to as the "phenomenological fallacy," is the mistake of supposing that when the subject describes his experience, when he describes how things look, sound, smell, taste, or feel to him, he is describing the literal properties of objects and events on a peculiar sort of internal cinema or television screen, usually referred to in the modern psychological literature as the "phenomenal field." If we assume, for example, that when a subject reports a green after-image he is asserting the occurrence inside himself of an object which is literally green, it is clear that we have on our hands an entity for which there is no place in the world of physics. In the case of the green after-image there is no green object in the subject's environment corresponding to the description that he gives. Nor is there anything green in his brain; certainly there is

[4] Sir Charles Sherrington, *The Integrative Action of the Nervous System* (Cambridge: Cambridge University Press, 1947), pp. xx–xxi.

nothing which could have emerged when he reported the appearance of the green after-image. Brain processes are not the sort of things to which color concepts can be properly applied.

The phenomenological fallacy on which this argument is based depends on the mistaken assumption that because our ability to describe things in our environment depends on our consciousness of them, our descriptions of things are primarily descriptions of our conscious experience and only secondarily, indirectly, and inferentially descriptions of the objects and events in our environments. It is assumed that because we recognize things in our environment by their look, sound, smell, taste, and feel, we begin by describing their phenomenal properties, i.e., the properties of the looks, sounds, smells, tastes, and feels which they produce in us, and infer their real properties from their phenomenal properties. In fact, the reverse is the case. We begin by learning to recognize the real properties of things in our environment. We learn to recognize them, of course, by their look, sound, smell, taste, and feel; but this does not mean that we have to learn to describe the look, sound, smell, taste, and feel of things before we can describe the things themselves. Indeed, it is only after we have learned to describe the things in our environment that we can learn to describe our consciousness of them. We describe our conscious experience not in terms of the mythological "phenomenal properties" which are supposed to inhere in the mythological "objects" in the mythological "phenomenal field," but by reference to the actual physical properties of the concrete physical objects, events, and processes which normally, though not perhaps in the present instance, give rise to the sort of conscious experience which we are trying to describe. In other words when we describe the after-image as green, we are not saying that there is something, the after-image, which is green; we are saying that we are having the sort of experience which we normally have when, and which we have learned to describe as, looking at a green patch of light.

Once we rid ourselves of the phenomenological fallacy we realize that the problem of explaining introspective observations in terms of brain processes is far from insuperable. We realize that there is nothing that the introspecting subject says about his conscious experiences which is inconsistent with anything the physiologist might want to say about the brain processes which cause him to describe the environment and his consciousness of that environment in the way he does. When the subject describes his experience by saying that a light which is in fact stationary, appears to move, all the physiologist or physiological psychologist has to do in order to explain the subject's introspective observations, is to show that the brain process which is causing the subject to describe his experience in this way, is the sort of process which normally occurs when he is observing an actual moving object and which therefore normally causes him to report the movement of an object in his environment. Once the mechanism whereby the individual describes what is going on in his environment has been worked out, all that is required to explain the individual's capacity to make introspective observations is an explanation of his ability to discriminate between those cases where his normal habits of verbal description are appropriate to the stimulus situation and those cases where they are not and an explanation of how and why, in those cases where the appropriateness of his normal descriptive habits is in doubt, he learns to issue his ordinary descriptive protocols preceded by a qualificatory phrase like "it appears," "seems," "looks," "feels," etc.[5]

[5] I am greatly indebted to my fellow-participants in a series of informal discussions on this topic which took place in the Department of Philosophy, University of Adelaide, in particular to Mr. C. B. Martin for his persistent and searching criticism of my earlier attempts to defend the thesis that consciousness is a brain process, to Prof. D. A. T. Gasking, of the University of Melbourne, for clarifying many of the logical issues involved, and to Prof. J. J. C. Smart for moral support and encouragement in what often seemed a lost cause.

2 *J. J. C. Smart*

Sensations and Brain Processes

⁂ J. J. C. Smart was born on September 16, 1920, in Cambridge, England, and was educated at the University of Glasgow and Oxford University. He is now Hughes Professor of Philosophy at the University of Adelaide. His major work has been on the philosophy of mind, the philosophy of science, and ethics. He has written several books, among them *Philosophy and Scientific Realism* and *Between Science and Philosophy*, and he is a frequent contributor to philosophical journals.

This paper[1] takes its departure from arguments to be found in U. T. Place's "Is Consciousness a Brain Process?" [2] I have had the benefit of discussing Place's thesis in a good many universities in the United States and Australia, and I hope that the present paper answers objections to his thesis which Place has not considered and that it presents his thesis in a more nearly unobjectionable form. This paper

FROM J. J. C. Smart, "Sensations and Brain Processes" in *The Philosophy of Mind*, V. C. Chappell, ed., © 1962. Reprinted by permission of Prentice-Hall, Inc., Englewood Cliffs, N.J.; the author; and the editors of *The Philosophical Review*, where an earlier version of the paper appeared.

[1] This is a very slightly revised version of a paper which was first published in the *Philosophical Review*, LXVIII (1959), pp. 141–56. Since that date there have been criticisms of my paper by J. T. Stevenson, *Philosophical Review*, LXIX (1960), pp. 505–10, to which I have replied in *Philosophical Review*, LXX (1961), pp. 406–07, and by G. Pitcher and by W. D. Joske, *Australasian Journal of Philosophy*, XXXVIII (1960), pp. 150–60, to which I have replied in the same volume of that journal, pp. 252–54.

[2] *British Journal of Psychology*, XLVII (1956), pp. 44–50; reprinted in this volume, pp. 21–31. Subsequent page references to Place's article are to the reprint in this volume.

is meant also to supplement the paper "The 'Mental' and the 'Physical,'" by H. Feigl,[3] which in part argues for a similar thesis to Place's.

Suppose that I report that I have at this moment a roundish, blurry-edged after-image which is yellowish towards its edge and is orange towards its center. What is it that I am reporting? One answer to this question might be that I am not reporting anything, that when I say that it looks to me as though there is a roundish yellowy-orange patch of light on the wall I am expressing some sort of *temptation*, the temptation to say that there *is* a roundish yellowy-orange patch on the wall (though I may know that there is not such a patch on the wall). This is perhaps Wittgenstein's view in the *Philosophical Investigations* (see §§ 367, 370). Similarly, when I "report" a pain, I am not really reporting anything (or, if you like, I am reporting in a queer sense of "reporting"), but am doing a sophisticated sort of wince. (See § 244: "The verbal expression of pain replaces crying and does not describe it." Nor does it describe anything else?)[4] I prefer most of the time to discuss an after-image rather than a pain, because the word "pain" brings in something which is irrelevant to my purpose: the notion of "distress." I think that "he is in pain" entails "he is in distress," that is, that he is in a certain agitation-condition.[5] Similarly, to say "I am in pain" may be to do more than "replace pain behavior": it may be partly to report something, though this something is quite nonmysterious, being an agitation-condition, and so susceptible of behavioristic analysis. The suggestion I wish if possible to avoid is a different one, namely that "I am in pain" is a genuine report, and that what it reports is an irreducibly psychical something. And similarly the suggestion I wish to resist is also that to say "I have a yellowish-orange after-image" is to report something irreducibly psychical.

Why do I wish to resist this suggestion? Mainly because of

[3] *Minnesota Studies in the Philosophy of Science,* II (Minneapolis: University of Minnesota Press, 1958), pp. 370–497.

[4] Some philosophers of my acquaintance, who have the advantage over me in having known Wittgenstein, would say that this interpretation of him is too behavioristic. However, it seems to me a very natural interpretation of his printed words, and whether or not it is Wittgenstein's real view it is certainly an interesting and important one. I wish to consider it here as a possible rival both to the "brain-process" thesis and to straight-out old-fashioned dualism.

[5] See Ryle, *The Concept of Mind* (London: Hutchinson's University Library, 1949), p. 93.

Occam's razor. It seems to me that science is increasingly giving us a viewpoint whereby organisms are able to be seen as physicochemical mechanisms:[6] it seems that even the behavior of man himself will one day be explicable in mechanistic terms. There does seem to be, so far as science is concerned, nothing in the world but increasingly complex arrangements of physical constituents. All except for one place: in consciousness. That is, for a full description of what is going on in a man you would have to mention not only the physical processes in his tissues, glands, nervous system, and so forth, but also his states of consciousness: his visual, auditory, and tactual sensations, his aches and pains. That these should be *correlated* with brain processes does not help, for to say that they are *correlated* is to say that they are something "over and above." You cannot correlate something with itself. You correlate footprints with burglars, but not Bill Sikes the burglar with Bill Sikes the burglar. So sensations, states of consciousness, do seem to be the one sort of thing left outside the physicalist picture, and for various reasons I just cannot believe that this can be so. That everything should be explicable in terms of physics (together of course with descriptions of the ways in which the parts are put together—roughly, biology is to physics as radio-engineering is to electromagnetism) except the occurrence of sensations seems to me to be frankly unbelievable. Such sensations would be "nomological danglers," to use Feigl's expression.[7] It is not often realized how odd would be the laws whereby these nomological danglers would dangle. It is sometimes asked, "Why can't there be psychophysical laws which are of a novel sort, just as the laws of electricity and magnetism were novelties from the standpoint of Newtonian mechanics?" Certainly we are pretty sure in the future to come across new ultimate laws of a novel type, but I expect them to relate simple constituents: for example, whatever ultimate particles are then in vogue. I cannot believe that ultimate laws of nature could relate simple constituents to configurations consisting of perhaps billions of neurons (and goodness knows how many

[6] On this point see Paul Oppenheim and Hilary Putnam, "Unity of Science as a Working Hypothesis," in *Minnesota Studies in the Philosophy of Science*, II (Minneapolis: University of Minnesota Press, 1958), pp. 3–36.

[7] Feigl, *op. cit.*, p. 428. Feigl uses the expression "nomological danglers" for the laws whereby the entities dangle: I have used the expression to refer to the dangling entities themselves.

billion billions of ultimate particles) all put together for all the world as though their main purpose in life was to be a negative feedback mechanism of a complicated sort. Such ultimate laws would be like nothing so far known in science. They have a queer "smell" to them. I am just unable to believe in the nomological danglers themselves, or in the laws whereby they would dangle. If any philosophical arguments seemed to compel us to believe in such things, I would suspect a catch in the argument. In any case it is the object of this paper to show that there are no philosophical arguments which compel us to be dualists.

The above is largely a confession of faith, but it explains why I find Wittgenstein's position (as I construe it) so congenial. For on this view there are, in a sense, no sensations. A man is a vast arrangement of physical particles, but there are not, over and above this, sensations or states of consciousness. There are just behavioral facts about this vast mechanism, such as that it expresses a temptation (behavior disposition) to say "there is a yellowish-red patch on the wall" or that it goes through a sophisticated sort of wince, that is, says "I am in pain." Admittedly Wittgenstein says that though the sensation "is not a something," it is nevertheless "not a nothing either" (§ 304); but this need only mean that the word "ache" has a use. An ache is a thing, but only in the innocuous sense in which the plain man, in the first paragraph of Frege's *Foundations of Arithmetic*, answers the question "What is the number one?" by "a thing." It should be noted that when I assert that to say "I have a yellowish-orange after-image" is to express a temptation to assert the physical-object statement "There is a yellowish-orange patch on the wall," I mean that saying "I have a yellowish-orange after-image" is (partly) the exercise of the disposition[8] which is the temptation. It is not to *report* that I have the temptation, any more than is "I love you" normally a report that I love someone. Saying "I love you" is just part of the behavior which is the exercise of the disposition of loving someone.

[8] Wittgenstein did not like the word "disposition." I am using it to put in a nutshell (and perhaps inaccurately) the view which I am attributing to Wittgenstein. I should like to repeat that I do not wish to claim that my interpretation of Wittgenstein is correct. Some of those who knew him do not interpret him in this way. It is merely a view which I find myself extracting from his printed words and which I think is important and worth discussing for its own sake.

Though for the reasons given above, I am very receptive to the above "expressive" account of sensation statements, I do not feel that it will quite do the trick. Maybe this is because I have not thought it out sufficiently, but it does seem to me as though, when a person says "I have an after-image," he *is* making a genuine report, and that when he says "I have a pain," he *is* doing more than "replace pain-behavior," and that "this more" is not just to say that he is in distress. I am not so sure, however, that to admit this is to admit that there are nonphysical correlates of brain processes. Why should not sensations just be brain processes of a certain sort? There are, of course, well-known (as well as lesser-known) philosophical objections to the view that reports of sensations are reports of brain-processes, but I shall try to argue that these arguments are by no means as cogent as is commonly thought to be the case.

Let me first try to state more accurately the thesis that sensations are brain-processes. It is not the thesis that, for example, "after-image" or "ache" means the same as "brain process of sort X" (where "X" is replaced by a description of a certain sort of brain process). It is that, in so far as "after-image" or "ache" is a report of a process, it is a report of a process that *happens to be* a brain process. It follows that the thesis does not claim that sensation statements can be *translated* into statements about brain processes.[9] Nor does it claim that the logic of a sensation statement is the same as that of a brain-process statement. All it claims is that in so far as a sensation statement is a report of something, that something is in fact a brain process. Sensations are nothing over and above brain processes. Nations are nothing "over and above" citizens, but this does not prevent the logic of nation statements being very different from the logic of citizen statements, nor does it insure the translatability of nation statements into citizen statements. (I do not, however, wish to assert that the relation of sensation statements to brain-process statements is very like that of nation statements to citizen statements. Nations do not just *happen to be* nothing over and above citizens, for example. I bring in the "nations" example merely to make a negative point: that the fact that the logic of A-statements is different from that of B-statements does not insure that A's are anything over and above B's.)

[9] See Place, *op. cit.*, p. 23, and Feigl, *op. cit.*, p. 390, near top.

REMARKS ON IDENTITY

When I say that a sensation is a brain process or that lightning is an electric discharge, I am using "is" in the sense of strict identity. (Just as in the—in this case necessary—proposition "7 is identical with the smallest prime number greater than 5.") When I say that a sensation is a brain process or that lightning is an electric discharge I do not mean just that the sensation is somehow spatially or temporally continuous with the brain process or that the lightning is just spatially or temporally continuous with the discharge. When on the other hand I say that the successful general is the same person as the small boy who stole the apples I mean only that the successful general I see before me is a time slice[10] of the same four-dimensional object of which the small boy stealing apples is an earlier time slice. However, the four-dimensional object which has the general-I-see-before-me for its late time slice is identical in the strict sense with the four-dimensional object which has the small-boy-stealing-apples for an early time slice. I distinguish these two senses of "is identical with" because I wish to make it clear that the brain-process doctrine asserts identity in the *strict* sense.

I shall now discuss various possible objections to the view that the processes reported in sensation statements are in fact processes in the brain. Most of us have met some of these objections in our first year as philosophy students. All the more reason to take a good look at them. Others of the objections will be more recondite and subtle.

Objection 1. Any illiterate peasant can talk perfectly well about his after-images, or how things look or feel to him, or about his aches and pains, and yet he may know nothing whatever about neurophysiology. A man may, like Aristotle, believe that the brain is an organ for cooling the body without any impairment of his ability to make true statements about his sensations. Hence the things we are talking about when we describe our sensations cannot be processes in the brain.

[10] See J. H. Woodger, *Theory Construction,* International Encyclopedia of Unified Science, II, No. 5 (Chicago: University of Chicago Press, 1939), p. 38. I here permit myself to speak loosely. For warnings against possible ways of going wrong with this sort of talk, see my note "Spatialising Time," *Mind,* LXIV (1955), pp. 239–41.

Reply. You might as well say that a nation of slugabeds, who never saw the Morning Star or knew of its existence, or who had never thought of the expression "the Morning Star," but who used the expression "the Evening Star" perfectly well, could not use this expression to refer to the same entity as we refer to (and describe as) "the Morning Star." [11]

You may object that the Morning Star is in a sense not the very same thing as the Evening Star, but only something spatiotemporally continuous with it. That is, you may say that the Morning Star is not the Evening Star in the strict sense of "identity" that I distinguished earlier.

There is, however, a more plausible example. Consider lightning.[12] Modern physical science tells us that lightning is a certain kind of electrical discharge due to ionization of clouds of water vapor in the atmosphere. This, it is now believed, is what the true nature of lightning is. Note that there are not two things: a flash of lightning and an electrical discharge. There is one thing, a flash of lightning, which is described scientifically as an electrical discharge to the earth from a cloud of ionized water molecules. The case is not at all like that of explaining a footprint by reference to a burglar. We say that what lightning really is, what its true nature as revealed by science is, is an electrical discharge. (It is not the true nature of a footprint to be a burglar.)

To forestall irrelevant objections, I should like to make it clear that by "lightning" I mean the publicly observable physical object, lightning, not a visual sense-datum of lightning. I say that the publicly observable physical object lightning is in fact the electrical discharge, not just a correlate of it. The sense-datum, or rather the having of the sense-datum, the "look" of lightning, may well in my view be a correlate of the electrical discharge. For in my view it is a brain state *caused* by the lightning. But we should no more confuse sensations of lightning with lightning than we confuse sensations of a table with the table.

In short, the reply to Objection 1 is that there can be contingent statements of the form "A is identical with B," and a person may well know that something is an A without knowing that it is a B. An illiterate peasant might well be able to talk about his sensations

[11] Cf. Feigl, *op. cit.*, p. 439.
[12] See Place, *op. cit.*, p. 27, also Feigl, *op. cit.*, p. 438.

without knowing about his brain processes, just as he can talk about lightning though he knows nothing of electricity.

Objection 2. It is only a contingent fact (if it is a fact) that when we have a certain kind of sensation there is a certain kind of process in our brain. Indeed it is possible, though perhaps in the highest degree unlikely, that our present physiological theories will be as out of date as the ancient theory connecting mental processes with goings on in the heart. It follows that when we report a sensation we are not reporting a brain-process.

Reply. The objection certainly proves that when we say "I have an after-image" we cannot *mean* something of the form "I have such and such a brain-process." But this does not show that what we report (having an after-image) is not *in fact* a brain process. "I see lightning" does not *mean* "I see an electrical discharge." Indeed, it is logically possible (though highly unlikely) that the electrical discharge account of lightning might one day be given up. Again, "I see the Evening Star" does not *mean* the same as "I see the Morning Star," and yet "The Evening Star and the Morning Star are one and the same thing" is a contingent proposition. Possibly Objection 2 derives some of its apparent strength from a "Fido"—Fido theory of meaning. If the meaning of an expression were what the expression named, then of course it *would* follow from the fact that "sensation" and "brain-process" have different meanings that they cannot name one and the same thing.

Objection 3.[13] Even if Objections 1 and 2 do not prove that sensations are something over and above brain-processes, they do prove that the qualities of sensations are something over and above the qualities of brain-processes. That is, it may be possible to get out of asserting the existence of irreducibly psychic processes, but not out of asserting the existence of irreducibly psychic *properties*. For suppose we identify the Morning Star with the Evening Star. Then there must be some properties which logically imply that of being the Morning Star, and quite distinct properties which entail

[13] I think this objection was first put to me by Professor Max Black. I think it is the most subtle of any of those I have considered, and the one which I am least confident of having satisfactorily met.

that of being the Evening Star. Again, there must be some properties (for example, that of being a yellow flash) which are logically distinct from those in the physicalist story.

Indeed, it might be thought that the objection succeeds at one jump. For consider the property of "being a yellow flash." It might seem that this property lies inevitably outside the physicalist framework within which I am trying to work (either by "yellow" being an objective emergent property of physical objects, or else by being a power to produce yellow sense-data, where "yellow," in this second instantiation of the word, refers to a purely phenomenal or introspectible quality). I must therefore digress for a moment and indicate how I deal with secondary qualities. I shall concentrate on color.

First of all, let me introduce the concept of a normal percipient. One person is more a normal percipient than another if he can make color discriminations that the other cannot. For example, if A can pick a lettuce leaf out of a heap of cabbage leaves, whereas B cannot though he can pick a lettuce leaf out of a heap of beetroot leaves, then A is more normal than B. (I am assuming that A and B are not given time to distinguish the leaves by their slight difference in shape, and so forth.) From the concept of "more normal than" it is easy to see how we can introduce the concept of "normal." Of course, Eskimos may make the finest discriminations at the blue end of the spectrum, Hottentots at the red end. In this case the concept of a normal percipient is a slightly idealized one, rather like that of "the mean sun" in astronomical chronology. There is no need to go into such subtleties now. I say that "This is red" means something roughly like "A normal percipient would not easily pick this out of a clump of geranium petals though he would pick it out of a clump of lettuce leaves." Of course it does not exactly mean this: a person might know the meaning of "red" without knowing anything about geraniums, or even about normal percipients. But the point is that a person can be *trained* to say "This is red" of objects which would not easily be picked out of geranium petals by a normal percipient, and so on. (Note that even a color-blind person can reasonably assert that something is red, though of course he needs to use another human being, not just himself, as his "color meter.") This account of secondary qualities explains their unimportance in physics. For obviously the discriminations and lack of discriminations made by a very complex neurophysiological mechanism are hardly likely to correspond to simple and nonarbitrary distinctions in nature.

I therefore elucidate colors as powers, in Locke's sense, to evoke certain sorts of discriminatory responses in human beings. They are also, of course, powers to cause sensations in human beings (an account still nearer Locke's). But these sensations, I am arguing, are identifiable with brain processes.

Now how do I get over the objection that a sensation can be identified with a brain process only if it has some phenomenal property, not possessed by brain processes, whereby one-half of the identification may be, so to speak, pinned down?

Reply. My suggestion is as follows. When a person says, "I see a yellowish-orange after-image," he is saying something like this: "*There is something going on which is like what is going on when* I have my eyes open, am awake, and there is an orange illuminated in good light in front of me, that is, when I really see an orange." (And there is no reason why a person should not say the same thing when he is having a veridical sense-datum, so long as we construe "like" in the last sentence in such a sense that something can be like itself.) Notice that the italicized words, namely "there is something going on which is like what is going on when," are all quasilogical or topic-neutral words. This explains why the ancient Greek peasant's reports about his sensations can be neutral between dualistic metaphysics or my materialistic metaphysics. It explains how sensations can be brain-processes and yet how a man who reports them need know nothing about brain-processes. For he reports them only very abstractly as "something going on which is like what is going on when. . . ." Similarly, a person may say "someone is in the room," thus reporting truly that the doctor is in the room, even though he has never heard of doctors. (There are not two people in the room: "someone" *and* the doctor.) This account of sensation statements also explains the singular elusiveness of "raw feels"—why no one seems to be able to pin any properties on them.[14] Raw feels, in my view, are colorless for the very same reason that *something* is colorless. This does not mean that sensations do not have plenty of properties, for if they are brain-processes they certainly have lots of neurological properties. It only

[14] See B. A. Farrell, "Experience," *Mind*, LIX (1950), pp. 170–98.

means that in speaking of them as being like or unlike one another we need not know or mention these properties.

This, then, is how I would reply to Objection 3. The strength of my reply depends on the possibility of our being able to report that one thing is like another without being able to state the respect in which it is like. I do not see why this should not be so. If we think cybernetically about the nervous system we can envisage it as able to respond to certain likenesses of its internal processes without being able to do more. It would be easier to build a machine which would tell us, say on a punched tape, whether or not two objects were similar, than it would be to build a machine which would report wherein the similarities consisted.

Objection 4. The after-image is not in physical space. The brain-process is. So the after-image is not a brain-process.

Reply. This is an *ignoratio elenchi*. I am not arguing that the after-image is a brain-process, but that the experience of having an after-image is a brain-process. It is the *experience* which is reported in the introspective report. Similarly, if it is objected that the after-image is yellowy-orange, my reply is that it is the experience of seeing yellowy-orange that is being described, and this experience is not a yellowy-orange something. So to say that a brain-process cannot be yellowy-orange is not to say that a brain-process cannot in fact be the experience of having a yellowy-orange after-image. There is, in a sense, no such thing as an after-image or a sense-datum, though there is such a thing as the experience of having an image, and this experience is described indirectly in material object language, not in phenomenal language, for there is no such thing.[15] We describe the experience by saying, in effect, that it is like the experience we have when, for example, we really see a yellowy-orange patch on the wall. Trees and wallpaper can be green,

[15] Dr. J. R. Smythies claims that a sense-datum language could be taught independently of the material object language ("A Note on the Fallacy of the 'Phenomenological Fallacy,'" *British Journal of Psychology*, XLVIII [1957], pp. 141–44). I am not so sure of this: there must be some public criteria for a person having got a rule wrong before we can teach him the rule. I suppose someone might *accidentally* learn color words by Dr. Smythies' procedure. I am not, of course, denying that we can learn a sense-datum language in the sense that we can learn to report our experience. Nor would Place deny it.

but not the experience of seeing or imagining a tree or wallpaper. (Or if they are described as green or yellow this can only be in a derived sense.)

Objection 5. It would make sense to say of a molecular movement in the brain that it is swift or slow, straight or circular, but it makes no sense to say this of the experience of seeing something yellow.

Reply. So far we have not given sense to talk of experiences as swift or slow, straight or circular. But I am not claiming that "experience" and "brain-process" mean the same or even that they have the same logic. "Somebody" and "the doctor" do not have the same logic, but this does not lead us to suppose that talking about somebody telephoning is talking about someone over and above, say, the doctor. The ordinary man when he reports an experience is reporting that something is going on, but he leaves it open as to what sort of thing is going on, whether in a material solid medium or perhaps in some sort of gaseous medium, or even perhaps in some sort of nonspatial medium (if this makes sense). All that I am saying is that "experience" and "brain-process" may in fact refer to the same thing, and if so we may easily adopt a convention (which is not a change in our present rules for the use of experience words but an addition to them) whereby it would make sense to talk of an experience in terms appropriate to physical processes.

Objection 6. Sensations are private, brain processes are *public.* If I sincerely say, "I see a yellowish-orange after-image," and I am not making a verbal mistake, then I cannot be wrong. But I can be wrong about a brain-process. The scientist looking into my brain might be having an illusion. Moreover, it makes sense to say that two or more people are observing the same brain-process but not that two or more people are reporting the same inner experience.

Reply. This shows that the language of introspective reports has a different logic from the language of material processes. It is obvious that until the brain-process theory is much improved and widely accepted there will be no *criteria* for saying "Smith has an experience of such-and-such a sort" *except* Smith's introspective reports.

So we have adopted a rule of language that (normally) what Smith says goes.

Objection 7. I can imagine myself turned to stone and yet having images, aches, pains, and so on.

Reply. I can imagine that the electrical theory of lightning is false, that lightning is some sort of purely optical phenomenon. I can imagine that lightning is not an electrical discharge. I can imagine that the Evening Star is not the Morning Star. But it is. All the objection shows is that "experience" and "brain-process" do not have the same meaning. It does not show that an experience is not in fact a brain process.

This objection is perhaps much the same as one which can be summed up by the slogan: "What can be composed of nothing cannot be composed of anything." [16] The argument goes as follows: on the brain-process thesis the identity between the brain-process and the experience is a contingent one. So it is logically possible that there should be no brain-process, and no process of any other sort either (no heart process, no kidney process, no liver process). There would be the experience but no "corresponding" physiological process with which we might be able to identify it empirically.

I suspect that the objector is thinking of the experience as a ghostly entity. So it is composed of something, not of nothing, after all. On his view it is composed of ghost stuff, and on mine it is composed of brain stuff. Perhaps the counter-reply will be[17] that the experience is simple and uncompounded, and so it is not composed of anything after all. This seems to be a quibble, for, if it were taken seriously, the remark "What can be composed of nothing cannot be composed of anything" could be recast as an a priori argument against Democritus and atomism and for Descartes and infinite divisibility. And it seems odd that a question of this sort could be settled a priori. We must therefore construe the word "composed" in a very weak sense, which would allow us to say that even an indivisible atom is composed of something (namely, itself). The dualist cannot really say that an experience can be composed of

[16] I owe this objection to Dr. C. B. Martin. I gather that he no longer wishes to maintain this objection, at any rate in its present form.
[17] Martin did not make this reply, but one of his students did.

nothing. For he holds that experiences are something over and above material processes, that is, that they are a sort of ghost stuff. (Or perhaps ripples in an underlying ghost stuff.) I say that the dualist's hypothesis is a perfectly intelligible one. But I say that experiences are not to be identified with ghost stuff but with brain stuff. This is another hypothesis, and in my view a very plausible one. The present argument cannot knock it down a priori.

Objection 8. The "beetle in the box" objection (see Wittgenstein, *Philosophical Investigations,* § 293). How could descriptions of experiences, if these are genuine reports, get a foothold in language? For any rule of language must have public criteria for its correct application.

Reply. The change from describing how things are to describing how we feel is just a change from uninhibitedly saying "this is so" to saying "this looks so." That is, when the naïve person might be tempted to say, "There is a patch of light on the wall which moves whenever I move my eyes" or "A pin is being stuck into me," we have learned how to resist this temptation and say "It *looks as though* there is a patch of light on the wallpaper" or "It *feels as though* someone were sticking a pin into me." The introspective account tells us about the individual's state of consciousness in the same way as does "I see a patch of light" or "I feel a pin being stuck into me": it differs from the corresponding perception statement in so far as it withdraws any claim about what is actually going on in the external world. From the point of view of the psychologist, the change from talking about the environment to talking about one's perceptual sensations is simply a matter of disinhibiting certain reactions. These are reactions which one normally suppresses because one has learned that in the prevailing circumstances they are unlikely to provide a good indication of the state of the environment.[18] To say that something looks green to me is simply to say that my experience is like the experience I get when I see something that really is green. In my reply to Objection 3, I pointed out the extreme openness or generality of statements which report experiences. This explains why there is no language of private

[18] I owe this point to Place, in correspondence.

qualities. (Just as "someone," unlike "the doctor," is a colorless word.)[19]

If it is asked what is the difference between those brain processes which, in my view, are experiences and those brain processes which are not, I can only reply that it is at present unknown. I have been tempted to conjecture that the difference may in part be that between perception and reception (in D. M. MacKay's terminology) and that the type of brain process which is an experience might be identifiable with MacKay's active "matching response." [20] This, however, cannot be the whole story, because sometimes I can perceive something unconsciously, as when I take a handkerchief out of a drawer without being aware that I am doing so. But at the very least, we can classify the brain processes which are experiences as those brain processes which are, or might have been, causal conditions of those pieces of verbal behavior which we call reports of immediate experience.

I have now considered a number of objections to the brain-process thesis. I wish now to conclude with some remarks on the logical status of the thesis itself. U. T. Place seems to hold that it is a straight-out scientific hypothesis.[21] If so, he is partly right and partly wrong. If the issue is between (say) a brain-process thesis and a heart thesis, or a liver thesis, or a kidney thesis, then the issue is a purely empirical one, and the verdict is overwhelmingly in favor of the brain. The right sorts of things don't go on in the heart, liver, or kidney, nor do these organs possess the right sort of complexity of structure. On the other hand, if the issue is between a brain-or-liver-or-kidney thesis (that is, some form of materialism) on the one hand and epiphenomenalism on the other hand, then the issue is not an empirical one. For there is no conceivable experiment which could decide between materialism and epiphenomenal-

[19] The "beetle in the box" objection is, *if it is sound*, an objection to *any* view, and in particular the Cartesian one, that introspective reports are genuine reports. So it is no objection to a weaker thesis that I would be concerned to uphold, namely, that if introspective reports of "experiences" are genuinely reports, then the things they are reports of are in fact brain processes.

[20] See his article "Towards an Information-Flow Model of Human Behaviour," *British Journal of Psychology*, XLVII (1956), pp. 30–43.

[21] *Op. cit.* For a further discussion of this, in reply to the original version of the present paper, see Place's note "Materialism as a Scientific Hypothesis," *Philosophical Review*, LXIX (1960), pp. 101–04.

ism. This latter issue is not like the average straight-out empirical issue in science, but like the issue between the nineteenth-century English naturalist Philip Gosse[22] and the orthodox geologists and paleontologists of his day. According to Gosse, the earth was created about 4000 B.C. exactly as described in *Genesis,* with twisted rock strata, "evidence" of erosion, and so forth, and all sorts of fossils, all in their appropriate strata, just as if the usual evolutionist story had been true. Clearly this theory is in a sense irrefutable: no evidence can possibly tell against it. Let us ignore the theological setting in which Philip Gosse's hypothesis had been placed, thus ruling out objections of a theological kind, such as "what a queer God who would go to such elaborate lengths to deceive us." Let us suppose that it is held that the universe just *began* in 4004 B.C. with the initial conditions just everywhere as they were in 4004 B.C., and in particular that our own planet began with sediment in the rivers, eroded cliffs, fossils in the rocks, and so on. No scientist would ever entertain this as a serious hypothesis, consistent though it is with all possible evidence. The hypothesis offends against the principles of parsimony and simplicity. There would be far too many brute and inexplicable facts. Why are pterodactyl bones just as they are? No explanation in terms of the evolution of pterodactyls from earlier forms of life would any longer be possible. We would have millions of facts about the world as it was in 4004 B.C. that just have to be *accepted.*

The issue between the brain-process theory and epiphenomenalism seems to be of the above sort. (Assuming that a behavioristic reduction of introspective reports is not possible.) If it be agreed that there are no cogent philosophical arguments which force us into accepting dualism, and if the brain process theory and dualism are equally consistent with the facts, then the principles of parsimony and simplicity seem to me to decide overwhelmingly in favor of the brain-process theory. As I pointed out earlier, dualism involves a large number of irreducible psychophysical laws (whereby the "nomological danglers" dangle) of a queer sort, that just have to be taken on trust, and are just as difficult to swallow as the irreducible facts about the paleontology of the earth with which we are faced on Philip Gosse's theory.

[22] See the entertaining account of Gosse's book *Omphalos* by Martin Gardner in *Fads and Fallacies in the Name of Science,* 2nd ed. (New York: Dover, 1957), pp. 124–27.

3 *J. J. C. Smart*

Man as a Physical Mechanism

MEN AND MECHANISMS

Descartes thought that while animals were mere machines, men were machines with souls. As Ryle has put it,[1] according to Descartes man is a ghost in a machine. At first sight the mere fact of consciousness seems to prove Descartes' point. For it would seem that however complicated we made an electronic computer, for example, it would not be conscious. It would appear therefore that man differs from a physical mechanism in some very fundamental way. However, if my conclusions in the last chapter* are correct these appearances are deceptive. There would seem to be no reason why a sufficiently complex electronic gadget should not be conscious or have experiences. If consciousness is a brain process, then presumably it could also be an electronic process. Provided the electronic process were of the same pattern as the appropriate neural process, it also would be a conscious experience.

According to Ryle, Descartes is wrong on another count as well. Not only is it incorrect to think of man as a ghost in a machine,

FROM chapter VI of J. J. C. Smart, *Philosophy and Scientific Realism.* Reprinted by permission of the author and Routledge & Kegan Paul Ltd.

[1] Gilbert Ryle, *The Concept of Mind* (New York: Barnes & Noble, 1949).

* The following selection contains several references to the previous chapter in the volume from which this selection was taken, *Philosophy and Scientific Realism.* Since the arguments in "Sensations and Brain Processes," the preceding article in the present volume, are similar in many ways to the arguments in the chapter referred to by Smart, the reader may construe those references as relating to the "Brain Process" paper.—J. O'C.

it is also incorrect to think of man as a machine at all, even a ghostless one. I think that Ryle must here be thinking of rather simple mechanisms: the reasons he gives for saying that we are not machines turn on the peculiar purposefulness, appropriateness, and adaptiveness of human, and indeed animal, behavior. To say that we have a mind is to say that we behave intelligently, not that we have a soul or "ghost." But is there any reason why a machine should not have the sort of purposefulness, appropriateness, and adaptiveness that is characteristic of human beings? I shall contend that we have no reason for thinking that a machine could not have the human sort of intelligence, and therefore that the antecedent scientific plausibility of physicalism should lead us to espouse the view that men are physical mechanisms. The hypothesis that I shall put forward is an old one in that it goes back at least to La Mettrie's *L'Homme Machine*,[2] but it has been enormously strengthened by recent developments in cybernetics, the theory of self-regulating mechanisms. Let us therefore look with a critical eye at some of the arguments which have been brought up against the mechanistic theory of man.

MECHANISMS AND MACHINES

My thesis is that man is a physical mechanism, and I frequently express this loosely in the form "man is a machine." It is clearly useful to use the word "machine" in this wide sense of "physical mechanism": this use of the word has respectable ancestry, as is testified to by the phrases "l'homme machine" and "the ghost in the machine" which were quoted on the last page. It is nevertheless important to remember that this is not the colloquial use of the word "machine." It is not even the case that all of the artifacts which are mechanisms are (in the colloquial sense) "machines." It is not normal to call a watch, a telescope, a wireless set, or a howitzer a machine. Looms and printing presses are clearly machines, and so, of course, are such things as mowing machines, sewing machines, and milking machines. What is the difference between those artificial mechanisms which we call "machines" and

[2] J. O. de La Mettrie, *L'Homme Machine*, critical edition with an introductory monograph and notes by A. Vartanian (Princeton, N.J.: Princeton University Press, 1960).

those which we do not call "machines"? It is not that the machines are mechanical, full of cog wheels and the like, while the others are not. A watch has cog wheels, but it is not a machine but an instrument. A calculating machine may be purely electronic, and yet it is indubitably a machine. I suggest that we tend to call a thing a machine if it replaces men, or possibly animals, in the performance of some function. Indeed, a similar definition of "machine" has been given by Louis Couffignal in his book *Les Machines à Penser*,[3] though I think as a stipulative definition rather than as an analysis of colloquial language. The loom replaces the hand weaver, the printing press replaces the scribe, the mowing machine replaces the man with the scythe, and the milking machine takes over the job of milking the cows. On the other hand, clocks, watches, wireless sets, and telescopes do not do better what was previously done by human beings. The wireless set, for example, has a function, but it does not replace a human being in the way in which the milking machine replaces the milkmaid. An interesting case is that of the gramophone. Normally it is not usual to call gramophones "machines," but in some quarters where the gramophone is used in lieu of a dance band it is beginning to be called a "record machine." Notice also how an aeroplane used to be called "a flying machine." This was in the days when flying was a sport rather like hunting, and the aeroplane was a sort of mechanical flying horse. Now that the aeroplane is no longer a substitute for a horse, but is a conveyance like a bus, a train, or a lorry, it is no longer called "a flying machine" but "a craft." A borderline case between machines and non-machines is that of machine guns and machine tools. These are not naturally called "machines" *simplicitur* because they require not just an operator but a soldier or craftsman who exercises skill by means of them. (Like the man with the scythe rather than like the man with the mowing machine.) But a fully automatic lathe would, I imagine, come to be called "a machine" purely and simply.

If this is right, then, that the colloquial meaning of the word "machine" is "that which replaces a man or an animal in the exercise of a function," we can see that there can be something

[3] Paris: Les Editions de Minuit, 1952. Couffignal says: "Nous désignons du nom de *machine* tout ensemble . . . capable de remplacer l'homme dans l'éxecution d'un ensemble d'opérations . . . proposé par l'homme" (p. 10).

absurd in saying that men are machines. It would be absurd to say that men are artifacts which do well or quickly tasks which were previously done badly or slowly by men. This, however, is in the colloquial sense of the word "machine." If we mean by "machine" simply "physical mechanism," then it is by no means obviously absurd to say that men are machines. The human brain has sometimes been compared to an electronic computer. Now computers are machines in the colloquial sense of the word: they are artifacts which replace clerks and human calculators. They replace men in *some* of the activities which men perform. It is not surprising, therefore, that men are in many respects unlike computers. This does not prove, however, that an artifact could not be made to perform all the functions, both computational and non-computational, which men perform. Later on in this chapter we shall discuss the possibility of our one day being able to build machines which possess mathematical ingenuity. These might naturally come to be called "thinking machines": they would replace the mathematician rather than the mere calculator. Such an artifact would nevertheless not replace men in *all* the functions which they perform. It should therefore not be surprising that it would not be in all respects like a man. This, however, will not go against the view that men are machines in the non-colloquial sense of "physical mechanism." Nor is it inconsistent with the supposition that it might one day be possible, though somewhat pointless, to build an artifact which behaved in every way just like a man.

The distinction between the colloquial sense of "machine" as "artifact made to perform some human function" and the wider sense of "physical mechanism" allows us to deal with some criticisms of the cybernetic view of man. Thus, Mario Bunge, in a very acute book,[4] has pointed out that a computing machine no more performs artificial thinking than a motor car performs artificial walking. W. Mays[5] has said that calculating machines "think by proxy." Now of course a calculating machine does whatever it does (I would rather say "calculate" than "think") "by proxy," and it is like a motor car in that it does a job *for us*. But this does not

[4] Mario Bunge, *Metascientific Queries* (Springfield, Ill.: Charles C. Thomas, 1959), p. 147.
[5] W. Mays, "The Hypothesis of Cybernetics," *British Journal for the Philosophy of Science,* II (1951), pp. 249–50.

affect the question of whether some other sort of artifact could think not by proxy but on its own account. There seem to be two different reasons for saying that artifacts could not think. One is that they would lack consciousness. However, if the results of the last chapter are accepted, then it is possible that an artifact could be built which would possess consciousness. The other reason for saying that machines could not think is that they could not possess ingenuity: calculating is something done according to a routine which can be completely programmed into a machine. A good human calculator can indeed calculate without thinking what he is doing, just as he may walk to his office without thinking what he is doing. (A bad calculator may have to think, even when doing something even as routine as calculating.) Since calculating can be done without thought, it is not surprising that calculating machines do not think. What about a machine which was able to exercise ingenuity? We shall investigate shortly whether it is possible that we should one day be able to build machines which possess ingenuity.

However ingenious a machine was, in other words however much we were able to turn over to it non-routine problems which baffled us, it might still be said that such a machine would be essentially different from a man. Such a machine would just be a physical mechanism, and it has been common in recent philosophy to stress the fact that not all questions are physical questions. For example, it has been pointed out that to sign a document is not just to make certain physical *movements*. A machine could make exactly the same movements as I do in signing my name, and yet would not have signed anything. Nor would it make any difference if the machine made exactly the same movements as I do in writing *its* name, supposing it had a name. The machine would still not have signed anything. We may concede the point at once. Many of our concepts, such as those of a signature, are clearly not physical concepts but legal or sociological ones. An isolated machine could not sign a document, because the notion of signing presupposes a set of legal and sociological rules. Before a machine could sign a document it would have to belong to a society of machines. Suppose, however, that there were a group of machines which were able to communicate with one another, for example by beams of light detected by photo-electric cells. Suppose also that these machines were so complex that they had evolved, or perhaps had built in to them, a set of rules of behavior and a legal and moral terminology whereby they controlled one another's behavior. Such machines could correctly be said to sign documents. Some of the questions which these machines might ask one another, such as whether a document had been correctly signed, would not be physical questions but legal ones. No doubt, for the machines to be able to work within a legal system, they would have to be responsible agents, that is, capable of perception, of thinking, of memory, and understanding. To assert dogmatically that a machine is not capable of all of these is simply to beg the issues in question in this chapter and in the previous chapter. It is not at all necessary for me to accept the view that signing is analyzable wholly in terms of physical movements of the hand. The right things would have to go on in the central nervous system or the electronic "brain," and the right sort of legal or quasi-legal conventions would have to be in existence. The machines would be machines none the less. The remark, therefore, that not all questions are physical questions is irrelevant to the problem of whether men are or are not machines, in the sense of physical mechanisms. This should not surprise us. How many philosophical mechanists, even those of the crude nineteenth-century variety, would have wished to say that legal questions are physical questions?

PROBLEM-SOLVING INGENUITY

We must now consider in what way it might be possible to build ingenuity into a machine. One particularly instructive type of ingenuity is the problem-solving ingenuity required in mathematics. Some mathematical questions, such as a problem in long division, can be answered in a routine way, without the need for ingenuity. For such problems we have an algorithm or set of rules, which always tells us what to do next. Algorithms can be programmed into computing machines. The application of an algorithm can be very tedious for human beings, and moreover, a machine, because of its colossal speed of operations, is able to answer questions which it would take years, or even more than a lifetime, for human beings to answer. There are, however, problems in mathematics for which there are no algorithms. Indeed, it can be proved for certain mathematical theories that not only has no algorithm or "decision procedure" been discovered for them but that there is none to be discovered. Logicians used to have to use ingenuity to prove theorems in the propositional calculus, but later it was discovered that an algorithmic method, namely the method of the truth tables, enabled us to check in a purely routine way whether or not a proposition was a theorem of the propositional calculus. Might the same thing one day happen in interesting branches of mathematics? It has been proved that this is not so. For these branches of mathematics no decision procedure will ever be found. Alonzo Church proved that even for the predicate calculus in logic there could be no decision procedure.[6] A machine which proved theorems in such a theory would certainly possess what in human beings we call ingenuity. Moreover, it would be natural, if we had such a machine, to call it a thinking machine. In a very real sense it would do our thinking for us, just as a milking machine milks our cows for us. Such a thinking machine would possess originality of the sort we ascribe to bright students or research workers, who have the knack of solving mathematical problems, though it would fall far short of the sort of creativeness possessed by men who create new branches of mathematics.

To fix our ideas, let us consider the possibility of making a machine which would be able to prove Fermat's last theorem, if indeed this theorem is provable. The case is peculiarly instructive, because at present we do not know whether the theorem *is* provable, or even whether it is true. It is also instructive because in spite of the difficulty, or perhaps impossibility, of proving it the proposition is very easy to state and to understand. It is a proposition of elementary number theory, the theory of the natural numbers 0, 1, 2, 3, ... The theorem is to the effect if x, y, z are integers and if n is an integer greater than 2, it is never the case that $x^n + y^n = z^n$. No integers for which $x^n + y^n = z^n$ and $n > 2$ have in fact been discovered, and most mathematicians would be prepared to guess that the theorem is in fact true. However, no proof of the theorem has ever been found, unless possibly by Fermat, the great seventeenth-century mathematician who conjectured the proof. He asserted in the margin of a book he had been reading

[6] For a survey of such questions see Martin Davis, *Computability and Unsolvability* (New York: McGraw-Hill, 1958).

that he had discovered a proof, but died without having disclosed the proof. Let us suppose that Fermat's theorem is true, and let us, furthermore, suppose for the sake of simplicity that there is a proof of it expressible entirely within elementary number theory. (It might, of course, turn out to be provable, but provable only within a wider system, such as the theory of the real numbers, even though it itself is a proposition expressible in elementary number theory. But let us for the present purposes suppose that there is a proof using only concepts of elementary number theory.) On these assumptions there is indeed a sense in which it is possible that a computer should discover the proof. Consider a rigidly formalized system of elementary number theory. It would be possible to program a computer so that it could check whether a given string of symbols constituted a sequence of well-formed sentences of the formalized system, and if it did whether it constituted a proof of Fermat's last theorem. This corresponds to the familiar fact that it is a routine matter to check whether a putative proof is a proof or not, whereas it is not a routine matter to discover such a proof.

The machine could now be set to check all sequences of symbols of length one (*i.e.* of one symbol only), then all sequences of length two, then all sequences of length three, and so on. (We can suppose all sequences of equal length to be ordered lexicographically.) If there is a proof within elementary number theory of Fermat's last theorem the machine will eventually come to it. On the other hand, if there is no proof the machine will go on for ever and we shall never know whether this is because there is no proof or whether it is because the machine has not gone on for long enough. We might try to get over this by programming the machine to test each string of symbols for being either a proof or a disproof. Even so, there might remain the possibility that the theorem is neither provable nor disprovable. Nevertheless, the human mathematician would be in as bad a fix, wondering whether he should give up his quest.

The above method of searching for the proof will, as I said, ultimately produce the proof if there is a proof to be found. But it is necessary to point out that this is so only for an idealized machine given infinite time to play with. No actual machine can keep going indefinitely: it will wear out. Moreover, we want to get a proof in a reasonable time: even the next million years is too long for us. It should be clear that ingenious human mathematicians must get their proofs by a very different method from our machine. Suppose that the alphabet in which we express elementary number theory contains 10 symbols. Then in order to test all sequences of symbols 1000 symbols long the machine would have to test 10^{1000} sequences, which would take even the fastest electronic computer far longer than the whole past history of the universe (5×10^9 years) according to one plausible cosmological hypothesis. Of course it is true that the above procedure could be drastically shortened. In many cases, for example, the machine would have to examine only one or two symbols of a sequence to rule out the possibility of the sequence constituting a sequence of well-informed sentences (and hence of constituting a proof of the theorem). Nevertheless, even with such drastic short cuts built in, it is probable that any such machine would take an impracticably long time by human standards.

How does the human problem solver do his job? The psychology of mathematical inventiveness is a little-understood subject: advances in the psychology of thinking and in the mechanization of thought processes are likely to come about through mutual influences between these subjects. But one obvious suggestion comes to mind. The mathematician who is casting about, trying to find the proof of some theorem, is likely to use strategies of proof which have worked in the past and to try small variations on them. To do this he must be able to recognize patterns and symmetries in formulae. Sometimes, for example, a tentatively chosen expression (say as a possible true lemma which may, if it can be proved, serve as a step towards the theorem to be proved) will be replaced by a more symmetrical or otherwise "pretty" looking one. It is not out of the question that a machine should be built to do all of these things.[7] Computers can already be programmed so as to learn from their mistakes. The problem of devising mechanical methods of shape recognition has in great part been solved, and so there seems no reason in principle why a machine should not be able to look out for,

[7] For recent thinking in this sort of direction see Dr. Marvin L. Minsky's article, "Some methods of artificial intelligence and heuristic programming," National Physical Laboratory Symposium on *Mechanisation of Thought Proccesses*, I (London: Her Majesty's Stationery Office, 1959), pp. 5–27. Many other papers and discussions in this symposium are also relevant to the present topic.

and profit from, symmetry and other *gestalt* properties of symbolic expressions. If the reader objects to the words "recognition" and "look out for" on the ground that these imply consciousness, let him for the moment replace them by suitable behavioristic equivalents. The problem of consciousness is not at issue in the present argument, though I should remind the reader that if the last chapter is on the right lines it should be possible, though unnecessary, to build consciousness into a machine. The problem of consciousness will be taken up again later in this chapter.

We may hope, then, that one day, by making use of abilities to learn from previous experience, and hence the ability to develop heuristic techniques, aided perhaps by the ability to recognize patterns and symmetries, we shall be able to construct a proof-finding machine. This machine, unlike the ordinarily programmed computer, would be non-moronic. It would possess abilities, which if found in a human being would be taken as evidence of intelligence and originality. Let us call the problem of designing such a machine the *ingenuity problem*. That we are at present very far from having solved the ingenuity problem is incontestable. Nevertheless, it is equally true to say that the progress we have made, and are likely to make, in this direction is far from negligible. There are certainly no cogent *a priori* arguments why the ingenuity problem should not be solvable. Philosophers in the past have been far too ready to say what could not be done. Not so long ago they frequently said that purposiveness could not be built into a machine, and yet nowadays purposive mechanisms are a commonplace of engineering, for example in the field of self-guided missiles. In the 1920s the psychologist William McDougall used to propound an animistic theory, the "hormic theory," to account for all types of purposiveness and adaptiveness, whether in human beings or in animals.[8] I suggest that anyone who takes a similar attitude with regard to *ingenuity* may find himself looking equally foolish.

If the ingenuity problem comes to be solved we shall have a complete reply to one possible argument against the mechanistic theory of mind. This objection stems from Church's theorem in mathematical logic. Church's theorem is to the effect that there is no decision procedure or algorithm for deciding whether or not any given sentence of the predicate calculus is a theorem of that calculus. (For those

[8] W. McDougall, *Outline of Psychology*, 13th ed. (London: Methuen, 1949), pp. 71–73.

readers who are unversed in logic, it does not matter for our present purposes what exactly the predicate calculus is. However, it is the most important part of logic, and with the addition of suitable axioms, *e.g.* for set theory, can be used to formalize any interesting mathematical theory.) A computing machine could indeed be programmed in such a way that it churned out theorems in the predicate calculus, and so, if it were given as much time as it wanted, it would eventually produce a proof of any given theorem of the predicate calculus. However, if a given sentence has not been churned out we do not know whether this is because the sentence is not a theorem or whether it is simply because the machine has not come to it yet. The machine will therefore tell us whether a given sentence is a theorem, if it is one, but it will be unable to tell us that a sentence is not a theorem if it is not one. It is possible to remedy this situation by adding on to our theorem churning machine another machine which churns out non-theorems. It can be proved, and is indeed a corollary of Church's theorem, that there could never be a non-theorem churning machine. This is in the very same sense that we could not square the circle. There is a demonstrable mathematical impossibility in the idea of a computer which simply churns out non-theorems of the predicate calculus. We can put this by saying that whereas the class of theorems of the predicate calculus is "canonical," the class of non-theorems is not canonical.

Often we can be either completely or pretty well convinced that a sentence of the predicate calculus is not a theorem: we may either have disproved it or we may, despite much ingenuity, have failed to prove it. With the mere machine which churns out theorems we cannot be so convinced. Maybe the sentence in which we are interested will be churned out, but not for millions of years yet. Indeed, with the churning-out machine we might not get many proofs of interesting theorems within a reasonable stretch of time. But if the ingenuity problem could be solved for machines a machine could be in as good a position as we are for discovering theorems and non-theorems of the predicate calculus. That is, in many cases it might be able to discover interesting theorems and non-theorems in a reasonable period of time. And if it failed to prove a theorem in a reasonable period of time it could put out as a "guess" that the theorem was not provable.

THE ARGUMENT FROM GÖDEL

Some writers, such as P. Rosenbloom,[9] J. G. Kemeny,[10] E. Nagel and J. R. Newman,[11] and, most recently, J. R. Lucas,[12] have argued that another famous theorem in mathematical logic, namely Gödel's theorem, shows, in a different way, that men are not machines. For short I shall call this argument 'the argument from Gödel'. It should be emphasized that this argument is a philosophical one based on Gödel's theorem, and I have no idea whether Gödel himself would wish to see his theorem used in this way. Gödel's theorem has an implication with respect to most parts of mathematics which is similar to that which Church's theorem has with respect to the predicate calculus, and the reply we must make is here similar to that which we made in the last paragraph. But Gödel's theorem raises, in the view of writers such as those whom I have just mentioned, another difficulty. This objection goes as follows. Gödel has shown that for any formalization of elementary number theory (the theory concerned only with the natural numbers 0, 1, 2, 3, etc.) there will be a sentence which is neither provable nor disprovable within the system. However, *we*, by means of an argument in the metalanguage, in which we talk not *with*, but *about*, the formal system, can show that this sentence is true. Thus, it would appear that no matter how many axioms and rules we program into a computing machine there will always be some sentence which the human being can prove, but the machine cannot.

The solution of the ingenuity problem would not by itself enable us to get round the above difficulty. The solution of the ingenuity problem only enables us to design a machine which will probably do in some specified finite time a task which the moronic machine could certainly do if given infinite time, *i.e.* as much time as it needed. The argument from Gödel's theorem purports to show that there is something that we can do and which the moronic machine could not do

[9] P. Rosenbloom, *Elements of Symbolic Logic* (New York: Dover, 1951), p. 208.
[10] J. G. Kemeny, *A Philosopher Looks at Science* (Princeton, N.J.: Van Nostrand, 1959), p. 224.
[11] E. Nagel and J. R. Newman, *Gödel's Proof* (London: Routledge & Kegan Paul, 1959), pp. 100–101.
[12] J. R. Lucas, "Minds, Machines and Gödel," *Philosophy*, XXXVI (1961), pp. 112–27.

even in infinite time. Equally, therefore, a non-moronic machine could not do it. The argument would seem to show, therefore, that we are not machines—not even non-moronic machines of the sort we envisaged when we considered the ingenuity problem.

The argument goes as follows. Consider some formal language L_0 adequate for elementary number theory. Gödel has shown that if L_0 is consistent then there is some closed arithmetical sentence[13] expressible in the symbolism of L_0 which cannot be proved or disproved in L_0. By reasoning which makes use of the syntax language of L_0, however, we can show that this proposition which is undecidable within L_0 is in fact true. (The syntax language of a language L is the language in which are expressed the axioms and rules of L. The syntax language could itself be axiomatized. In the present case "semantics language" might be a better term than "syntax language," since the language must be able to define "true.") Though a computing machine T_0 can be specified which will prove or disprove all provable or disprovable sentences of L_0 it will not, even given infinite time, prove the Gödelian undecidable sentence of L_0 which nevertheless *we*, by ascent to the syntax language, can show to be true. Of course, by adjoining the syntax language of L_0 to L_0 we get a more powerful language L_1: corresponding to which there will be a machine T_1, which given infinite time could prove or disprove all the decidable propositions of L_1, including the already mentioned undecidable sentence of L_0. Nevertheless, there will similarly be some Gödelian undecidable proposition of L_1, which we can prove by ascending to the syntax language of L_1. And so on. It looks as though however far we go up the sequence of languages L_0, L_1, L_2, . . . and of the corresponding machines T_0, T_1, T_2, . . . there will always be some proposition which the machine cannot prove (even given infinite time) but which we can prove.

The rule for constructing the sequence of languages L_0, L_1, L_2, . . . could even be built into a machine. This would be a machine T_ω corresponding to a language L_ω. Nevertheless, in L_ω there would

[13] A closed arithmetical sentence is one without free variables. Thus "for any x and any y, $x + y \geqslant x$" is a closed sentence of elementary number theory. "$x < 7$" is not a closed sentence. It contains the free variable "x." It is rather trivial that such sentences containing free variables are neither provable nor disprovable in elementary number theory. They do not express truths or falsehoods, though they are *true of* some numbers, *false of* others. "$x < 7$" is true of 6, false of 8. We can think of an open sentence as a predicate.

be an undecidable sentence provable only in a language $L_{1+\omega}$. The process could indeed be carried on through the constructible ordinals. So equally is it with the human being. We must note that any one of our languages must contain an axiom to the effect that the language next lower down the hierarchy is consistent. But what is our justification for adding such an axiom? Of course, you can bet your boots that elementary number theory is consistent, but betting your boots is not the same proof. In the previous paragraph I have talked of "proving" the truth of the undecidable sentence of L_0 by ascending to the syntax language of L_0. But since such a proof would need such an axiom as "that L_0 is consistent," it would be better to say simply that by an argument in the syntax language we "convince ourselves" that the undecidable sentence is true. We are here concerned with something less than rigorous proof, for we do not know that arithmetic is consistent. I neglect here, however, the technical and controversial question of how much weight should be put on Gentzen's proof of the consistency of arithmetic, which makes use of so-called *transfinite* methods. It will not affect the goodness or badness of the solution to our problem which I propose in the next section.

AN INDUCTIVE MACHINE

If we became able to solve the ingenuity problem, discussed earlier in this chapter, we should be able to design a machine, which when programmed to prove and disprove propositions in a language *L*, could by observation of its own linguistic behavior ascertain the syntactical and semantical rules of *L*. This ascertainment would, of course, be inductive in nature, and so would not be possessed of full mathematical rigor. (I am here using "inductive" in the sense in which we contrast "inductive" and "deductive" logic, not in the sense of "mathematical induction.") However, in this respect the machine would be neither better nor worse off than a human being. It is true that in some cases the syntax and semantics of a language L_n is given in a language L_{n+1} in the form of explicit rules, but then the syntax and semantics of L_{n+1} must be known intuitively or given in the form of rules expressed in a language L_{n+2}, and so on. Sooner or later we must stop at a language whose rules are known "intuitively," which means in fact that they have to be ascertained, perhaps unconsciously, by empirical observation of linguistic behavior. This empirical ascertainment of the rules of language (whether in the human being or the machine) is, mathematically speaking, a bit of "cheating," and this provides a way of getting round the argument from Gödel. Suppose that we have a machine programmed for a language L_0 and also with built into it a capacity to learn empirically such things as the rules of its own behavior. By ascertaining the rules of its own language L_0 it can convert itself into an L_1 machine, and hence it can go on to ascertain the rules of L_1 and convert itself into an L_2 machine, and so it can go up the hierarchy of languages as long as the capacity of its storage units is not exhausted. Until this point is reached it can convert itself from an L_n machine to an L_{n+1} machine, so that it is then able to prove the Gödelian undecidable sentence of L_n. At any moment there will be true propositions which it cannot prove, but which it can prove at a later moment when it has converted itself to a machine of greater logical power. Ultimately it will exhaust its storage capacity, but equally the human being will also, literally, become exhausted.

This method of getting round the argument from Gödel seems to me to be a perfectly plausible one.[14] It depends on the possibility of machines which can learn from experience. It is admittedly beyond our present technological powers to make a machine of the sort required, but there does not seem to me to be any *a priori* or physical reason why such a machine should not exist.

CREATIVITY AND FREEDOM

Nothing that has been said so far bears on the question of whether a machine could be capable of the higher flights of mathematical creativity. Solution of the ingenuity problem would enable us, in theory at least, to design a problem-solving machine. Now a machine which was able to produce for us a proof of some well-known unproved theorem, such as Fermat's last theorem, would indeed do something which, if it were done by a human being, would be deserving of very high honor. Nevertheless, even this sort of feat would not be regarded by most mathematicians as comparable to that of inaugurating a new branch of mathematics, such as, for example, the Galois theory of

[14] Since writing this I have noticed a hint in the same direction in F. H. George, *The Brain as a Computer* (London: Pergamon Press, 1961), p. 3, and in his *Cognition* (London: Methuen, 1962), p. 209.

equations or the theory of recursive functions. Those mathematicians who invent, or help to invent, such quite new branches of mathematics are possessed of a creativity of a very high order. Nevertheless, the mere fact that at present we do not know how to make a machine with creativity of this sort does not provide a very strong argument that machines with this sort of creativity are impossible. After all, it is not so long since purposive mechanisms or machines which are capable of shape recognition, such as the new machines which can scan a printed page and feed the equivalent of the letters on it directly into a computer, would have seemed quite inconceivable. There are certainly no apparently knock-down arguments like the arguments from Church's theorem and from Gödel's theorem, and we have seen cause to reject these. Unless an argument is a cogent *a priori* one of this sort it seems to be no better than an appeal to our present technological ignorance. Its propounders may be no better based than those who denied the possibility of a heavier-than-air flying machine.

We must agree, nevertheless, that there is often much loose talk about computers.[15] As a reply to such loose talk, it may be said that a machine does not calculate: it is we who calculate by means of it. It is indeed a valid point that what we ordinarily call "calculating" is: (*a*) something which we do consciously, and (*b*) something which is set in the context of our whole language and way of life. This certainly shows that our ordinary calculating machines do not really "calculate," but it does not prove that a more complex machine, which was (*a*) conscious and (*b*) capable of subtle linguistic and interpersonal (or inter-machine) behavior, could not properly be said to do so. Again, consider the notion of "reading." It is, in a sense, incorrect to say that existing "reading machines" really read. Consider a machine which is able to scan a printed page and feed the sequence of letters on it into a computer in the form of series of electrical impulses. This is not truly a reading machine if the connotation of "reading" includes that of "understanding" or even "consciousness." But it would be doing that part of reading which is done by a person who reads a novel to a dim-sighted friend, yet so inattentively that he is not conscious of the words he is reading. Such a person would indeed be doing little more than converting the printed symbols into the appropriate sounds. (At any rate if the words were written in a

[15] As pointed out by Bunge, *op. cit.*

phonetic alphabet: to build a machine which would do the same with ordinary written English would be more difficult.) The exaggerations of the cyberneticians who use psychological vocabulary in connection with computers and the like should not cause us to go to the opposite extreme and deny that such psychological language could be perfectly applied to a sufficiently complex machine.

Sometimes it is felt that our alleged immediate intuition of freedom in action is incompatible with the idea of man as a machine. However, I see no absurdity in the conception of a machine which has free will. That is a machine might make use of the information at its disposal to compute what its next move should be, and might be made so as to put the result of this computation into execution. Such a machine would do something equivalent to deliberation in any sense in which this concept is at all clear.

Why is it that we find it useful to distinguish some acts as "free" and others as "not free"? Consider a very simple case. Suppose young Tommy has not done his homework, and the teacher has to decide whether to punish him or not. It may be that Tommy has not done his homework because he is too stupid. Then there is no point in punishing him or blaming him. Caning a stupid boy does not make him less stupid. On the other hand, Tommy may not have done his homework because he was lazy. In this case the teacher might quite reasonably punish him. The threat of punishment can make a lazy boy less lazy. Similar considerations apply in the case of physical restraints. If a man does not come home to dinner on time because he gets stuck in a lift there is not much point in his wife expostulating with him. He will as a result be no more likely in future to extricate himself from encarceration. But if a man is late for dinner because he called at a bar, then there is some point in his wife's expostulation. Maybe it will tend to make him mend his ways. (Of course, if expostulation drives him all the more into bars, then it would equally be reasonable for the wife to cease her nagging!) Similar considerations explain why it may be reasonable to treat as not guilty those men who commit crimes as a result of some mental disease. If a man commits a crime because he is an extreme paranoiac, then there is little point in punishing him. Rational considerations, threats, and the like will not have the least effect on him, nor will his punishment have an effect (as an example) on other paranoiacs. Non-paranoiacs, of course, will not be reassured, because they will know that they have no such let-out themselves. A lot of the provisions in ordinary criminal law can be made intelligible in this sort of way. Perhaps not all can be, because law depends partly on tradition and common feeling, and so may not always be rationally justifiable.

In the above ways, then, we can make a perfectly sensible distinction between free and unfree actions, and this distinction is in great part co-extensive with that which is made in common life by unreflecting people. This distinction is by no means incompatible with determinism. It is because reasoning, persuasion, and threats can be causal factors in determining human behavior that it is reasonable to reason, to persuade, and to threaten. Consider now an electric machine which was so complex that it could be influenced by reason, persuasion, or threats. Such a machine might be deterministic. If it were, and if we could have complete knowledge of the characteristics of the machine and of the information being fed into it, we could predict what it would do.[16] Alternatively, we could conceive of an unpredictable machine. Suppose it contained a Geiger counter whereby it was able to pick up isolated chance effects on the quantum level, and that as a result its behavior was partly undetermined. Such a machine would be like the human being according to those philosophers who have thought that the indeterminacy of quantum mechanics provided a loop-hole for free will in human beings. Such philosophers make several mistakes. The first is the mistake of supposing that the human brain is likely to be triggered off by effects on the quantum level. Even a single neuron is a huge macroscopic object by the standards of quantum mechanics, and furthermore, the failure to fire of an odd neuron is unlikely to affect behavior. There is almost certainly a great deal of redundancy in the human brain, and any thought or action almost certainly depends on the mass behavior of a large number of neurons.[17] This sort of redundancy is in fact, to a much lesser extent, built

[16] Unless it is in strong interaction with us—in which case it would be influenced by our predictions, and interesting logical difficulties arise. See K. R. Popper, "Indeterminism in Quantum Physics and in Classical Physics," *British Journal for the Philosophy of Science*, I (1950–51), pp. 117–33 and 173–95. See also G. F. Dear, "Determinism in Classical Physics," *ibid.*, II (1960–61), pp. 289–304.

[17] As D. M. MacKay has pointed out in his talk "Brain and Will," *Listener*, LVII (1957), pp. 788–89.

into certain computing machines, when it is necessary that they should work in a reliable way even though they have unreliable components.

If we think of the human brain as a machine it is plausible to think of it as a deterministic machine. Actually the operation of a deterministic machine could be quite indistinguishable from that of an indeterministic machine. Consider first an indeterministic machine which behaved in one or another of two ways according to whether it did or did not pick up some indeterministic quantum effect for which the probability was ½. Consider, secondly, an exactly similar machine, except that instead of having a device for picking up a quantum effect whose probability was ½ it had a device for scanning a table of random numbers and that it behaved in one or another of two ways according to whether the number scanned was odd or even. The behavior of the two machines would be quite indistinguishable.

If a machine is capable of making choices and of being influenced by punishment and reward, then it has in essence all that is needed for free will.

In the case of free actions, in the above sense, we say that a man "could have" done otherwise. What does "could have" mean here? There is admittedly a *possible* sense in which we might use the words "could have," according to which a man, if he is a deterministic mechanism, could not have done otherwise than he in fact has done. The sense is that from a precise description of the initial conditions (the input to his sense organs and his present brain state) and of the mode of functioning of his nervous system, it could in principle be deduced what his immediate action would be. Indeed, if the universe as a whole were deterministic, then Laplace's superhuman calculator[18] could from a complete description of its state at time t_0 and from a knowledge of sufficient laws of nature predict what its state will be at any other time t_1. In this sense of "could have" a man perhaps could never do other than he in fact does. But is this strained and metaphysical sense of "could have" the one which is important when we ordinarily talk of free will, when we say that on some occasions a man could have done otherwise than he in fact did?

[18] Marquis P. S. de Laplace, A *Philosophical Essay on Probabilities*, translated from the 6th French edition by F. W. Truscott and F. L. Emory (New York: Dover, 1951), p. 4.

I suggest that in the contexts in which we ordinarily say that a man "could have" or "could not have done otherwise" we are using "could have" in quite another sense. This other, common, non-metaphysical sense of "could have" may be elucidated by means of the following example. Suppose that I drop an ink pot on to the floor. For some reason it does not break. I say: "It did not break, and what's more, it could have broken." A stone, however, "could not have broken." What is the difference here? The difference is that within a very wide range of initial conditions I can predict that the stone will not break. Whether it falls on a sharp end or on a blunt face, whether it is dropped from two feet or ten feet, whether it is dropped with a spinning motion, or without a spinning motion, it still will not break. With the ink pot, in some cases it will break and in some cases it will not break. It may be that in some cases we are unable to predict whether it will break or not. It depends on what *exactly* the initial conditions are. Of course, a sufficiently knowledgeable and powerful calculator who knew the exact elasticity and strength of the glass of the ink pot, the exact velocity with which it leaves my hand as it is dropped, the exact distance to the ground, and so on, could perhaps in *every* case predict whether it will break or not. The words "it could have broken" and "it could not have broken" are useful simply because of our imprecise knowledge of initial conditions and of our limited powers of computation. In the case of the stone even we can predict that it will not break. Within a fairly wide margin of error, here, the initial conditions do not matter.

I suggest that the "could have" in "he could have done otherwise" is analogous to the "could have" in "the ink pot could have broken." There is a slight qualification to be made to this. It is as natural to say that "the ink pot *might* have broken" as it is to say that "it *could* have broken." But it is more natural to say that a criminal "could have" behaved virtuously than it is to say simply that he "might have" done so. The difference is, I suggest, as follows. The initial conditions which are unknown to us are of two sorts. In the first place, there are those which make up the external stimuli. In the second place, there are those which specify a person's internal state. It is when our ability to predict, on the basis of a set of initial conditions, what a man will do, is due to unsureness about the *internal* initial conditions that we tend to say "could have." "Could," unlike "might," carries suggestions of the possibility of internal effort.[19] Whether the ink pot breaks or not depends on the precise motions with which we dropped it and the precise characteristics of the floor on which it falls. With "he could have done otherwise" we are presupposing not only a range of possible external initial conditions but also that the internal state of the man may vary from time to time. An additional uncertainty has crept in. But to admit this is in no way to say anything incompatible with the possibility that men are deterministic mechanisms.

One of the sorts of variable initial condition that may perhaps determine a man to do one action rather than another are social pressures such as threats and promises, praise and blame. This is why the question of whether or not a man "could have done otherwise" is important in practical ethics and in criminal law. Once more we have nothing incompatible with the view of man as a deterministic machine.[20]

A special case of the view I have been concerned to refute, namely that determinism is incompatible with free will, is the contention that if determinism is true our assertions occur only because of *causes*, and not because they are based on *good reasons*. As a corollary it has sometimes been asserted that naturalism is self-refuting.[21] It has been argued that if a complete causal explanation of human behavior were possible, then if this behavior were a piece of so-called reasoning we should have no reason to accept its conclusion. For it is well known that when we find that someone has said something because he has been hypnotized to do so, or because he has a lesion in his brain, or because he is feeling liverish, we discount what he says. In short, when we are able to give a causal explanation of a person's verbal behavior we regard it as irrational and we regard his conclusions as unfounded. Saying something because of causes therefore seems to be incompatible with saying something because of reasons. Now if nat-

[19] See D. J. O'Connor, "Possibility and Choice," *Aristotelian Society Supplementary Volume 34* (1960), pp. 1–24, esp. p. 19.

[20] See R. E. Hobart, "Free Will as Involving Determinism," *Mind*, XLIII (1934), pp. 1–27.

[21] As by J. B. S. Haldane, *Possible Worlds* (London: Evergreen, 1940), p. 209, and by C. S. Lewis, *Miracles* (London: Bles, 1947), ch. 3. But later repudiated by Haldane in "I Repent an Error," *Literary Guide* (April, 1954). For further criticism of the argument see A. G. N. Flew, "The Third Maxim," *Rationalist Annual* (1955), pp. 63–66. Further discussion by E. Gellner, "Determinism and Validity," *ibid.* (1957), pp. 68–79, Flew, "Determinism and Validity Again," *ibid.* (1958), pp. 39–51.

uralism were true the naturalist's own arguments would be determined by material causes in his brain, not by reasons. So if naturalism is true we have no reason to believe in the validity of the naturalist's argument that it is true, and the argument is therefore self-refuting.

The fallacy in the above reasoning consists in the supposition that if a complete causal explanation of behavior is possible, then that behavior must be irrational, *i.e.* in the supposition that acting from causes and acting from reasons are mutually exclusive.

How do we decide whether an argument is based on *good reasons*? We apply various tests for validity. Thus, if a man says that most of the students in the university like sport and that most of them work hard, and that therefore most of the students both like sport and work hard, we refute him by pointing out that the inference does not hold, perhaps by citing an example of an inference which is of the same form and which has true premises but a false conclusion. (For example: most of the positive integers less than ten are greater than four, and most of the positive integers less than ten are less than six, but it is not the case that most of the positive integers less than ten are both greater than four and less than six.) In refuting the man in this way we do not in the least concern ourselves with the causes or lack of causes of his making his inference.

Why, then, do we sometimes discount a person's remark because we can assign some cause for it, such as hypnotism, neurosis, a bad liver, or a lesion of the brain? It is surely because we have noticed that frequently these conditions are associated with irrationality. To have made this discovery we must have had *independent* criteria of rationality and irrationality. Presumably in a great many cases, when people do not have bad livers, brain lesions, neuroses, or post-hypnotic states, but have, it may be, red hair and freckles, they argue quite correctly. That is, we find no correlation between red hair and irrationality or between freckles and irrationality. Moreover, conditions such as hypnotism and brain lesions only lead us to *suspect* irrationality: however bad a man's brain lesion was or however much he had been hypnotized, if we checked his argument and found that it obeyed the laws of logic and had well-attested premises we should have to pay as much attention to it as if it had been propounded by anyone else.

If determinism is true, then all arguments are caused. From this it follows that some causally determined arguments must be good arguments. For among these causally determined arguments must be some which have passed the independent tests for rationality. It follows that the argument that naturalism is self-refuting is not valid. This may forcibly be brought out by comparing correct deduction with correct computation. Consider an adding machine which is set to add 137 to 428. If it functions correctly it will produce the answer 565. But of course it may not function correctly. A tooth may be missing from a certain gear wheel, and in consequence it may produce the answer 555. A causal explanation of the failure will be quite easy. On the other hand, if we know the way in which the machine is constructed we can equally give a causal explanation of its success if no tooth is missing and it *does* produce the answer 565. If it were not for these causes it would not function correctly. Even if we do not have a full understanding of the working of a machine we may still suspect that it will function incorrectly if we find a tooth missing on a certain cog wheel. We may have observed in the past that machines with such a tooth missing have often given wrong answers. Similarly, we may have observed that the political prognostications of liverish men are frequently unreliable. This does not mean that there is not some causal explanation of the correct prognostications of normal men, any more than the fact that the missing tooth provides a causal explanation of the malfunctioning of the adding machine implies that there is no causal explanation of the correct functioning of a good adding machine. The moral for the argument that naturalism is self-refuting should be obvious.

When a mathematical logician theorizes about computing machines he discusses idealised machines called Turing[22] machines. These could in principle be realized in a number of ways, either electronically or mechanically (with toothed wheels and so on) or even as a cardboard "toy," or as human beings proceeding according to rigidly laid down rules. The actual "hardware" or physical realization is mathematically irrelevant. What matters is that there should be a number of states, a tape that can be scanned, and rules to the effect that if such and such a symbol is on the scanned part of the tape the machine proceeds to move to the right or left or stay put, to erase the symbol or print such and such a new one, and to change into a new state. The whole

[22] After A. M. Turing. See his paper "On Computable Numbers, with an Application to the Entscheidungsproblem," *Proceedings of the London Mathematical Society*, Series 2, XLII (1937), pp. 230–65; Correction, *ibid.*, XLIII (1937), pp. 544–46.

arithmetical notion of computability can be mirrored in terms of such machine states and machine instructions. Hilary Putnam has called machine states as thus abstractly defined "logical states," and has suggested that old-fashioned introspective psychology was really an attempt to discover a theory of the mind in terms of logical states. These logical states are not non-physical or "ghostly" states: they are abstractions from the physical and from the non-physical too. (Even immaterial souls could function as Turing machines.) The logical states are simply neutral between various possible realizations: the fact that we might discuss the mind in terms of such logical states no more implies that the mind is not a function of the physical than does the possibility of treating an electronic computer as though it were an abstract Turing machine imply that the computer is not a piece of solid hardware. Putnam interestingly suggests that introspective psychology did not fail, as has often been thought, because of methodological reasons: it failed for empirical reasons—as he says "the mental states and 'impressions' of human beings do not form a causally closed system to the extent to which the 'configurations' of a Turing machine do." [23] (It is hard to treat the human brain as a computer, partly because of its immense complexity, but mainly because of the continual stream of incoming "information," so that its "program" is continually changing.)

The possibility of a "logical description" of a computer does not confer a ghost on the computer. It is tempting to think that the mind-body problem is an outcome of the same sort of confusion as we would get if we confused the "logical" and "physical" descriptions of a computing machine. Nevertheless, there is the additional trouble of dealing with *consciousness*. I hope, however, that this was dealt with, with some approximation to satisfactoriness, in our previous chapter. . . .

[23] Hilary Putnam, "Minds and Machines," in Sidney Hook, ed., *Dimensions of Mind* (New York: Collier, 1961), pp. 138–64. This also contains an elegant refutation, different from mine, of the argument from Gödel. My solution, though mathematically less satisfying, can perhaps be defended as being probably more closely related to the way in which the human brain actually works. A rather different argument, of the "mathematical" sort, has been suggested to me by W. V. Quine. See the last paragraph of my paper "Gödel's Theorem, Church's Theorem, and Mechanism," *Synthese*, XIII (1961), pp. 105–10.

4 *Norman Malcolm*

Scientific Materialism and the Identity Theory

Norman Malcolm was born on June 11, 1911, in Selden, Kansas. He was educated at the University of Nebraska, Harvard, and Cambridge, and is now Professor of Philosophy at Cornell. His chief interests are in epistemology, the philosophy of psychology, and metaphysics. He is the author of *Dreaming*; *Ludwig Wittgenstein: A Memoir*; and *Knowledge and Certainty*; and he frequently contributes articles to leading philosophical journals.

I

My main topic will be, roughly speaking, the claim that mental events or conscious experiences or inner experiences are brain processes.[1] I hasten to say, however, that I am not going to talk about "mental events" or "conscious experiences" or "inner experiences." These expressions are almost exclusively philosophers' terms, and I am not sure that I have got the hang of any of them. Philosophers are not in agreement in their use of these terms. One philosopher will say, for example, that a pain in the foot is a mental event, whereas another will say that a pain *in the foot* certainly is not a *mental* event.

I will avoid these expressions, and concentrate on the particular

FROM *Dialogue*, III (1964), pp. 115–25. Reprinted by permission of the author and the editors.

[1] This paper was read at the Sixtieth Annual Meeting of the American Philosophical Association, Eastern Division. It is a reply to Professor J. J. C. Smart's essay, "Materialism," published in *The Journal of Philosophy*, LX, No. 22 (October, 1963).

example of *sudden thoughts.* Suddenly remembering an engagement would be an example of suddenly thinking of something. Suddenly realizing, in a chess game, that moving this pawn would endanger one's queen, would be another example of a sudden thought. Professor Smart says that he wishes to "elucidate thought as an inner process," [2] and he adds that he wants to identify "such inner processes with brain processes." He surely holds, therefore, that thinking and thoughts, including sudden thoughts, are brain processes. He holds also that conscious experiences (pp. 656 and 657), illusions (p. 659), and aches and pains (p. 654) are brain processes, and that love (p. 652) is a brain state. I will restrict my discussion, however, to sudden thoughts.

My first inclination, when I began to think on this topic, was to believe that Smart's view is false—that a sudden thought certainly is not a brain process. But now I think that I do not know what it *means* to say that a sudden thought is a brain process. In saying this I imply, of course, that the proponents of this view also do not know what it means. This implication is risky for it might turn out, to my surprise and gratification, that Smart will explain his view with great clarity.

In trying to show that there is real difficulty in seeing what his view means, I will turn to Smart's article "Sensations and Brain Processes." [3] He says there that in holding that a sensation is a brain process he is "using 'is' in the sense of strict identity" (p. 37). "I wish to make it clear," he says, "that the brain process doctrine asserts identity in the *strict* sense" (p. 37). I assume that he wishes to say the same about the claimed identity of a thought with a brain process. Unfortunately he does not attempt to define this "strict sense of identity," and so we have to study his examples.

One of his examples of a "strict identity" is this: 7 is identical with the smallest prime number greater than 5 (p. 37). We must remember, however, that one feature of "the identity theory," as I shall call it, is that the alleged identity between thoughts, sensations, etc., and brain processes, is held to be *contingent*. Since the identity of 7 with the smallest prime greater than 5 is *a priori* and relates to

[2] Smart, *op. cit.*, p. 657.
[3] J. J. C. Smart, "Sensations and Brain Processes," *The Philosophical Review*, April 1959; republished in *The Philosophy of Mind*, V. C. Chappell, ed., Prentice-Hall, 1962; reprinted in this volume, pp. 32–47. Subsequent page references to Smart's article are to the reprint in this volume.

timeless objects, it does not provide me with any clue as to how I am to apply the notion of "strict identity" to temporal events that are *contingently* related. The example is unsatisfactory, therefore, for the purpose of helping me to deal with the question of whether thoughts are or are not "strictly identical" with certain brain processes.

Let us move to another example. Smart tells us that the sense in which the small boy who stole apples is the same person as the victorious general, is *not* the "strict" sense of "identity" (p. 37). He thinks there is a mere spatio-temporal continuity between the apple-stealing boy and the general who won the war. From this *non*-example of "strict identity" I think I obtain a clue as to what he means by it. Consider the following two sentences: "General De Gaulle is the tallest Frenchman"; "The victorious general is the small boy who stole apples." Each of these sentences might be said to express an identity: yet we can see a difference between the two cases. Even though the victorious general *is* the small boy who stole apples, it is possible for the victorious general to be in this room at a time when there is *no* small boy here. In contrast, if General De Gaulle *is* the tallest Frenchman, then General De Gaulle is not in this room unless the tallest Frenchman is here. It would be quite natural to say that this latter identity (if it holds) is a *strict* identity, and that the other one is not. I believe that Smart would say this. This suggests to me the following rule for his "strict identity": If something, *x*, is in a certain place at a certain time, then something, *y*, is strictly identical with *x* only if *y* is in that same place at that same time.

If we assume that Smart's use of the expression "strict identity" is governed by the necessary condition I have stated, we can possibly understand why he is somewhat hesitant about whether to say that the Morning Star is strictly identical with the Evening Star. Smart says to an imaginary opponent: "You may object that the Morning Star is in a sense not the very same thing as the Evening Star, but only something spatio-temporally continuous with it. That is, you may say that the Morning Star is not the Evening Star in the strict sense of 'identity' that I distinguished earlier" (p. 38). Instead of rebutting this objection, Smart moves on to what he calls "a more plausible example" of strict identity. This suggests to me that Smart is not entirely happy with the case of the Stars as an example of strict identity. Why not? Perhaps he has some inclination to feel that the planet that is both the Morning and Evening Star, is not the Morning Star *at the same time* it is the Evening Star. If this were so, the suggested necessary condition for "strict identity" would not be satisfied. Smart's hesitation is thus a further indication that he wants his use of the expression "strict identity" to be governed by the rule I have stated.

Let us turn to what Smart calls his "more plausible" example of strict identity. It is this: Lightning is an electric discharge. Smart avows that this is truly a strict identity (p. 37 and pp. 38–39). This example provides additional evidence that he wants to follow the stated rule. If an electrical discharge occurred in one region of the sky and a flash of lightning occurred simultaneously in a different region of the sky, Smart would have no inclination to assert (I think) that the lightning was strictly identical with the electric discharge. Or if electrical discharges and corresponding lightning flashes occurred in the same region of the sky, but not at the same time, there normally being a perceptible interval of time between a discharge and a flash, then Smart (I believe) would not wish to hold that there was anything more strict than a systematic correlation (perhaps causal) between electric discharges and lightning.[4]

I proceed now to take up Smart's claim that a sudden thought is strictly identical with some brain process. It is clear that a brain process has spatial location. A brain process would be a mechanical, chemical or electrical process in the brain substance, or an electric discharge from the brain mass, or something of the sort. As Smart puts it, brain processes take place "inside our skulls." [5]

Let us consider an example of a sudden thought. Suppose that when I am in my house I hear the sound of a truck coming up the driveway and it suddenly occurs to me that I have not put out the milk bottles. Now is this sudden thought (which is also a sudden

[4] Mr. U. T. Place, in his article "Is Consciousness a Brain Process?" (reprinted in this volume, pp. 21–31; subsequent page references to Place's article are to the reprint in this volume), also defends the identity theory. An example that he uses to illustrate the sense of identity in which, according to him, "consciousness" could turn out to be a brain process is this: "A cloud is a mass of water droplets or other particles in suspension" (pp. 23 and 26). I believe that Place would not be ready to hold that this is a genuine identity, *as contrasted with* a systematic and/or causal correlation, if he did not assume that in the very same region of space occupied by a cloud there is, at the very same time, a mass of particles in suspension.

[5] "Materialism," *loc. cit.*, p. 654.

memory) literally inside my skull? I think that in our ordinary use of the terms "thought" and "thinking," we attach no meaning to the notion of determining the bodily location of a thought. We do not seriously debate whether someone's sudden thought occurred in his heart, or his throat, or his brain. Indeed, we should not know what the question meant. We should have no idea what to look for to settle this "question." We do say such a thing as "He can't get the thought out of his head"; but this is not taken as giving the location of a thought, any more than the remark "He still has that girl on the brain," is taken as giving the location of a girl.

It might be replied that *as things are* the bodily location of thoughts is not a meaningful notion; but if massive correlations were discovered between thoughts and brain processes then we might *begin* to locate thoughts in the head. To this I must answer that our philosophical problem *is* about how things are. It is a question about our *present* concepts of thinking and thought, not about some conjectured future concepts.[6]

The difficulty I have in understanding Smart's identity theory is the following. Smart wants to use a concept of "strict identity." Since there are a multitude of uses of the word "is," from the mere fact that he tells us that he means "is" in the sense of "strict identity," it does not follow that he has explained which use of "is" he intends. From his examples and non-examples, I surmise that his so-called "strict identity" is governed by the necessary condition that if x occurs in a certain place at a certain time, then y is strictly identical with x only if y occurs in the same place at the same time. But if x is a brain process and y is a sudden thought, then this condition

[6] Mr. Jerome Shaffer proposes an ingenious solution to our problem in "Could Mental States Be Brain Processes?" *The Journal of Philosophy*, LVIII, No. 26 (December 21, 1961). He allows that at present we do not attach any meaning to a bodily location of thoughts. As he puts it, we have no "rules" for asserting or denying that a particular thought occurred in a certain part of the body. But why could we not *adopt* a rule, he asks? Supposing that there was discovered to be a one-to-one correspondence between thoughts and brain processes, we could *stipulate* that a thought is located where the corresponding brain process is located. Nothing would then stand in the way of saying that thoughts are *identical* with those brain processes! Although filled with admiration for this philosophical technique, I disagree with Shaffer when he says (*ibid.*, p. 818) that the adopted convention for the location of thoughts would not have to be merely an elliptical way of speaking of the location of the corresponding brain processes. Considering the origin of the convention, how could it amount to anything else?

for strict identity is not (and cannot be) satisfied. Indeed, it does not even make sense to set up a test for it. Suppose we had determined, by means of some instrument, that a certain process occurred inside my skull at the exact moment I had the sudden thought about the milk bottles. How do we make the further test of whether my *thought* occurred inside my skull? For it would have to be a *further* test: it would have to be logically independent of the test for the presence of the brain process, because Smart's thesis is that the identity is *contingent*. But no one has any notion of what it would mean to test for the occurrence of the thought inside my skull *independently* of testing for a brain process. The idea of such a test is not intelligible. Smart's thesis, as I understand it, requires this unintelligible idea. For he is not satisfied with holding that there is a systematic correlation between sudden thoughts and certain brain processes. He wants to take the additional step of holding that there is a "strict identity." Now his concept of strict identity either embodies the necessary condition I stated previously, or it does not. If it does not, then I do not know what he means by "strict identity," over and above systematic correlation. If his concept of strict identity does embody that necessary condition, then his concept of strict identity cannot be meaningfully applied to the relationship between sudden thoughts and brain processes. My conclusion is what I said in the beginning: the identity theory has no clear meaning.

II

I turn now to a different consideration. A thought requires circumstances or, in Wittgenstein's word, "surroundings" (*Umgebung*). Putting a crown on a man's head is a coronation, only in certain circumstances.[7] The behavior of exclaiming, "Oh, I have not put out the milk bottles," or the behavior of suddenly jumping up, rushing to the kitchen, collecting the bottles and carrying them outside —such behavior expresses the thought that one has not put out the milk bottles, *only in certain circumstances.*

The circumstances necessary for this simple thought are complex. They include the existence of an organized community, of a practice of collecting and distributing milk, of a rule that empty bottles will not be collected unless placed outside the door, and so on. These

[7] *Investigations,* Sec. 584.

practices, arrangements and rules could exist only if there was a common language; and this in turn would presuppose shared activities and agreement in the use of language. The thought about the milk bottles requires a background of mutual purpose, activity and understanding.

I assume that if a certain brain process were strictly identical with a certain thought, then the occurrence of that brain process would be an absolutely sufficient condition for the occurrence of that thought. If this assumption is incorrect, then my understanding of what Smart means by "strict identity" is even *less* than I have believed. In support of this assumption I will point out that Smart has never stated his identity theory in the following way: *In certain circumstances* a particular brain process is identical with a particular thought. His thesis has not carried such a qualification. I believe his thesis is the following: A particular brain process is, *without qualification,* strictly identical with a particular thought. If this thesis were true it would appear to follow that the occurrence of that brain process would be an absolutely sufficient condition for the occurrence of that thought.

I have remarked that a necessary condition for the occurrence of my sudden thought about the milk bottles is the previous existence of various practices, rules and agreements. If the identity theory were true, then the surroundings that are necessary for the existence of my sudden thought would also be necessary for the existence of the brain process with which it is identical.[8] That brain process would not have occurred unless, for example, there was or had been a practice of delivering milk.

This consequence creates a difficulty for those philosophers who, like Smart, hold both to the identity theory and also to the viewpoint that I shall call "scientific materialism." According to the latter viewpoint, the furniture of the world "in the last resort" consists of "the ultimate entities of physics." [9] Smart holds that everything in

[8] It is easy to commit a fallacy here. The circumstances that I have mentioned are *conceptually* necessary for the occurrence of my thoughts. If the identity theory were true it would not follow that they were *conceptually* necessary for the occurrence of the brain process that is identical with that thought. But it would follow that those circumstances were necessary for the occurrence of the brain process *in the sense* that the brain process *would not* have occurred in the absence of those circumstances.

[9] "Materialism," *loc. cit.*, p. 651.

the world is "explicable in terms of physics." [10] It does not seem to me that this can be true. My sudden thought about the milk bottles was an occurrence in the world. That thought required a background of common practices, purposes and agreements. But a reference to a practice of (*e.g.*) delivering milk could not appear in a proposition of physics. The word "electron" is a term of physics, but the phrase "a practice of delivering milk" is not. There could not be an explanation of the occurrence of my thought (an explanation taking account of all the necessary circumstances) which was stated solely in terms of the entities and laws of physics.

My sudden thought about the milk bottles is not unique in requiring surroundings. The same holds for any other thought. No thought would be explicable wholly in the terms of physics (and/or biology) because the circumstances that form the "stage-setting" for a thought cannot be described in the terms of physics.

Now if I am right on this point, and if the identity theory were true, it would follow that none of those *brain processes* that are identical with thoughts could be given a purely physical explanation. A philosopher who holds both to the identity theory and to scientific materialism is forced, I think, into the self-defeating position of conceding that many brain processes are not explicable solely in terms of physics.[11] The position is self-defeating because such a philosopher regards a brain process as a *paradigm* of something wholly explicable in terms of physics.

A defender of these two positions might try to avoid this outcome by claiming that the circumstances required for the occurrence of a thought, do themselves consist of configurations of ultimate particles (or of their statistical properties, or something of the sort). I doubt, however, that anyone knows what it would mean to say, for example, that the *rule* that milk bottles will not be collected unless placed outside the door, is a configuration of ultimate particles.

[10] "Sensations and Brain Processes," p. 34.

[11] I believe this argument is pretty similar to a point made by J. T. Stevenson, in his "Sensations and Brain Processes: A Reply to J. J. C. Smart," *The Philosophical Review* (October, 1960), p. 507. Smart's view, roughly speaking, is that unless sensations are identical with brain processes they are "nomological danglers." Stevenson's retort is that by insisting that sensations are identical with brain processes we have not got rid of any nomological danglers. He says: "Indeed, on Smart's thesis it turns out that brain processes are danglers, for now brain processes have all those properties that made sensations danglers."

At the very least, this defence would have to assume a heavy burden of explanation.

III

There is a further point connected with the one just stated. At the foundation of Smart's monism there is, I believe, the desire for a homogeneous system of explanation. Everything in the world, he feels, should be capable of the same *kind* of explanation, namely, one in terms of the entities and laws of physics. He thinks we advance toward this goal when we see that sensations, thoughts, etc., are identical with brain processes.

Smart has rendered a service to the profession by warning us against a special type of fallacy. An illustration of this fallacy would be to argue that a sensation is not a brain process because a person can be talking about a sensation and yet not be talking about a brain process.[12] The verb "to talk about" might be called an "intentional" verb, and this fallacy committed with it might be called "the intentional fallacy." Other intentional verbs would be "to mean," "to intend," "to know," "to predict," "to describe," "to notice," and so on.

It is easy to commit the intentional fallacy, and I suspect that Smart himself has done so. The verb "to explain" is also an intentional verb and one must beware of using it to produce a fallacy. Suppose that the Prime Minister of Ireland is the ugliest Irishman. A man might argue that this cannot be so, because someone might be explaining the presence of the Irish Prime Minister in New York and yet not be explaining the presence in New York of the ugliest Irishman. It would be equally fallacious to argue that since the Irish Prime Minister and the ugliest Irishman *are* one and the same person, therefore, to explain the presence of the Prime Minister *is* to explain the presence of the ugliest Irishman.

I wonder if Smart has not reasoned fallaciously, somewhat as follows: If a sudden thought *is* a certain brain process, then to *explain* the occurrence of the brain process *is* to explain the occurrence of the thought. Thus there will be just one kind of explanation for both thoughts and brain processes.

The intentional fallacy here is transparent. If a thought is iden-

[12] Smart, "Sensations and Brain Processes," p. 37.

tical with a brain process, it does not follow that to explain the occurrence of the brain process is to explain the occurrence of the thought. And in fact, an explanation of the one differs in *kind* from an explanation of the other. The explanation of why someone *thought* such and such, involves different assumptions and principles and is guided by different interests than is an explanation of why this or that process occurred in his brain. These explanations belong to different *systems* of explanation.

I conclude that even if Smart were right in holding that thoughts are strictly identical with brain processes (a claim that I do not yet find intelligible) he would not have established that there is one and the same explanation for the occurrence of the thoughts and for the occurrence of the brain processes. If he were to appreciate this fact then, I suspect, he would no longer have any *motive* for espousing the identity theory. For this theory, even if true, would not advance us one whit toward the single, homogenous system of explanation that is the goal of Smart's materialism.

IV

I shall close by taking note of Smart's conceptual experiment with a human brain kept alive *in vitro*.[13] What is supposed to be proved by this experiment? That for thinking, pain, and so-called "mental experience" in general, what goes on in the brain is more "important" or "essential" than behavior. How is this proved? By the supposed fact that the experimental brain has thoughts, illusions, pains, and so on, although separated from a human body.

Could this supposed fact be a fact? Could a *brain* have thoughts, illusions or pains? The senselessness of the supposition seems so obvious that I find it hard to take it seriously. No experiment could establish this result for a brain. Why not? The fundamental reason is that a brain does not sufficiently resemble a human being.[14]

What can have led Smart to suppose that a brain can have thoughts? The only explanation which occurs to me is that he thinks that if my thought is in my brain, then my brain has a thought. This would be like thinking that if my invitation to dinner is in my pocket, then my pocket has an invitation to dinner. One bad joke deserves another.

[13] "Materialism," *loc. cit.*, pp. 659–60.
[14] Cf. Wittgenstein, *Investigations*, sections 281 and 283.

5 *Paul Feyerabend*

Materialism and the Mind-Body Problem

Paul Feyerabend was born on January 13, 1924, in Vienna, Austria. In 1951, he received his Ph.D. from the University of Vienna. He is now Professor of Philosophy at the University of California at Berkeley. His major interests are the philosophy of science and the theory of knowledge. He is the author of *Explanation, Reduction, and Empiricism*, and *Problems of Empiricism*, and is co-editor of *Mind, Matter, and Method.*

(1) This paper has a twofold purpose. First, it defends materialism against a certain type of attack which seems to be based upon a truism but which is nevertheless completely off the mark. And secondly it intends to put philosophy in its proper place. It occurs only too often that attempts to arrive at a coherent picture of the world are held up by philosophical bickering and are perhaps even given up before they can show their merits. It seems to me that those who originate such attempts ought to be a little less afraid of difficulties; that they ought to look through the arguments which are presented against them; and that they ought to recognize their irrelevance. Having disregarded irrelevant objections they ought then to proceed to the much more rewarding task of developing their point of view *in detail*, to examine its fruitfulness and thereby to get fresh insight, not only into some generalities, but into very concrete and detailed processes. To encourage such development from the abstract to the concrete, to contribute to the invention of fur-

FROM *The Review of Metaphysics*, XVII (1963), pp. 49–66. Reprinted by permission of the author and the editors.

ther ideas, this is the proper task of a philosophy which aspires to be more than a hindrance to progress.

(2) The crudest form of materialism will be taken as the basis of argument. If *it* can successfully evade the objections of some philosophers, then a more refined doctrine will be even less troubled.

Materialism, as it will be discussed here, assumes that the only entities existing in the world are atoms, aggregates of atoms and that the only properties and relations are the properties of, and the relations between such aggregates. A simple atomism such as the theory of Democritos will be sufficient for our purpose. The refinements of the kinetic theory, or of the quantum theory, are outside the domain of discussion. And the question is: Will such a cosmology give a correct account of human beings?

(3) The following reason is put forth why this question must be answered in the negative: human beings, apart from being material, have *experiences;* they *think;* they *feel* pain; etc., etc. These processes cannot be analyzed in a materialistic fashion. Hence, a materialistic psychology is bound to fail.

The most decisive part of this argument consists in the assertion that experiences, thoughts, etc. are not material processes. It is customary to support this assertion in the following manner.

(4) There are statements which can be made about pains, thoughts, etc., which cannot be made about material processes; and there are other statements which can be made about material processes but which cannot be made about pains, thoughts, etc. This impossibility exists because the attempt to form such statements would lead to results which are either *false,* or else to results which are *meaningless.*

Let us consider meaninglessness first. Whether or not a statement is meaningful depends on the grammatical rules guiding the corresponding sentence. The argument appeals to such rules. It points out that the materialist, in stating his thesis, is violating them. Note that the particular *words* he uses are of no relevance here. Whatever the *words* employed by him, the resulting *system of rules* would have a structure incompatible with the structure of the idiom in which we usually describe pains and thoughts. This incompatibility is taken to refute the materialist.

It is evident that this argument is incomplete. An incompatibility between the materialistic language and the rules implicit in some other idiom will criticize the former only if the latter can be shown to possess certain advantages. Nor is it sufficient to point out that the idiom on which the comparison is based is in *common use.* This is an irrelevant historical accident. Is it really believed that a vigorous propaganda campaign which makes everyone speak the materialistic language will turn materialism into a correct doctrine? The choice of the language that is supposed to be the basis of criticism must be supported by better reasons.

(5) As far as I am aware there is only one further reason that has been offered: it is the *practical success* of ordinary English which makes it a safe basis for argument. "Our common stock of words" writes J. L. Austin ("A Plea for Excuses") "embodies all the distinctions men have found worth drawing, and the connexions they have found worth marking, in the lifetime of many generations: these surely are likely to be more numerous, more sound, since they have stood up to the long test of the survival of the fittest, and more subtle . . . than any that you or I are likely to think up. . . ." [1] This reason is very similar, and almost identical, with a certain point of view in the philosophy of science. Ever since Newton it has been assumed that a theory which is confirmed to a very high degree is to be preferred to more tentative general ideas and it has been, and still is, believed that such general ideas must be removed in order not to hinder the course of factual discovery. "For if the possibility of hypotheses," writes Newton (reply to a letter by P. Pardies), "is to be the test of truth and reality of things, I see not how certainty can be obtained in any science; since numerous hypotheses may be devised, which shall seem to overcome new difficulties." [2] I mention this parallel in order to show that philosophical points of view which *prima facie* seem to bear the stamp of revolutionary discoveries, especially to those who are not too well acquainted with the history of ideas, may in the end turn out to be nothing but uncritical repetitions of age-old prejudices. However, it must also be emphasized, in all fairness to the scientists, that the parallel does not go very far.

[1] *Proceedings of the Aristotelian Society*, 1956–57. Article reprinted in *Philosophical Papers*, Urmson and Warnock, eds. (Oxford, 1961), p. 130.

[2] *Isaak Newton's Papers and Letters on Natural Philosophy*, I. B. Cohen, ed. (Cambridge, 1958), p. 106.

Scientific theories are constructed in such a way that they can be *tested.* Every application of the theory is at the same time a most sensitive investigation of its validity. This being the case there is indeed some reason to trust a theory that has been in use for a considerable time and to look with suspicion at new and vague ideas. The suspicion is mistaken, of course, as I shall try to point out presently. Still, it is not completely foolish to have such an attitude. At least *prima facie* there seems to be a grain of reason in it.

The situation is very different with "common idioms." First of all, such idioms are adapted not to *facts,* but to *beliefs.* If these beliefs are widely accepted; if they are intimately connected with the fears and the hopes of the community in which they occur; if they are defended, and reinforced with the help of powerful institutions; if one's whole life is somehow carried out in accordance with them —then the language representing them will be regarded as most successful. At the same time it is clear that the question of the truth of the beliefs has not been touched.

The second reason why the success of a "common" idiom is not at all on the same level as is the success of a scientific theory lies in the fact that the use of such an idiom, *even in concrete observational situations,* can hardly ever be regarded as a *test.* There is no attempt, as there is in the sciences, to conquer new fields and to try the theory in them. And even on familiar ground one can never be sure whether certain features of the descriptive statements used are *confronted* with facts, and are thereby *examined;* or whether they do not simply function as *accompanying noises.* Some more recent analyses concerning the nature of facts seem to show that the latter is the case. It is clear that the argument from success is then inapplicable.

Assume thirdly—and now I am well aware that I am arguing contrary to fact—that the idiom to which reference is made in the above argument *is* used in a testable fashion and that the parallel, alluded to above, with scientific method is a legitimate one. Is it *then* possible to reject materialism by reference to the success of a nonmaterialistic language?

The answer is NO and the reason which I have explained in detail in my "Explanation, Reduction, and Empiricism" (in Vol. III of the *Minnesota Studies in the Philosophy of Science*)[3] as well as in "Problems of Empiricism" (in Vol. II of the *Pittsburgh Studies*

[3] Minneapolis, 1962.

in the Philosophy of Science)[4] is as follows: in order to discuss the weaknesses of an all-pervasive system of thought such as is expressed by the "common" idiom, it is not sufficient to compare it with "the facts." Many such facts are formulated in terms of the idiom and therefore already prejudiced in its favor. Also there are many facts which are inaccessible, *for empirical reasons*, to a person speaking a certain idiom and which become accessible only if a different idiom is introduced. This being the case, the construction of alternative points of view and of alternative languages which radically differ from the established usage, far from precipitating confusion, *is a necessary part of the examination of this usage* and must be carried out *before* a final judgment can be made. More concretely: if you want to find out whether there *are* pains, thoughts, feelings in the sense indicated by the common usage of these words, then you must become (among other things) a materialist. Trying to eliminate materialism by reference to the common idiom, therefore, means putting the cart before the horse.

(6) The argument presented so far has some further features which are in need of criticism. Let us take it for granted that incompatibility with ordinary (or other) usage and the meaninglessness arising from it is a sufficient reason for eliminating a point of view. Then it must still be made clear that while the grammar of the *primitive terms* of the point of view may be incompatible with accepted usage, the grammar of the *defined terms* need not be so incompatible. The same applies to the "grain" of both: it has sometimes been objected that a sensation is a very simple thing, whereas a collection of atoms has a much more complex structure (it is "spotty"). This is correct. But there are still *properties* of such collections which do not participate in their "grain." The density of a fluid is an example. The fluid itself has the same "grain" as a heap of atoms. The density has not. It ceases to be applicable in domains where the fine structure of the fluid becomes apparent. There are infinitely many other properties of this kind. The defender of the customary point of view has therefore much too simple an idea of the capabilities of materialism. He overlooks that materialism might even be able to provide him with the synonyms he wants; he over-

[4] Pittsburgh, 1963.

looks that the materialistic doctrine might be able to satisfy his (*irrelevant*) demand for at least partial agreement of grammar.

(7) While the argument from meaninglessness is wholly based upon language, the argument from falsity is not. That a thought cannot be a material process is, so it is believed, established *by observation.* It is by observation that we discover the difference between the one and the other and refute materialism. We now turn to an examination of this argument.

(8) To start with we must admit that the difference does exist. Introspection does indicate, in a most decisive fashion, that my present thought of Aldebaran is not localized whereas Aldebaran is localized; that this thought has no color whereas Aldebaran has a very definite color; that this thought has no parts whereas Aldebaran consists of many parts exhibiting different physical properties. Is this character of the introspective result proof to the effect that thoughts cannot be material?

The answer is NO and the argument is the truism that what *appears to be* different does not need to *be* different. Is not the seen table very different from the felt table? Is not the heard sound very different from its mechanical manifestations (Chladni's figures; Kundt's tube, etc., etc.)? And if despite this difference of appearance we are allowed to make an identification, postulating an object in the outer world (the physical table, the physical sound), then why should the observed difference between a thought and the impression of a brain process prevent us from making another identification, postulating this time an object in the inner (material) world, viz., a brain process? It is of course quite possible that such a postulate will run into trouble and that it will be refuted by independent tests (just as the earlier identification of comets with atmospheric phenomena was refuted by independent tests). The point is that the *prima facie* observed difference between thoughts and the appearance of brain processes does *not* constitute such trouble. It is also correct that a language which is based upon the assumption that the identification has already been carried out would differ significantly from ordinary English. But this fact can be used as an argument against the identification only *after* it has been shown that the new language is *inferior* to ordinary

English. And such disproof should be based upon the *fully* developed materialistic idiom and *not* on the bits and pieces of materialese which are available to the philosophers of today. It took a considerable time for ordinary English to reach its present stage of complexity and sophistication. The materialistic philosopher must be given *at least* as much time. As a matter of fact he will need more time as he intends to develop a language which is fully testable, which gives a coherent account of the most familiar facts about human beings *as well as* of thousands more recondite facts which have been unearthed by the physiologists. I also admit that there are people for whom even the reality of the external world and the identifications leading to it constitute a grave problem. My answer is that I do not address *them*, but that I presuppose a minimum of reason in my readers; I assume they are realists. And assuming this I try to point out that their realism need not be restricted to processes outside their skin—unless of course one already *presupposes* what is to be established by the argument, that things inside the skin are very different from what goes on outside. Considering all this I conclude that the argument from observation is invalid.

(9) It is quite entertaining to speculate about some results of an identification of what is observed by introspection with brain processes. Observation of microprocesses in the brain is a notoriously difficult affair. Only very rarely is it possible to investigate them in the living organism. Observation of dead tissue, on the other hand, is applied to a structure that may differ significantly from the living brain. To solve the problems arising from this apparent inaccessibility of processes in the living brain we need only realize that the living brain *is already connected with a most sensitive instrument*—the living human organism. Observation of the reactions of this organism, introspection included, may therefore be much more reliable sources of information concerning the living brain than any other "more direct" method. Using a suitable identification-hypothesis one might even be able to say that introspection leads to a *direct observation* of an otherwise quite inaccessible and very complex process *in the brain*.

(10) Against what has been said above it might, and has been, objected that in the case of thoughts, sensations, feelings, the distinction between what they *are* and what they *appear to be* does

not apply. Mental processes are things with which we are *directly acquainted.* Unlike physical objects whose structure must be unveiled by experimental research and about whose nature we can make only more or less plausible conjectures, they can be known completely, and with certainty. Essence and appearance coincide here, and we are therefore entitled to take what they seem to be as a direct indication of what they are. This objection must now be investigated in some detail.

(11) In order to deal with all the prejudices operating in the present case, let us approach the matter at a snail's pace. What are the reasons for defending a doctrine like the one we have just outlined? If the materialist is correct, then the doctrine is false. It *is* then possible to test statements of introspection by physiological examination of the brain, and reject them as being based upon an introspective mistake. Is such a possibility to be denied? The doctrine we are discussing at the present moment thinks it is. And the argument is somewhat as follows.

When I am in pain, then there is no doubt, no possibility of a mistake. This certainty is not simply a psychological affair, it is not due to the fact that I am too strongly convinced to be persuaded of the opposite. It is much more related to a logical certainty: there is no possibility whatever of criticizing the statement. I might not show any physiological symptoms—but I never meant to include them into my assertion. I might not even show pain behavior—but this is not part of the content of my statement either. Now if the difference between essence and appearance were applicable in the case of pains, then such certainty could not be obtained. It *can* be obtained as has just been demonstrated. Hence, the difference does not apply and the postulation of a common object for mental processes and impressions of physiological processes cannot be carried out.

(12) The first question which arises in connection with this argument concerns the *source* of this certainty of statements concerning mental processes. The answer is very simple: it is their *lack of content* which is the source of their certainty. Statements about physical objects possess a very rich content. They are vulnerable because of the existence of this content. Thus, the statement "there is a table in front of me" leads to predictions concerning my tactual

sensations; the behavior of other material objects (a glass of brandy put in a certain position will remain in this position and will not fall to the ground; a ball thrown in a certain direction will be deflected); the behavior of other people (they will walk around the table; point out objects on its surface); etc. Failure of any one of these predictions may force me to withdraw the statement. This is not the case with statements concerning thoughts, sensations, feelings; or at least there is the impression that the same kind of vulnerability does not obtain here. The reason is that their content is so much poorer. No prediction, no retrodiction can be inferred from them, and the need to withdraw them can therefore not arise. (Of course, lack of content is only a *necessary* condition of their empirical certainty; in order to have the character they possess, statements about mental events must also be such that in the appropriate circumstances their production can be achieved with complete ease; they must be *observational* statements. *This* characteristic they share with many statements concerning physical objects.)

(13) The second question is how statements about physical objects *obtain* their rich content and how it is that the content of mental statements as represented in the current argument is so much poorer.

One fairly popular answer is by reference to the "grammar" of mental statements and of physical statements respectively. We mean by pains, thoughts, etc., processes which are accessible only to one individual and which have nothing to do with the state of his body. The content of "pain," or of "thinking of Vienna" is low because "pain," "thought" are mental terms. If the content of these terms were enriched, and thereby made similar to the content of "table," they would cease to function in the peculiar way in which mental terms do as a matter of fact function, and "pain," for example, would then cease to mean what is meant by an ordinary individual who in the face of the absence of physiological symptoms, of behavioral expression, of suppressed conflicts still maintains that he is in pain. This answer may be correct, and it will be taken to be correct for the sake of argument. However, in order to defeat the materialist it must also be shown that a language structured in this way will describe the world more correctly, and more efficiently than any language the materialist could develop.

No such proof is available. The argument from "common" usage and, for that matter, from any established usage is therefore irrelevant.

(14) There is only one point on which this argument may possess some force, and this point concerns the use of *words:* having shown that a materialistic pain and an "ordinary" pain would be two very different things indeed, the defender of the established usage may forbid the materialist to employ the word "pain" which for him rightfully belongs to the ordinary idiom. Now, quite apart from the fact that this would mean being very squeamish indeed, and unbearably "proper" in linguistic matters, the desired procedure *cannot be carried out.* The reason is that changes of meaning occur too frequently, and that they cannot be localized in time. Every interesting discussion, that is every discussion which leads to an advance of knowledge terminates in a situation where some decisive change of meaning has occurred. Yet it is not possible, or it is only very rarely possible, to say *when* the change took place. Moreover a distinction must be drawn between the *psychological circumstances* of the production of a sentence, and the *meaning* of the statement that is connected with that sentence. A new theory of pains will not change the pains; nor will it change the causal connection between the occurrence of pains and the production of "I am in pain," except perhaps very slightly. It *will* change the *meaning* of "I am in pain." Now it seems to me that observational terms should be correlated with causal antecedents and *not* with meanings. The causal connection between the production of a "mental" sentence and its "mental" antecedent is very strong. It has been taught in the very youth. It is the basis of all observation concerning the mind. To sever this connection is a much more laborious affair than a change of connections with meaning. The latter connections change all the time anyway. It is therefore much more sensible to establish a one-to-one connection between observational terms and their causal antecedents, than between such terms and the always variable *meanings.* This procedure has great advantages and can do no harm. An astronomer who wishes to determine the rough shape of the energy output (dependence on frequency) of a star by looking at it will hardly be seduced into thinking that the word "red" which he uses for announcing his results refers to sensations. Linguistic sensi-

tivity may be of some value. But it should not be used to turn intelligent people into nervous wrecks.

(15) Another reply to the question of section 13 which is *prima facie* satisfactory is that we know quite a lot about physical objects and that we know much less about mental events. We use this knowledge not only on the relatively rare occasions when we answer questions involving it, but we infuse it also into the notions with which we describe material objects: a table *is* an object which deflects a ball thrown at it; which supports other objects; which is seen by other people; and so on. We let this knowledge become part of the language we speak by allowing the laws and theories it contains to become the grammatic rules of this language. This reply would seem to be supported by the fact that objects of a relatively unknown kind always give rise to fewer predictions and that the statements concerning them are therefore relatively safe. In many such cases the only tests available are the reports of others which means that mass-hallucinations can still count as confirming evidence.

Now this reply, however plausible, does not take into account that a considerable amount is known about mental processes also, and this not only by the psychologist, or the physiologist, but even by the common man, be he now British, or a native of Ancient Greece, or of Ancient Egypt. Why has *this* knowledge not been incorporated into the mental notions? Why are these notions still so poor in content?

(16) Before answering the question we must first qualify it. It is quite incorrect to assume that the relative poverty of mental notions is a common property of all languages. Quite the contrary, we find, that people have at all times objectivized mental notions in a manner very similar to the manner in which we today objectivize materialistic notions. They did this mostly (but not always—the witchcraft theory of the Azande constituting a most interesting *materialistic* exception) in an objective-*idealistic* fashion and can therefore be easily criticized, or smiled about, by some progressive thinkers of today. In our present discussion such criticism is off the mark. We have *admitted*, in section 8, that the materialistic type of objection may at some future time run into trouble. What we wanted to defend was the *initial* right to carry it out and it was

this *initial* right that was attacked by reference to "common usage." Considering this context, it is important to point out that there is hardly any interesting language, used by a historical culture, which is built in accordance with the idea of acquaintance. This idea is nothing but a philosophical invention. It is now time to reveal the motives for such an invention.

(17) We start the discussion with a still further argument intending to show that and why the knowledge we may possess about mental events must not be incorporated into the mental terms and why their content must be kept low. This argument is apparently factual and it consists in pointing out *that there is knowledge by acquaintance,* or, alternatively, that there are things which can be known by acquaintance; we *do* possess direct and full knowledge of our pains, of our thoughts, of our feelings, at least of those which are immediately present and not suppressed.

This argument is circular. If we possess knowledge by acquaintance with respect to mental states of affairs, if there seems to be something "immediately given," then this is the *result* of the low content of the statements used for expressing this knowledge. Had we enriched the notions employed in these statements in a materialistic (or an objective-idealistic) fashion *as we might well have done,* then we would not any longer be able to say that we know mental processes by acquaintance. Just as with material objects we would then be obliged to distinguish between their nature and their appearance, and each judgment concerning a mental process would be open to revision by further physiological (or behavioral) inquiry. The reference to acquaintance cannot therefore justify our reluctance to use the knowledge we possess concerning mental events, their causes, their physiological concomitants (as their physiological content will be called *before* the materialistic move) for enriching the mental notions.

(18) What has just been said deserves repetition. The argument which we attacked was as follows: there is the *fact* of knowledge by acquaintance. This fact refutes materialism which would exclude such a fact. The attack consisted in pointing out that although knowledge by acquaintance may be a fact (which was, however, doubted in section 16), this fact is the result of certain peculiarities of the language spoken *and therefore alterable.* Materialism (and,

for that matter, also an objective spiritualism like the theory of the *ba* or Hegel's spiritualism) recognizes the fact and suggests that it be altered. It therefore clearly cannot be refuted by a repetition of the fact. What must be shown is that the *suggestion* is undesirable, and that acquaintance is desirable.

(19) We have here discovered a rather interesting feature of philosophical arguments. The argument from acquaintance presents what seems to be fact of nature, viz. our ability to acquire secure knowledge of our own states of mind. We have tried to show that this alleged fact of nature is the result of the way in which any kind of knowledge (or opinion) concerning the mind has been incorporated, or is being incorporated into the language used for describing facts: this knowledge, this opinion is not used for *enriching* the mental concepts; it is rather used for making predictions in terms of the still unchanged, and poor concepts. Or, to use terms from technical philosophy, this knowledge is interpreted instrumentalistically, and not in a realistic fashion. The alleged fact referred to above is therefore a projection, into the world, of certain peculiarities of our way of building up knowledge. Why do we (or why do philosophers who use the language described) proceed in this fashion?

(20) They proceed in this fashion because they hold a certain philosophical theory. According to this theory, which has a very long history and which influences even the most sophisticated and the most "progressive" contemporary philosophers (with the possible exception of Popper and Wittgenstein), the world consists of two domains, the domain of the outer, physical world, and the domain of the inner, or mental world. The outer world can be experienced, but only indirectly. Our knowledge of the outer world will therefore forever remain hypothetical. The inner world, the mental world, on the other hand, can be directly experienced. The knowledge gained in this fashion is complete, and absolutely certain. This, I think, is the philosophical theory behind the method we described in the last section.

Now I am not concerned here with the question of whether this theory is correct or not. It is quite possible that it is true (though I am inclined to doubt this, especially in view of the fact that it presents what should be the result of a decision, viz., the richness or the poverty of the content of a statement and its corresponding property of being either hypothetical, or certain, *as a fact of nature* and thereby confounds the basic distinction between the *ought* and the *is*). What I *am* interested in here is the way in which the theory is *presented.* It is not presented as a hypothesis which is open to criticism and which can be rationally discussed. In a certain sense it is not even presented. It is rather incorporated into the language spoken in a fashion which makes it inaccessible to empirical criticism—whatever the empirical results, they are not used for enriching the mental concepts which will therefore forever refer to entities knowable by acquaintance.

This procedure has two results. It hides the theory and thereby removes it from criticism. And it creates what looks like a very powerful fact supporting the theory. As the theory is hidden, the philosopher can even *start* with this fact and reason from it, thereby providing a kind of inductive argument for the theory. It is only when we examine what independent support there exists for this alleged fact that we discover that it is not a fact at all but rather a reflection of the way in which empirical results are handled. We discover that "we were ignorant of our . . . activity and therefore regarded as an alien object what had been constructed by ourselves" (Kuno Fischer in his account of Kant's theory of knowledge).[5]

This is an excellent example of the circularity of philosophical argumentation even in those cases where such argumentation is based upon what seems to be an uncontrovertible fact of nature ("inner" nature, that is). This example is a warning that we should not be too impressed by empirical arguments but that we should first investigate the source of their apparent success. Such an investigation may discover a fatal circularity and thereby destroy the force of the argument. It is quite obvious that a circularity of this kind cannot be removed by considering further *empirical* evidence. But it can be removed by an examination of the *methodological* tenability of the procedure described. We now give a brief outline of such an examination.

(21) There are some philosophers who agree that the *fact* of acquaintance cannot be used as an argument against the materialist (or any other kind of "internal realist"). Their reasons are not

[5] *Immanuel Kant und seine Lehre* (Heidelberg, 1889), p. 10.

those given above but rather the realization that none of the situations described in the ordinary idiom, in any ordinary idiom, can be known by acquaintance. Realizing this they will look for arguments which remain valid in the face of adverse facts, and they will therefore appeal to norms rather than to facts. They usually suggest the construction of an *ideal language* containing statements of the desired property. In this they are guided by the idea that our knowledge must possess a solid, that is an incorrigible foundation. The construction of such a language has sometimes been represented as a task of immense difficulty and as worthy of a great mind. I submit that this means vastly overestimating it. Of course, if this task is meant to be the discovery of *already existing* statements of the ordinary language which possess the desired property (Russell's "canoid patch of colour" indicates that he conceived his task in this fashion), then it is perhaps impossible to carry it out. It may also be impossible to give an account of complex perceptions in terms of simple sensible elements (the investigations of the *Gestalt* school of psychology most definitely indicate that such composition from psychological elements will be an extremely difficult matter). But why should the attempt to find a safe observation language be impeded by such inessential restrictions? What we want is a series of observation statements leading to knowledge by acquaintance. Such statements can be obtained *immediately* by a philosophical laboratory assistant, by taking any observation statement and eliminating its predictive and retrodictive content as well as all consequences concerning public events occurring simultaneously. The resulting string of signs will still be observational, it will be uttered on the same objective occasion as was its predecessor, but it will be incorrigible, and the object described by it will be 'known' by acquaintance. This is how acquaintance can be achieved. Now let us investigate some consequences of this procedure.

(22) Such an investigation is hardly ever carried out with due circumspection. What happens usually is this: One starts with a sentence which has a perfectly good meaning, such as "I am in pain." One interprets it as a statement concerning what can be known by acquaintance. One overlooks that such an interpretation drastically changes the original meaning of the sentence and one retains in this fashion the illusion that one is still dealing with a

meaningful statement. Blinded by this illusion one cannot at all understand the objection of the opponent who takes the move towards the "given" seriously and who is incapable of getting any sense out of the result. Just investigate the matter in some detail. Being in pain I say "I am in pain" and, of course, I have some independent idea as to what pains are. They do not reside in tables and chairs; they can be eliminated by taking drugs; they concern only a single human being (hence, being in pain I shall not get alarmed about my dog); they are not contagious (hence, being in pain I shall not warn people to keep away from me). This idea is shared by everyone else and it makes people capable of understanding what I intend to convey. But now I am not supposed to let any one of these ideas contribute to the meaning of the *new* statement, expressed by the same sentence, about the immediately given; I am supposed to free this meaning of all that has just been said; not even the idea that a dreamt pain and a pain really felt are different must now be retained. If all these elements are removed, then what do I mean by the new statement resulting from this semantical canvas cleaning? I may utter it on the occasion of pain (in the normal sense); I may also utter it in a dream with no pain present, and I may be equally convinced that this is the right thing to do. I may use it metaphorically, connecting it with a thought (in the usual sense) concerning the number two; or I may have been taught (in the usual sense of the word) to utter it when I have pleasant feelings and therefore utter it on these occasions. Clearly all these usages are now legitimate, and all of them describe the "immediately given pain." Is it not evident that using this new interpretation of the sentence I am not even in principle able to derive enlightenment from the fact that Herbert has just uttered it? Of course, I can still treat it as a *symptom* of the occurrence of an event which in the ordinary speech would be expressed in the very same fashion, viz., by saying "I am in pain." But in this case I provide my own interpretation which is very different from the interpretation we are discussing at the present moment. And we have seen that according to this interpretation the sentence cannot be taken to be the description of anything definite. It therefore means nothing; it cannot be understood by anyone (except in the sense in which a person looking at someone else's distorted face "understands" what is going on —but then he does his own interpreting); and it is completely inadequate as a "foundation of knowledge" or as a measure of factual meaning. Now if the Given were a reality, then this would mean the end of rational, objective knowledge. Not even revelation could then teach us what admittedly cannot be known in principle. Language and conversation, if it existed, would become comparable to a cat-serenade, all expression, nothing said, nothing understood. Fortunately enough, the "given" is but the reflection of our own unreason and it can be eliminated by building up language in a more sensible fashion. This finishes our discussion of the argument from acquaintance.

(23) To sum up: we have discussed three arguments against materialism. The first argument points out that materialism is not the ontology of ordinary English. We are given the reasons why this argument would be irrelevant even if ordinary English should turn out to be a highly successful *testable* idiom. The second argument refers to results of observation. We have pointed out that results of observation are in need of *interpretation* and that no reason has been given why a materialistic interpretation should be excluded. The third argument was by reference to the fact of "acquaintance." We have shown, first, that this fact is not unchangeable and second that if it were a *fact* knowledge would be impossible. I am not aware of any other philosophical arguments against materialism (clearly all considerations of synonymy or co-extensionality belong to what we have above called the first argument). There is, therefore, not a single reason why the attempt to give a purely physiological account of human beings should be abandoned, or why physiologists should leave the "soul" out of their considerations.

(24) A common feature of all the discussed arguments is this: they try to criticize a theory *before* this theory has been developed in sufficient detail to be able to show its power. And they make established modes of thinking and of expression the basis of this criticism. We have pointed out that the only way of discovering the faults of established modes of thinking is by resolutely trying out a different approach. It would seem to me that the task of philosophy, or of any enterprise interested in the advance, rather than the embalming of knowledge, would be to encourage the development of such new modes of approach, to participate in their improvement rather than to waste time in showing, what is obvious anyway, that they are different from the established ways of thinking.

6 *Thomas Nagel*

Physicalism

Thomas Nagel was born on July 4, 1937, in Belgrade, Yugoslavia. He was educated at Cornell, Oxford, and Harvard universities. He is Assistant Professor of Philosophy at Princeton University. His special interests are in ethics and the philosophy of mind, and he has contributed articles to leading philosophical journals.

I

It is the purpose of this paper to examine the reasons for believing that physicalism cannot possibly be true.[1] I mean by physicalism the thesis that a person, with all his psychological attributes, is nothing over and above his body, with all its physical attributes. The various theories which make this claim may be classified according to the identities which they allege between the mental and the physical.[2] These identities may be illustrated by the standard example of a quart of water which is identical with a collection of molecules, each containing two atoms of hydrogen and one of oxygen.

All states of the water are states of that collection of molecules: for the water to be in a particular bottle is for those molecules to be in that bottle; for the water to be frozen is for the molecules to be arranged in a space lattice, with strong intermolecular attractive

FROM *The Philosophical Review*, LXXIV (July, 1965), pp. 339–56. Reprinted by permission of the author and the editors.

[1] An earlier version of this paper was read at the Pacific Division A.P.A. meetings in Seattle, September 5, 1964.

[2] I shall not consider behaviorism or reductionism of any kind.

force and relatively weak individual vibratory motion; for the water to be boiling is for the molecules to have a kinetic energy sufficient to produce a vapor pressure equal to the atmospheric pressure; and so forth. In addition to general identities like these, there will be particular ones.[3] One such is the identity between an individual splash of the water and a particular sudden displacement of certain of the molecules—an identity which does not imply that a splash is always identical with that particular type of displacement. In all of these cases we can say something like the following: that the water's splashing is not anything over and above the displacement of those molecules; they are the same occurrence.

It is not clear whether every physicalist theory must assert the identity of each person with his body, nor is the connection between this identity and that of psychological with physical states easy to describe. Still, we can specify a range of possible views in terms of the latter relation alone. (1) An implausibly strong physicalism might assert the existence of a general identity between each psychological condition and a physical counterpart. (2) A weaker view would assert some general identities, particularly on the level of sensation, and particular identities for everything that remains. (3) A still weaker view might not require that a physical condition be found identical even in the particular case with every psychological condition, especially if it were an intensional one. (4) The weakest conceivable view would not even assert any particular identities, but of course it is unclear what other assertion by such a theory about the relation between mental and physical conditions might amount to a contention of physicalism.

I am inclined to believe that some weak physicalist theory of the third type is true, and that any plausible physicalism will include some state and event identities, both particular and general. Even a weak view, therefore, must be defended against objections to the possibility of identifying *any* psychological condition with a physical one. It is with such general objections that we shall be occupied.

I shall contend that they fail as objections to physicalism, but

[3] Any identity both of whose terms are universal in form will be called general, even if their specification involves reference to particulars. Thus, "Water is H_2O," "For water to be frozen is for its molecules to be in condition *F*," and "For *this* water to be frozen is for its molecules to be in condition *F*" are all general identities. On the other hand, "This water's (now) being frozen is its molecules' being in condition *F*" is a particular identity.

I shall also contend that they fail to express properly the real source of unhappiness with that position. This conclusion is drawn largely from my own case. I have always found physicalism extremely repellent. Despite my current belief that the thesis is true, this reaction persists, having survived the refutation of those common objections to physicalism which I once thought expressed it. Its source must therefore lie elsewhere, and I shall make a suggestion about that later.[4] First, however, it will be necessary to show why the standard objections fail, and what kind of identity can hold between mental and physical phenomena.

II

Since Smart refuted them, it has presumably become unnecessary to discuss those objections which rest on the confusion between identity of meaning and identity in fact.[5] We may concentrate rather on two types of objection which seem still to be current.

The first is that physicalism violates Leibniz' law, which requires that if two things are identical they have all their nonintensional and nonmodal properties in common. It is objected that sensory impressions, pains, thoughts, and so forth have various properties which brain states lack, and vice versa. I shall eventually propose a modification of Leibniz' law, since I do not believe that in its strict form it governs the relation asserted by the identity thesis. At this point, however, the thesis may be defended without resorting to such methods, through a somewhat altered version of a device employed by Smart, and earlier by U. T. Place.[6]

Instead of identifying thoughts, sensations, afterimages, and so

[4] In Sec. V; of the other sections, II attempts to rebut some standard objections, and III contains a general discussion of identity whose results are applied to physicalism in IV.

[5] J. J. C. Smart, "Sensations and Brain Processes," *Philosophical Review*, LXVIII (1959), pp. 141–56; republished in V. C. Chappell, ed., *The Philosophy of Mind*, (Englewood Cliffs, N.J.: Prentice-Hall, 1962); reprinted in this volume, pp. 32–47. Subsequent page references to Smart's article are to the reprint in this volume. See also Smart's book, *Philosophy and Scientific Realism* (London, 1963), and his article "Materialism," *Journal of Philosophy*, LX (1963), pp. 651–62, for further discussion of the identity thesis.

[6] U. T. Place, "Is Consciousness a Brain Process?" *British Journal of Psychology*, XLVII (1956), republished in Chappell, *op. cit.*; reprinted in this volume, pp. 21–31. Subsequent page references to Place's article are to the reprint in this volume. My formulation of the physical side of the identity differs from Smart's, and I do not accept his psychological reductionism.

forth with brain processes, I propose to identify a person's having the sensation with his body's being in a physical state or undergoing a physical process. Notice that both terms of this identity are of the same logical type, namely (to put it in neutral terminology) a subject's possessing a certain attribute. The subjects are the person and his body (not his brain), and the attributes are psychological conditions, happenings, and so forth, and physical ones. The psychological term of the identity must be the person's having a pain in his shin rather than the pain itself, because although it is undeniable that pains exist and people have them, it is also clear that this describes a condition of one entity, the person, rather than a relation between two entities, a person and a pain. For pains to exist *is* for people to have them. This seems to me perfectly obvious, despite the innocent suggestions of our language to the contrary.

So we may regard the ascription of properties to a sensation simply as part of the specification of a psychological state's being ascribed to the person. When we assert that a person has a sensation of a certain description *B*, this is not to be taken as asserting that there exist an x and a y such that x is a person and y is a sensation and $B(y)$, and x *has* y. Rather we are to take it as asserting the existence of only one thing, x, such that x is a person, and moreover $C(x)$, where C is the attribute "has a sensation of description *B*." The specification of this attribute is accomplished in part by the ascription of properties to the sensation; but this is merely part of the ascription of that psychological state to the person. This position seems to me attractive independently of physicalism, and it can be extended to psychological states and events other than sensations. Any ascription of properties to them is to be taken simply as part of the ascription of other attributes to the person who has them—as *specifying* those attributes.

I deviate from Smart in making the physical side of the identity a condition of the body rather than a condition of the brain,[7] because it seems to me doubtful that anything without a body of some conventional sort could be the subject of psychological states.[8]

[7] One might alternatively make it a physical condition of the *person*, so that the two identified attributes would be guaranteed the same subject. I cannot say how such a change would affect the argument.

[8] Cf. Norman Malcolm, "Scientific Materialism and the Identity Theory," *Dialogue*, III (1964); reprinted in this volume, pp. 72–81. Subsequent page references to Malcolm's article are to the reprint in this volume.

I do not mean to imply that the presence of a particular sensation need depend on the condition of any part of one's body outside of the brain. Making the physical term of the identity a bodily rather than a brain state merely implies that the brain is *in* a body. To identify the person's having a pain with the brain's being in state X rather than with the body's containing a brain in state X would imply, on the other hand, that if the individual's brain could have been in that state while the rest of his body was destroyed, he would still have been in the corresponding psychological state.

Given that the terms of the identity are as specified, nothing obliges us to identify a sensation or a pain or a thought with anything physical, and this disposes of numerous objections. For although I may have a visual sense impression whose attributes of form and color correspond closely to those which characterize the "Mona Lisa," my *having* the sense impression does not possess those attributes, and it is therefore no cause for worry that nothing in my brain looks like the "Mona Lisa." Given our specification of the psychological side of the identity, the demands on the physical side are considerably lessened. The physical equivalents of auditory impressions may be silent, those of olfactory impressions odorless, and so forth.

Most important, we can be rid of the stubbornest objection of this type, that having to do with location.[9] Brain processes are located in the brain, but a pain my be located in the shin and a thought has no location at all. But if the two sides of the identity are not a sensation and a brain process, but my *having* a certain sensation or thought and my body's *being* in a certain physical state, then they will both be going on in the same place—namely, wherever I (and my body) happen to be. It is important that the physical side of the identity is not a brain process, but rather my *body's* being in that state which may be specified as "having the relevant process going on in its brain." *That* state is not located in the brain; it has been located as precisely as it can be when we have been told the precise location of that of which it is a state—namely, my body. The same is true of my having a sensation: that

[9] Malcolm, *op. cit.*, pp. 75–77. See also Jerome Shaffer, "Could Mental States Be Brain Processes?," *Journal of Philosophy*, LVIII (1961). Shaffer thinks the difficulty can be got over, but that this depends on the possibility of a *change* in our concept of mental states, which would make it meaningful to assign them locations.

is going on wherever I happen to be at the time, and its location cannot be specified more precisely than mine can. (That is, even if a pain is located in my right shin, I am *having* that pain in my office at the university.) The location of bodily sensations is a very different thing from the location of warts. It is phenomenal location, and is best regarded as one feature of a psychological attribute possessed by the *whole* person rather than as the spatial location of an event going on in a part of him.

The other type of objection which I shall discuss is that physicalism fails to account for the privacy or subjectivity of mental phenomena. This complaint, while very important, is difficult to state precisely.

There is a trivial sense in which a psychological state is private to its possessor, namely, that since it is his, it cannot be anyone else's. This is just as true of haircuts or, for that matter, of physiological conditions. Its triviality becomes clear when we regard thoughts and sensations as conditions of the person rather than as things to which the person is related. When we see that what is described as though it were a relation between two things is really a condition of one thing, it is not surprising that only one person can stand in the said relation to a given sensation or feeling. In this sense, bodily states are just as private to their possessor as the mental states with which they may be equated.

The private-access objection is sometimes expressed epistemologically. The privacy of haircuts is uninteresting because there is lacking in that case a special connection between possession and knowledge which is felt to be present in the case of pains. Consider the following statement of the privacy objection.[10] "When I am in a psychological state—for example, when I have a certain sensation—it is logically impossible that I should fail to know that I am in that state. This, however, is not true of any bodily state. Therefore no psychological state is identical with any bodily state." As it

[10] See Kurt Baier, "Smart on Sensations," and J. J. C. Smart, "Brain Processes and Incorrigibility," *Australasian Journal of Philosophy*, XL (1962). This is regarded as a serious difficulty by Smart and other defenders of physicalism. See D. M. Armstrong, "Is Introspective Knowledge Incorrigible?," *Philosophical Review*, LXXII (1963), pp. 418–19. On the other hand, Hilary Putnam has argued that all the problems about privacy and special access which can be raised about persons can be raised about machines as well. See his paper, "Minds and Machines," in Sidney Hook, ed., *Dimensions of Mind* (New York: New York University Press, 1960).

happens, I believe that the first clause of this objection—namely, the incorrigibility thesis—is false, but I do not have to base my attack on that contention, for even if the incorrigibility thesis were true it would not rule out physicalism.

If state *x* is identical with state *y* it does not follow by Leibniz' law that if I know I am in state *x* then I know I am in state *y*, since the context is intensional. Therefore neither does it follow from "If I am in state *x* then I know I am in state *x*" that if I am in state *y* I know I am in state *y*. All that follows is that if I am in state *y* I know I am in state *x*. Moreover, this connection will not be a necessary one, since only one of the premises—the incorrigibility thesis—is necessary. The other premise—that *x* is identical with *y*—is contingent, making the consequence contingent.[11]

There may be more to the special-access objection than this, but I have not yet encountered a version of it which succeeds. We shall later discuss a somewhat different interpretation of the claim that mental states are subjective.

III

Let us now consider the nature of the identity which physicalism asserts. Events, states of affairs, conditions, psychological and otherwise, may be identical in a perfectly straightforward sense which conforms to Leibniz' law as strictly as does the identity between, say, the only horse in Berkeley and the largest mammal in Berkeley. Such identities between events may be due to the identity of two things referred to in their descriptions—for example, my being kicked by the only horse in Berkeley and my being kicked by the largest mammal in Berkeley—or they may not—for example, the sinking of the Titanic and the largest marine disaster ever to occur in peacetime. Whether they hold between things, events, or conditions, I shall refer to them as *strict* identities.

We are interested, however, in identities of a different type—

[11] It is worth noting that if two mental states are necessarily connected, this connection must be mirrored on the level of the physical states with which we identify them. Although the connection between the physical states need not be a logically necessary one, that would be a desirable feature in a physicalistic theory, and it seems in fact to be present in the example of water and molecules: the water's being frozen necessarily includes its being cold, and the specification of the molecular state which *is* its being frozen entails that the molecules will have a low average kinetic energy—which is in fact the same thing as the water's being cold.

between psychological and physical events, or between the boiling of water and the activity of molecules. I shall call these theoretical identities[12] and shall concentrate for the moment on their application to events and attributes rather than to things, although they hold between things as well. It is a weaker relation than strict identity, and common possession of causal and conditional attributes is crucial for its establishment.[13] Strict identities are likely to be established in other ways, and we can infer the sameness of all causal and conditional attributes. Thus, if being kicked by the only horse in Berkeley gave me a broken leg, then being kicked by the largest mammal in Berkeley had the same effect, given that they are the same creature; and if it is the case that I should not have been kicked by the only horse in Berkeley if I had stayed in my office that afternoon, then it follows that if I had stayed in my office I should not have been kicked by the largest mammal in Berkeley.

But if we lack grounds such as these, we must establish sameness of conditional attributes independently, and this depends on the discovery of general laws from which the particular conditionals follow. Our grounds for believing that a particular quart of water's boiling is the same event as a collection of molecules' behaving in a certain way are whatever grounds we may have for believing that all the causes and effects of one event are also causes and effects of the other, and that all true statements about conditions under which the one event would not have occurred, or about what would have happened if it had not, or about what would happen if it continued, and so forth, are also true of the other.

This is clearly more than mere constant conjunction; it is a fairly strong requirement for identity. Nevertheless it is weaker than the

[12] Following Hilary Putnam, *op. cit.*, who says that the "is" in question is that of theoretical identification. The word "identity" by itself is actually too strong for such cases, but I shall adopt it for the sake of convenience.

[13] An attribute, for our purposes, is signified by any sentence frame containing one free variable (in however many occurrences) where this may be a variable ranging over objects, events, and so forth. (One gets a particular instance of an attribute by plugging in an appropriate particular for the variable and converting to gerundival form.) Thus all three of the following are attributes: ". . . is boiling," ". . . will stop boiling if the kettle is taken off the fire," and ". . . will stop if the kettle is taken off the fire." A particular quart of water has the second of these attributes if and only if that water's boiling has the third, where this can be described as the possession of the third attribute by a particular instance of the first.

standard version of Leibniz' law in that it does not require possession by each term of *all* the attributes of the other. It does not require that the complex molecular event which we may identify with my being kicked by the only horse in Berkeley be independently characterizable as ridiculous—for example, on the grounds that the latter event was ridiculous and if the former cannot be said to be ridiculous, it lacks an attribute which the latter possesses. There are some attributes from the common possession of which the identity follows, and others which either do not matter or which we cannot decide whether to ascribe to one of the terms without first deciding whether the identity in question holds.

To make this precise, I shall introduce the notion of independent ascribability. There are certain attributes such as being hot or cold, or boiling or offensive, which cannot significantly be ascribed to a collection of molecules per se. It may be that such attributes *can* be ascribed to a collection of molecules, but such ascription is dependent for its significance on their primary ascription to something of a different kind, like a body of water or a person, with which the molecules are identical. Such attributes, I shall say, are not independently ascribable to the molecules though they may be dependently ascribable. Similarly, the property of having eighty-three trillion members is not independently ascribable to a quantity of water, though it may be possessed by a collection of H_2O molecules. Nevertheless, there is in such cases a class of attributes which are independently ascribable to both terms, and the condition for theoretical identity may be stated as follows: that the two terms should possess or lack in common all those attributes which can be independently ascribed to each of them individually—with the qualification that nothing is by this criterion to be identical with two things which are by the same criterion distinct.[14] Actually this will serve as a condition for identity in general; a strict identity will simply be one between terms sufficiently similar in type to allow independent ascription to both of *all* the same attributes, and will include such cases as the sinking of the Titanic being the largest marine disaster ever to occur in peacetime, or the morning star

[14] The qualification takes care of such possibly problematic claims as that I am the square root of 2, for although it may be that we share all attributes which can be independently ascribed to each of us, I also share those attributes with the square root of 3, whose attributes clearly contradict those of the square root of 2.

being the evening star. The identities I have characterized as theoretical hold across categories of description sufficiently different to prohibit independent ascription to both terms of all the same attributes, although, as I have observed, such ascriptions may be meaningful as *consequences* of the identity.

The question naturally arises, to what extent do particular theoretical identities depend on corresponding general ones? In the examples I have given concerning the case of water, the dependence is obvious. There the particular identities have simply been instances of general ones, which are consequences of the same theory that accounts for the common possession of relevant attributes in the particular cases. Now there is a technical sense in which every particular theoretical identity must be an instance of a general identity, but not all cases need be like that of water. Although it is essential that particular identities must follow from general laws or a general theory, this does not prevent us from distinguishing between cases in which, for example, the molecular counterpart of a macroscopic phenomenon is always the same, and those in which it varies from instance to instance. The common possession of conditional attributes can follow for a particular case from general laws, without its being true that there is a general correlation between macroscopic and microscopic phenomena of that type. For example, it may at the same time follow from general laws that types of microscopic phenomena other than the one present in this case would also share the requisite conditional properties.

The technical sense in which even in such cases the particular identity must be an instance of a general one is that it must be regarded as an instance of the identity between the macroscopic phenomenon and the disjunction of all those microscopic phenomena which are associated with it in the manner described, via general laws. For suppose we have a type of macroscopic phenomenon A and two types of microscopic phenomena *B* and C so associated with it. Suppose on one occasion particular cases of A and *B* are occurring at the same place and time, and so forth, and suppose it is asserted that since it follows from general laws that they also have all their conditional attributes in common, A is in this case identical in the specified sense with *B*. They do not, however, have common the conditional attribute $F(X)$, defined as follows: "If C and not *B*, then *X*." That is, $F(A)$ but not $F(B)$.

Therefore, we must identify the occurrence of *A* even in this case with the occurrence of the disjunction *B* or *C*. This does not prevent us, however, from introducing as a subsidiary sense of identity for particular cases that in which *A* is *B* because the disjunction *B* or *C* which is properly identical with *A* is in fact satisfied by *B*. There is of course a range of cases between the two kinds described, cases in which the disjuncts in the general identity consist of conjunctions which overlap to a greater or lesser degree, and this complicates the matter considerably.[15] Nevertheless we can, despite the technicality, differentiate roughly between particular identities which are in a narrow sense instances of general identities and those which are not—that is, which are instances only of radically disjunctive general identities. Henceforth when I refer to general identities I shall be excluding the latter.

I have concentrated on identities between states, events, and attributes because it is in such terms that physicalism is usually conceived, but if it is also part of physicalism to hold that people are their bodies, it becomes appropriate to inquire into the relation between the theoretical identity of things and the theoretical identity of their attributes. Unfortunately, I do not have a general answer to this question. The case of strict identity presents no problem, for there every attribute of one term is strictly identical with the corresponding attribute of the other; and in our standard example of theoretical identity, each attribute of the water seems to be theoretically identical with some attribute of the molecules, but not vice versa. This may be one (asymmetrical) condition for the theoretical identity of things. It is not clear, however, whether the identity of things must always be so closely tied to the identity of their attributes. For example, it might be that everything we could explain in terms of the water and

[15] A fuller treatment would have to include a discussion of the nonsymmetrical relation ". . . consists of . . ." which is distinct from identity. A macroscopic event (the freezing of some water, for example) may be identical with a microscopic event *A* described in general terms (average kinetic energy, spatial ordering, and the like) while at the same time consisting of a very specific collection *B* of microscopic events with which it is not identical, since if one of them (the motion of a particular molecule) had been different, that particular complex of microscopic events would not have occurred though both *A* and the macroscopic event would have. (Presumably in such cases the occurrence of *B* entails the occurrence of *A*, but more than that needs to be said about the relation between the two.) The same concept applies to the relation between World War II and the immense collection of actions and events of which it consisted, or that between the Eiffel Tower and the girders and rivets which make it up.

its attributes could be explained in terms of the batch of molecules and their attributes, but that the two systems of explanation were so different in structure that it would be impossible to find a single attribute of the molecules which explained all and only those things explained by a particular attribute of the water.

Whether or not this is true of water, the possibility has obvious relevance to physicalism. One might be able to define a weak criterion of theoretical identity which would be satisfied in such a case, and this might in turn give sense to an identification of persons with their bodies which did not depend on the discovery of a single physical counterpart for every psychological event or condition. I shall, however, forgo an investigation of the subject; this general discussion of identity must remain somewhat programmatic.

IV

It provides us with some things to say, however, about the thesis of physicalism. First, the grounds for accepting it will come from increased knowledge of (a) the explanation of mental events and (b) the physiological explanation of happenings which those mental events in turn explain. Second, in view of the condition of independent ascribability, physicalism need not be threatened by the difficulty that although anger may be, for example, justified, it makes no sense to say this of a physical state with which we may identify it. Third, it does not require general identities at every level: that is, there need not be, either for all persons or even for each individual, a specific physical state of the body which is *in general* identical with intending to vote Republican at the next election, or having a stomach-ache, in order that physicalism be true. It seems likely that there will be general identities of a rough kind for nonintensional states, such as having particular sensations or sensory impressions, since the physical causes of these are fairly uniform. But one can be practically certain that intensional mental states, even if in each particular case they are identical with some physical state, will not have general physical counterparts, because both the causes and the effects of a given belief or desire or intention are extremely various on different occasions even for the same individual, let alone for different persons. One might as easily hope to find a general equivalent, in molecular terms, of a building's collapsing or a bridge's being unsafe—yet each instance of such an event or circumstance is identical with some microscopic phenomenon.

The relation of intensional mental states to physical states may be even more involved than this. For one thing, if it should be the case that they are dispositional in a classical sense, then physicalism requires only that the events and states to which they are the dispositions be identical with physical events and states. It does not require that they be identical with any additional independent physical state, existing even when the disposition is not being exercised. (In fact, I do not believe that dispositions operate according to the classical Rylean model, and this will affect still further the way in which the identity thesis applies to dispositional mental states; but this is not the place for a discussion of that issue.)

There is still another point: many intensional predicates do not just ascribe a condition to the person himself but have implications about the rest of the world and his relation to it. Physicalism will of course not require that these be identical simply with states of the person's body, narrowly conceived. An obvious case is that of knowledge, which implies not only the truth of what is known but also a special relation between this and the knower. Intentions, thoughts, and desires may also imply a context, a relation with things outside the person. The thesis that all states of a person are states of his body therefore requires a liberal conception of what constitutes a state—one which will admit relational attributes. This is not peculiar to mental states: it is characteristic of intensional attributes wherever they occur. That a sign says that fishing is forbidden does not consist simply in its having a certain geometrically describable distribution of black paint on its surface; yet we are not tempted here to deny that the sign is a piece of wood with paint on it, or to postulate a noncorporeal substance which is the subject of the sign's intensional attributes.

Even with all these qualifications, however, it may be too much to expect a specific physical counterpart for each particular psychological phenomenon. Thus, although it may be the case that what explains and is explained by a particular sensation can also explain and be explained by a particular neurological condition, it may also be that this is not precisely true of an intention, but rather that the various connections which we draw between causes and effects via the intention can be accounted for in terms of many different physical conditions, some of which also account for connections which in psychological discourse we draw via states other than the intention, and no subset of which, proper or improper, accounts for all and only those connections which the intention explains. For this reason a thoroughgoing physicalism might have to fall back on a criterion for identity between things not dependent on the identity of their attributes—a criterion of the sort envisaged at the end of the previous section.

Obviously any physicalistic *theory,* as opposed to the bare philosophical thesis of physicalism, will be exceedingly complex. We are nowhere near a physical theory of how human beings work, and I do not know whether the empirical evidence currently available indicates that we may expect with the advance of neurology to uncover one. My concern here has been only to refute the philosophical position that mental-physical identity is *impossible,* and that *no* amount of further information could constitute evidence for it.

V

Even if what might be called the standard objections have been answered, however, I believe that there remains another source for the philosophical conviction that physicalism is impossible. It expresses itself crudely as the feeling that there is a fundamental distinction between the subjective and the objective which cannot be bridged. Objections having to do with privacy and special access represent attempts to express it, but they fail to do so, for it remains when they have been defeated. The feeling is that I (and hence any "I") cannot be a mere physical object, because I possess my mental states: I am their *subject,* in a way in which no physical object can possibly be the subject of its attributes. I have a type of internality which physical things lack; so in addition to the connection which all my mental states do admittedly have with my body, they are also mine—that is, they have a particular *self* as subject, rather than merely being attributes of an object. Since any mental state must have a self as subject, it cannot be identical with a mere attribute of some object like a body, and the self which is its subject cannot therefore be a body.

Why should it be thought that for *me* to have a certain sensation —to be in a certain mental state—cannot consist merely in a physical object's being in some state, having some attribute? One might put it as follows. States of my body, physical states, are, admittedly, physical states of me, but this is not simply because they are states of that body but because in addition it is my body. And its being my body consists in its having a certain relation, perhaps a causal one, to the subject of my mental states. This leads naturally to the conclusion that I, the subject of my mental states, am something else—perhaps a mental substance. My physical states are only derivatively mine, since they are states of a body which is mine in virtue of being related in the appropriate way to my psychological states. But this is possible only if those psychological states are mine in an original, and not merely derivative, sense; therefore *their* subject cannot be the body which is derivatively mine. The feeling that physicalism leaves out of account the essential subjectivity of psychological states is the feeling that nowhere in the description of the state of a human body could there be room for a physical equivalent of the fact that *I* (or any self), and not just that body, am the subject of those states.

This, so far as I can see, is the source of my uneasiness about physicalism. Unfortunately, whatever its merits, it is no more an argument against physicalism than against most other theories of mind, including dualism, and it therefore provides us with no more reason for rejecting the former in favor of the latter than do the standard objections already discussed. It can be shown that if we follow out this type of argument, it will provide us with equally strong reasons for rejecting any view which identifies the subject of psychological states with a substance and construes the states as attributes of that substance. A noncorporeal substance seems safe only because in retreating from the physical substance as a candidate for the self, we are so much occupied with finding a subject whose states are originally, and not just derivatively, mine—one to which the physical body can be related in a way which explains how *it* can be mine—that we simply postulate such a subject without asking ourselves whether the same objections will not apply to it as well: whether indeed any substance can possibly meet the requirement that its states be *underivatively* mine.

The problem can be shown to be general in the following way: consider everything that can be said about the world without employing any token-reflexive expressions.[16] This will include the description

[16] I.e., expressions *functioning* as token reflexives. Such words of course lose this function in quotation and in certain cases of *oratio* (or *cogitatio*) *obliqua:* e.g., "John Smith thinks that he is Napoleon."

of all its physical contents and their states, activities, and attributes. It will also include a description of all the persons in the world and their histories, memories, thoughts, sensations, perceptions, intentions, and so forth. I can thus describe without token-reflexives the entire world and everything that is happening in it—and this will include a description of Thomas Nagel and what he is thinking and feeling. But there seems to remain one thing which I cannot say in this fashion—namely, which of the various persons in the world *I* am. Even when everything that can be said in the specified manner has been said, and the world has in a sense been completely described, there seems to remain one fact which has not been expressed, and that is the fact that I am Thomas Nagel. This is not, of course, the fact ordinarily conveyed by those words, when they are used to inform someone else who the *speaker* is—for that could easily be expressed otherwise. It is rather the fact that *I* am the subject of *these* experiences; this body is my body; the subject or center of my world is this person, Thomas Nagel.

Now it follows from this not only that a sensation's being mine cannot consist simply in its being an attribute of a particular body; it follows also that it cannot consist in the sensation's being an attribute of a particular soul which is joined to that body; for nothing in the specification of that soul will determine that *it* is mine, and I am *that* person. So long as we construe psychological states as attributes of a substance, no matter what substance we pick, it can be thrown, along with the body, into the "objective" world; its states and its relation to a particular body can be described completely without touching upon the fact that I am that person.[17] It turns out therefore that, given the requirements which led us to reject physicalism, the quest for the self, for a substance which *is* me and whose possession of a psychological attribute will *be* its being mine, is a quest for something which could not exist. The only possible conclusion is that the self is not a substance, and that the special kind of possession which characterizes the relation between me and my psychological states cannot be represented as the possession of certain attributes by a subject, no matter what that subject may be. The subjectivity of the true psychological subject is of a different kind from that of the mere subject of attributes. And if I am to extend this to cases other than my own, I must conclude that for no person is it the case that his having a par-

[17] Cf. Wittgenstein, *Tractatus*, 5.64.

ticular sensation consists in some occupant of the world having a particular attribute or being in a certain state.

I shall not discuss the reasons for rejecting this position. My attitude toward it is precisely the reverse of my attitude toward physicalism, which repels me although I am persuaded of its truth. The two are of course related, since what bothers me about physicalism is the thought that I cannot be a mere physical object, cannot in fact be anything *in* the world at all, and that my sensations and so forth cannot be simply the attributes of some substance.

But if we reject this view (as it seems likely that we must) and accept the alternative that a person is something in the world and that his mental states are states of that thing, then there is no a priori reason why it should not turn out to be a physical body and those states physical states. We are thus freed to investigate the possibility, and to seek the kind of understanding of psychological states which will enable us to formulate specific physicalistic theories as neurology progresses.

POSTSCRIPT, 1968

I now believe that theoretical identity is not distinct from strict identity, and that the device by which I formerly defined theoretical identity can be used to explain how Leibniz's law is satisfied by identities whose terms are of disparate types. Suppose boiling is independently ascribable to a quart of water but not to the molecules which compose it. Nevertheless, we can say that the molecules are boiling if they bear a certain relation to the water and the water is boiling. The relation in question, call it R, is simply that which I formerly described as theoretical identity. It holds between a and b if (i) they possess or lack in common all those attributes which can be independently ascribed to each of them individually (call this relation S), and (ii) neither a nor b bears relation S to any third term which does not bear relation S to the other.[1] Let F range over nonintensional and nonmodal attributes, and let us symbolize the modal statement "F is independently ascribable (truly or falsely) to a" as I(F,a). Then

(1) $S(a,b) \equiv df\ (F)\ (I(F,a) \cdot I(F,b) \cdot \supset \cdot F(a) \equiv F(b))$

(2) $R(a,b) \equiv df$ (i) $S(a,b)$ & (ii) a true statement results whenever a name or definite description is substituted for "x" in the schema $S(a,x) \equiv S(b,x)$

I claim that a true statement results whenever names or definite descriptions are substituted for 'x' and 'y' in the following schema:

(3) $(F)\ (I(F,x) \cdot F(x) \cdot R(x,y) \cdot \supset F(y))$

If this is correct, then when a and b are related by R they will share all the attributes independently ascribed to either of them. By Leibniz's law, therefore,

(4) $R(a,b) \equiv a = b$

[1] Condition (ii) is added for the reason cited in footnote 14 of my 1965 paper.

7 *W. V. Quine*

On Mental Entities

W. V. Quine was born on June 25, 1908, in Akron, Ohio, and attended Oberlin College. In 1931, he received his Ph.D. from Harvard University, where he is now Edgar Pierce Professor of Philosophy. Quine is one of the most influential philosophers of the twentieth century, especially in logic and the philosophy of language. He is the author of many books; among them are *Methods of Logic, From a Logical Point of View,* and *Word and Object.*

A question which is very much in the air is whether we should affirm or deny that there are such things as *sensations,* these being conceived as immediate, subjective experiences. I shall touch on this question, but not just yet. For a while it will be convenient to talk as if there are.

Falling in thus uncritically with the usage of old-fashioned epistemology and introspective psychology, let us consider, to begin with, the process of language. It has been the fashion in recent philosophy, both that of some of the English analysts and that of some of the logical positivists, to think of the terms of science and ordinary language as having some sort of hidden or implicit definitions which carry each such term back finally to terms relating to immediate experience. Now this view is clearly unrealistic. A better description, though countenancing the notion of immediate experience still, is

FROM *Proceedings* of the American Academy of Arts and Sciences, LXXX (Boston, 1951). Reprinted by permission of the author and the editors. Presented at Cambridge, Mass., November 18, 1952, in a colloquium of the Institute for the Unity of Science.

as follows. On the one hand we have language, as an infinite totality of said or appropriately sayable phrases and sentences. On the other hand we have our sense experience, which, by a process of psychological association or conditioned response, is keyed in with the linguistic material at numerous and varied places. The linguistic material is an interlocked system which is tied here and there to experience; it is not a society of separately established terms and statements, each with its separate empirical definition. There is no separate meaning, in terms of direct experience, for the statement that there is a table here, or that there is a planet somewhere in outer space. The statement that there is the planet may be keyed with our sense experience by our seeing the planet, or by our merely noting perturbations in the orbits of other planets. And even the statement that there is a table right here may be keyed with our sense experience through touch *or* sight *or* hearsay. Again the statement that I have cut my finger may be tied with experience either by sight or by pain or both. I have often argued that it is mistaken to try to distinguish even between those scientific statements which are true by virtue of the meanings of our terms and those which are true or probable by inductive evidence. As Pierre Duhem urged, it is the system as a whole that is keyed to experience. It is taught by exploitation of its heterogeneous and sporadic links with experience, and it stands or falls, is retained or modified, according as it continues to serve us well or ill in the face of continuing experience.

We get the system, in its main lines, from our forebears. As children learning the language, we get on to various simple terms and key phrases by direct association with appropriate experiences. When we have progressed a bit with this kind of learning, we learn further usages contextually. Eventually we are in a position to receive traditional doctrine a whole chapter at a time. Finally some men venture to revise the tradition here and there, for the sake of greater simplicity or better experiential links; and these are scientists.

So much for the individual's mastery of language and lore; but what of the origins of all this in the race? It would be irrational to suppose that those origins were rational. The prehistory of science was probably a composite of primitive unconscious symbolism of the Freudian kind, confusions of sign and object, word magic, wishful thinking, and a lazy acquiescence in forms whose motivation had been long forgotten. Biases in our conceptual schemes may have great utility in the systematizing of science, and therewith high survival value, despite humble origins in the random workings of unreason—just as chance mutations in the chromosome may launch a sturdy and efficient new race. Natural selection through the ages tends to favor the happy accidents at the expense of the unpropitious ones, in the evolution of ideas as in the evolution of living species.

As scientists we accept provisionally our heritage from the dim past, with intermediate revisions by our more recent forebears; and then we continue to warp and revise. As Neurath has said, we are in the position of a mariner who must rebuild his ship plank by plank while continuing to stay afloat on the open sea.

How do we decide on such retentions and revisions? To be more specific: how do we decide, apropos of the real world, what things there *are?* Ultimately, I think, by considerations of simplicity plus a pragmatic guess as to how the overall system will continue to work in connection with experience. We posit molecules, and eventually electrons, even though these are not given to direct experience, merely because they contribute to an overall system which is simpler as a whole than its known alternatives; the empirical relevance of the notion of molecules and electrons is indirect, and exists only by virtue of the links with experience which exist at *other* points of the system. Actually I expect that tables and sheep are, in the last analysis, on much the same footing as molecules and electrons. Even these have a continuing right to a place in our conceptual scheme only by virtue of their indirect contribution to the overall simplicity of our linguistic or conceptual organization of experience; for note that even tables and sheep are not direct sensations.

The notion of macroscopic objects, tables and sheep, differs from that of molecules and electrons mainly, from an epistemological point of view, in point of degree of antiquity. Molecules were posited consciously in historic times, whereas the positing of the external objects of common sense is an original trait of human nature. Men have believed in something very like our common-sense world of external objects as long, surely, as anything properly describable as language has existed; for the teaching of language and the use of it for communication depend on investing linguistic forms with intersubjectively fixed references. It would be senseless to speak of a motive for this archaic and unconscious posit, but we can significantly speak of its function and its survival value; and in these respects the hypothesis of common-sense external objects is quite like that of molecules and electrons.

Because the notion of external macroscopic objects is so fundamental both to the origins of language and to the continued learning of language, we may be pretty sure that it is here to stay, though electrons and other more hypothetical entities may, with the continued revisions of science, come and go. Experience is continually reminding us that it is over the external macroscopic objects that there is least semantical misunderstanding between speakers; it is naturally to tables and sheep and the like that we keep returning when there is trouble about new concepts.

Epistemologists, put off by the fact that macroscopic objects are epistemologically on the same footing as molecules and electrons, have looked to sense data—the raw content of sensation itself—as a more ultimate realm of entities. The ensuing difficulties are notorious. They may be seen most vividly if to begin with we think about memory. Our present data of our own past experiences are, on this theory, some sort of faint present replicas of past sense impressions; faint echoes of past sensation accompanying the blare of present sensation. Now it takes little soul-searching to persuade oneself that such double impressions, dim against bright, are rather the exception than the rule. Ordinarily we do not remember the trapezoidal sensory surface of a desk, as a color patch extending across the lower half of the visual field; what we remember is *that* there was a desk meeting such-and-such approximate specifications of form and size in three-dimensional space. Memory is just as much a product of the past positing of extra-sensory objects as it is a datum for the positing of past sense data.

What has been said just now of memory applies in some degree to the stream of sensory experience generally. It would be increasingly apparent from the findings of the Gestalt psychologists, if it were not quite apparent from everyday experience, that our selective awareness of present sensory surfaces is a function of present purposes and past conceptualizations. The contribution of reason cannot be viewed as limited merely to conceptualizing a presented pageant of experience and positing objects behind it; for this activity reacts, by selection and emphasis, on the qualitative make-up of the pageant itself in its succeeding portions. It is not an instructive oversimplification, but a basic falsification, to represent cognition as a discernment of regularities in an unadulterated stream of experience. Better to conceive of the stream itself as polluted, at each succeeding point of its course, by every prior cognition.

So the notion of pure sense datum is a pretty tenuous abstraction, a good deal more conjectural than the notion of an external object, a table or a sheep. It is significant that when we try to talk of the subjective we borrow our terminology from the objective: I feel as if I were falling, I have a sinking sensation, I feel on top of the world, I see pink elephants (better: I feel as if I were really seeing real pink elephants), etc. Even the terms which we have come to regard as strictly and immediately sensory, like 'red', are obviously objective in reference in the first instance: we learn the word 'red' by being confronted with an external object which our parent calls red, just as we learn the word 'sheep' by being confronted with an external object which our parent calls a sheep. When, at a certain stage of epistemological sophistication, we transfer the word 'red' to an alleged datum of immediate subjective sense experience, we are doing just what we do when we say we have a sinking sensation: I feel *as if* I were really, externally falling, and I feel *as if* I were really confronted by an external red object.

I suggest that it is a mistake to seek an immediately evident reality, somehow more immediately evident than the realm of external objects. Unbemused by philosophy, we would all go along with Dr. Johnson, whose toe was his touchstone of reality. Sheep are real, unicorns not. Clouds are real, the sky (as a solid canopy) not. Odd numbers are perhaps real, but prime even numbers other than 2 not. Everything, of course, is real; but there are sheep and there are no unicorns, there are clouds and there is (in the specified sense of the term) no sky, there are odd numbers and there are no even primes other than 2. Such is the ordinary usage of the word 'real', a separation of the sheep from the unicorns. Failing some aberrant definition which is certainly not before us, this is the only usage we have to go on.

The crucial insight of empircism is that any evidence for science has its end points in the senses. This insight remains valid, but it is an insight which comes after physics, physiology, and psychology, not before. Epistemologists have wanted to posit a realm of sense data, situated somehow just me-ward of the physical stimulus, for fear of circularity: to view the physical stimulation rather than the sense datum as the end point of scientific evidence would be to make physical science rest for its evidence on physical science. But if with

Neurath we accept this circularity, simply recognizing that the science of science is a science, then we dispose of the epistemological motive for assuming a realm of sense data. May we then make a clean sweep of mental entities?

I urged earlier that we decide what things there are, or what things to treat as there being, by considerations of simplicity of the overall system and its utility in connection with experience, so to speak. I say "so to speak" because I do not want to force the issue of recognizing experience as an entity or composite of entities. I have talked up to now as if there were such entities; I had to talk some language, and I uncritically talked this one. But the history of the mind-body problem bears witness to the awkwardness of the practice. We are virtually bound, as remarked earlier, to hold to an ontology of external objects; but it is moot indeed whether the positing of additional objects of a mental kind is a help or a hindrance to science. Or perhaps not so moot. At any rate it is moot or else it is clear that they are a hindrance.

To repudiate mental entities is not to deny that we sense or even that we are conscious; it is merely to report and try to describe these facts without assuming entities of a mental kind. What is spoken of in terms of the residual posited objects of science and common sense as my cut finger is keyed into our nervous responses in various ways; nerves from my eye and other eyes are involved, and nerves from my finger. Some persons are so situated as to be accessible to the stimuli which are most closely relevant to the phrase 'Quine's cut finger' and some are not. A dozen of us are in a position for the appropriate stimulation of the eye, and one of us for the appropriate stimulation of the finger.

None of us is oriented to external objects quite like anyone else, for we occupy different positions, and while we exchange positions the objects age. None of us learned his words quite like anyone else. But we use them in sufficient systematic agreement for fair communication—which is no accident, since language is subject to the law of survival of the fittest. We manage to talk effectively about other people's cut fingers because of a pattern of habits connecting with present and past stimulation of the eye together with past stimulation, under optically similar circumstances, of our own fingers. The same is true of pain—but no argument against construing pain as a state of the physical organism. If we repudiate mental entities as entities, there ceases to be an iron curtain between the private and the public; there remains only a smoke screen, a matter of varying degrees of privacy of events in the physical world. Consciousness still retains a place, as a state of a physical object, if—following the suggestion made by Professor Deutsch in addressing this institute last year—we construe consciousness as a faculty of responding to one's own responses. The responses here are, or can be construed as, physical behavior. It is not the purpose of this view to leave any aspect of life out of account. The issue is merely whether, in an ideal last accounting of everything or a present practical accounting of everything we can, it is efficacious so to frame our conceptual scheme as to mark out a range of entities or units of a so-called mental kind in addition to the physical ones. My hypothesis, put forward in the spirit of a hypothesis of natural science, is that it is not efficacious.

8 *Wilfrid Sellars*

The Identity Approach to the Mind-Body Problem

Wilfrid Sellars was born on May 20, 1912, in Ann Arbor, Michigan. He was educated at the University of Michigan, the University of Buffalo, Oxford, and Harvard, and is now Professor of Philosophy and Resident Professor of the Philosophy of Science at the University of Pittsburgh. His special interests are the theory of knowledge, ethics, and the history of philosophy. He is the author of *Science, Perception, and Reality* and *Philosophical Perspectives,* and he is the co-editor of *Readings in Ethical Theory.*

I

1. My primary aim in this paper is to set the stage for a discussion of some of the central themes in the so-called "identity approach" to the mind-body problem.[1] I have particularly in mind Herbert Feigl's elaborate statement and defence of this approach in Volume II of the *Minnesota Studies.*[2] A secondary, but more constructive, purpose is to bring out some of the reasons which incline me to think that the theory is either very exciting but false, or true but relatively uninteresting.

FROM *The Review of Metaphysics,* XVIII (1965), pp. 430–51. Reprinted by permission of the author and the editors.

[1] This paper was prepared for and presented at the Boston Colloquium for the Philosophy of Science, April 10, 1963. I am also grateful to my colleagues at the University of Pittsburgh who forced me to clarify key passages in the argument.

[2] Herbert Feigl, "The 'Mental' and the 'Physical,'" *Minnesota Studies in the Philosophy of Science,* II (1957), pp. 370–498.

2. I shall begin with a preliminary formulation of the identity theory which will highlight the topics I propose to discuss. Roughly put, the theory claims that what it calls "raw feels"—a technical expression which is intended to cover impressions and images pertaining to the external senses, as well as bodily sensations and feelings in a more usual sense—are identical with "brain states." It hastens to add that in speaking of "raw feels" as identical with "brain states" it does not simply mean that the very same logical subjects which have "raw feel" characteristics also have "brain state" characteristics, or that "raw feel" characteristics do not occur apart from "brain state" characteristics, but rather that the very characteristics themselves are identical. As Feigl puts it, "raw feel" universals are identical with certain "brain state" universals.

3. This rough and ready formulation of what is actually a highly sophisticated philosophical thesis blocks out three topics with which any attempt to assess the identity theory must come to grips. Each of these topics turns out on the most cursory inspection to involve highly controversial issues which are at the very center of the philosophical stage. I shall not attempt to resolve all or, indeed, any of these issues. My aim will rather be to thread my way through them in such a way as to bring out the common ground I share with the identity theory and thus make possible a meaningful joining of issues.

4. It will not have passed unnoticed in this particular climate of opinion that the identity theory as formulated above is committed to the idea that it makes sense to speak of the identity of attributes or universals. This is the first of the thorny topics on which *something* must be said. This may be the place, but it is not the time to develop a theory of abstract entities.[3] I shall simply mobilize some of the preanalytic strands which any theory must take into account, and develop them in a way which gives the claim that "raw feel" universals are identical with certain "brain state" universals at least the appearance of being in keeping with the spirit of a scientifically oriented philosophy.

5. Universals, then, are a subset of abstract entities. Their distinctive feature is that they are expressed in language by predicates (e.g. 'red') or by predicative expressions (e.g. '3 feet long,' 'between red and yellow in color'). I shall say that predicates (under which term

[3] For the main outlines of the view I would defend, see "Abstract Entities," *Review of Metaphysics*, XVII (1963).

I shall usually include predicative expressions) 'stand for' or 'express' universals. Universals may be referred to as well as stood for or expressed. But predicates do not *refer to* universals; indeed, they are not referring expressions at all. Among the expressions which refer to universals, a particularly important role is played by those which are formed from predicates or predicative expressions which stand for or express the universals to which reference is made; thus

Triangularity
Being three feet long
Being between red and yellow in color

6. Universals are public objects. They are identities not only with respect to their many instances, but also with respect to the many minds which think in terms of them, and the many languages which give expression to them. This inter-subjective and inter-linguistic character must be accounted for by any adequate theory of abstract entities. Equally important, and even more "platonistic" in tone is the distinction which must be drawn between those universals which have been "discovered" or come to be "known" and those which have not, and, within the sphere of the former, between those which are effectively taken account of by our language and those which are not. To unpack this a bit, I shall assume that a universal is "discovered" or comes to be "known" in the course of coming to know what *use* a predicate would have to have in order to stand for or express it. The universal is *effectively taken account of* by our language if our language contains a predicative expression which actually has this use.[4]

7. Notice, therefore, that while we can refer to unknown or undiscovered universals (I drop the quotation marks from these metaphorically used terms) and to universals which are not effectively taken account of by our language, only universals which are effectively taken account of by our language can be referred to by referring expressions formed from predicates which stand for or express them. Thus, although we can *refer to* the as yet unknown property of persons which would explain their telekinetic powers (supposing them to have such), our language contains no predicate which stands for or expresses this property.

[4] For the difference between these two stages compare a newly minted theory which is still but a candidate for espousal, with an accepted theory which is in day-to-day use.

8. Against this background, the following criterion for the identity of two universals can be formulated:

> Two universals are identical if, were a language to contain predicative expressions which stand for or express them, these predicative expressions would either independently have the same use, or one would be a definitional abbreviation of the other.

9. Clearly, much of the burden of the above distinctions is borne by the word "use" and the phrase "the same use." My general strategy is clear. It is to connect "realistic" talk about universals with "nominalistic" talk about linguistic expressions. My further strategy would be to connect talk about the use of expressions with talk about uniformities in the occurrence of linguistic inscriptions, and, therefore, to build a bridge to "behavioral criteria of synonymy." But that is strategy for a war and not a battle. Here I shall limit myself to pointing out that the patterns of use I have primarily in mind are (1) the reporting or observation pattern; (2) the consequence pattern. The latter is, roughly, the pattern which would find its explicit formulation in what Carnap calls 'transformation rules,' L-transformation rules, P-transformation rules and others. I add "and others" to Carnap's list because it is not clear that it is an exhaustive classification. Other possible candidates are "bridge laws" and "correspondence rules."

10. I pointed out above that we can refer to universals for which we have no corresponding predicates. There are two types of case, one of which is, for our purposes, uninteresting. Thus there is a sense in which it can be said that there are color universals for which we have no predicates. We can imagine that we had no predicate for the color between red and yellow. It should be noticed, however, that while we might not have had the predicate "orange" we might well have had the predicate expression "between red and yellow in color." And, indeed, for a person to be in the logical space of color is for him to know how to use predicate expressions adequate to the job of *introducing* predicates in the narrower sense, such as "orange."

11. The interpretation of statements asserting the identity of universals where the logical space of the universals is in this sense familiar is relatively straightforward. Consider, for example the schema:

> The universal which. . . . = the universal which. . . .

We can distinguish two forms the descriptions might take: (a) Each locates a universal with respect to a point outside the logical space of the universal located. Thus,

The color of Plato's beard = the color of your father's moustache.

Here, if we have the relevant information we can go from one of the descriptions either directly to an illustrating name of the universal, i.e. a name formed appropriately from the predicative expression which stands for it, thus

The color of Plato's beard = orange (i.e. being orange)

or to a description which locates the universal with respect to the logical space to which it belongs, thus

The color of Plato's beard = the color between red and yellow

(b) This last identity statement gives us an example of the second form the descriptions might take. In it at least one of them locates a universal in a manner internal to the logical space to which it belongs. From an identity statement of this form, for example the above, we can move, given that we have a predicate—say, 'orange'—which expresses the universal located as between red and yellow, to an identity statement

The color of Plato's beard = orange

in which a *description* is identified with a *nominatum* as in the paradigm of identification:

The author of Waverly = Scott.

If we do not have such a predicate, we at least have the predicate expression 'between red and yellow in color,' and could *introduce* a predicate having the use of 'orange'—which does not mean that the latter would be "short for" 'between red and yellow in color' any more than proper names are "short for" their criteria.

12. But the important case of referring to universals for which we have no corresponding predicates is that in which we refer to what I have called unknown or undiscovered universals. Consider, thus,

A. The property which an adequate theory of telekinesis—if we but had it—would ascribe to persons having this power.

Contrast this with

B. The property which the theory (current) of chemical interactions assigns to catalysts.

In B it is implied that we have a predicate in our language which stands for or expresses the property in question. Not so in case A. There the property in question is referred to by relating it to the properties expressed by the predicates of the science of telekinesis at its operational and instantially inductive level. The logical space of these empirical constructs is not that of the properties to which access would be gained by constructing a sound theory of telekinetic phenomena.

13. In general, then, the universals which it is the task of theoretical science to "discover" are referred to *via* a reference to the unborn or undeveloped theory, the predicates of which would stand for or express them, and, therefore, *via* a reference to the logical space of the empirical properties of the phenomena to be explained by the theory.

14. Yet the predicates of even sketchily developed theories express or stand for universals. Here it is essential to note that as a theory develops, its predicates cannot, in general, be said to continue to stand for or express the same universals. This brings me to a fundamental point which adds an element of symmetry to our previous classification of universals. To the classification (which highlights the temporal dimension)

1. Not yet discovered.
2. Discovered or known:
   a. Not yet effectively taken account of by our language
   b. Effectively taken account of by our language

we must now add a third heading under 2

   c. No longer effectively taken account of by our language

and a new major category:

3. Lost, or, so to speak, undiscovered universals

15. These considerations strongly suggest that the objective or "platonistic" status I am ascribing to universals might be construed in a Peircean way as relative to the continuing scientific community. Thus, if on hearing the above proliferation of universals, one is tempted to expostulate, 'which of these universals really exist!' I would reply by calling Peirce's characterization of a true proposition

as one that the continuing scientific community would ultimately accept—and then changing the subject.

II

16. Now if thc claims of the identity theory are placed in the framework of the above distinctions, it is clear that the theory can scarcely intend to assert the identity of "raw feel" universals with certain "brain state" universals which are effectively taken account of by existing language. For on the above analysis, this would involve that some "brain state" predicates currently have the same use as "raw feel" predicates. And this is obviously not the case. The claim must, surely, rather be that among the universals which would find expression in the predicates of a to-be-developed "brain state" theory, some are identical with "raw feel" universals.

17. At first sight, this is hardly much better. For, it might be urged, how could any predicates in a "brain state" theory have the same use as "raw feel" predicates? After all, the latter doesn't even presuppose the knowledge that there are such things as brains! But before we take up this and other objections, we must explore the notion of a "raw feel" universal.

III

18. The "rawness" of "raw feels" is their non-conceptual character. The sense in which "raw feels" (e.g. a feeling of warmth) are "of something" is not to be assimilated to the intentionality of thoughts. To say that they are non-conceptual is, of course, not to deny that they can be referred to and characterized by the use of concepts, or even, directly responded to by concepts in direct self-knowledge. 'Non-conceptual' does not mean non-conceptualized.

19. The word "feel" in the expression "raw feel" is an extension to all sense modalities of a use of the word "feel" which has its ultimate source in such contexts as

1. He felt the hair on the back of his neck bristle.

In this primary context, 'to feel' is clearly a cousin of 'to see,' and feeling in this sense can properly be classified as a mode of perception. Notice that feeling in this sense is conceptual; a propositional attitude. One would, perhaps, be more comfortable about this remark if the example had been,

2. He felt that the hair on the back of his neck was bristling.

The relation between 1 and 2 is an interesting and important topic in the philosophy of perception. I shall simply assume on the present occasion that 1 is a stronger form of 2 which emphasizes the non-inferential character of the experience.

20. Notice that to ascribe a perceptual propositional attitude to a person in the form

3. He perceived that-p

is to endorse the proposition involved in the attitude. We can, however, ascribe the same propositional attitude in a non-endorsing way by using such locutions as

4. He thought he perceived that-p
5. It seemed to him that he perceived that-p
6. It appeared to him that-p
7. He was under the (perceptual) impression that-p

None of these is *completely* neutral with respect to endorsement. They all tend to imply the falsity of the proposition involved in the attitude, and have other overtones which are irrelevant to my purpose. I shall make a technical use of 7 in which it will imply neither the truth nor the falsity of the proposition involved in the perceptual propositional attitude. In this usage the statements

8. He was under the tactual impression that the hair at the back of his neck was bristling
9. He was under the visual impression that there was a red and triangular physical object in front of him

ascribe perceptual propositional attitudes while making no commitment concerning the truth or falsity of the proposition involved in the attitude.

21. Now a classical theme in the philosophy of perception is that the truth of statements such as 9 imply the occurrence of something which is variously called a '(visual) sensation' (a sensation of a red triangle) or a '(visual) impression' (an impression of a red triangle), where this occurrence is understood to be a non-conceptual episode which *somehow* has the perceptible qualities which the corresponding conceptual episode, i.e. the propositional attitude takes to be

exemplified in the world of perceptible things. Thus, the fact that a person is under the visual impression that a certain stick in water is bent is taken to imply that he is having a visual impression of a bent object. I shall assume that this is true. This does not mean that I accept the "sense datum inference," for it should not be assumed that to have a visual impression is to sense a sense datum as these terms are used in classical sense-datum theories.

22. Notice that visual impressions are classified by the use of the word "of" followed by the phrase which would appear in the statement of the propositional attitudes which imply their occurrence; thus

> Impression of a red and triangular object

corresponds to

> Impression that there is a red and triangular object in front of one

The idea that there are such non-conceptual episodes was put to use in explaining, for example, how a straight stick (in water) can look bent, and a red object (in green light) look black. It was postulated that the propositional attitude expressed by

> He is under the visual impression that there is a black object in a certain place

involves, among other things, (a) the occurrence of an impression of a black object, (b) the occurrence of the thought that there is a black object in a certain place, and thought (or perceptual judgment, as it was called) being evoked by the impression. Roughly speaking, *impressions that* were construed as conceptual responses to *impressions of*. To this was added the idea that while in standard conditions viewing red objects results in an impression of a red object, and viewing bent objects results in an impression of a bent object, in non-standard conditions (e.g. viewing a straight stick in water) the viewing of an object that is not bent may result in an impression of a bent object, and the viewing of an object that is not red may result in an impression of a red object.

23. Although the examples I have been using come from vision, exactly the same distinctions were in the case of feeling. Here 'feelings of . . .' are the counterparts of 'visual impressions of . . .' We can

therefore understand the philosophical use of the expression "raw feel" as an extension to all modes of perception of an expression which stands for the non-conceptual kind of episode which explains why a person can be under the impression that he is being pricked by something sharp when in fact this is not the case.

24. I pointed out in 22 that sense impressions or raw feels are classified according to the perceptible qualities which are ascribed to some part of the world by the perceptual propositional attitudes which they evoke, and which characterize their standard causes. As I see it, the "of" phrases in

Sense impression of a red triangle
Raw feel of being pricked by a sharp object

are adjectives which, in addition to classifying raw feels *extrinsically* by their causes and effects, also classify them with reference to their intrinsic character.

25. How are we to understand the intrinsic character of raw feels? Obviously the sense impression of red triangle is not, in the literal sense, either red or triangular; nor is the raw feel of being pricked by a sharp object a being pricked by a sharp object. The most that can be said is that the families of qualities and relations which intrinsically characterize raw feels or sense impressions correspond in a certain way to the families of qualities and relations which characterize perceptible objects and processes.[5] I shall return to this point later. For the moment I shall simply say that the logical space of the qualities and relations which characterize raw feels is, in certain respects, isomorphic with the logical space of the perceptible qualities and relations of physical objects and processes. It would be useful, therefore, to introduce predicates for raw feels which are formed from predicates which stand for perceptible qualities and relations by adding the subscript 's'. Thus a triangular$_s$ impression or raw feel would be one which in standard conditions is brought about by view-

[5] The scholastics took the different, and ultimately unsatisfactory tack of holding that the characteristics are the same, but that the mode of exemplification is different. For an analysis of the Thomist-Aristotelian approach to this question see my "Being and Being Known," *Proceedings of the American Catholic Philosophical Association* (1960), reprinted as Chapter II of *Science, Perception and Reality* (London: Routledge & Kegan Paul, 1963).

ing a triangular object and which, *ceteris paribus*, results in being under the impression that a triangular object is before one.[6]

26. It will have been noticed that even my characterization of the intrinsic properties of raw feels has been, so to speak, extrinsic. For I characterized them in terms of their correspondence with the perceptible qualities and relations of physical objects and processes. It might be inferred from this that I think of our access to the logical space of impressions as indirect, as based upon a prior access to the logical space of perceptible qualities and relations. I shall postpone taking a stand of my own on this matter, and limit myself for the moment to pointing out that the type of identity theory I am examining rejects this suggestion and insists that our access to the logical space of sense impressions or raw feels is direct and, indeed, is the presupposition of our access to the logical space of physical objects and processes. It insists, indeed, that the qualities and relations of "raw feels" are "directly given" and that physical objects and their properties are "existential hypotheses" whose reality is guaranteed by the fine job they do of saving the appearances.

27. Finally a categorical point about raw feels which is implicit in the preceding remarks. They are construed as "pure episodes" and are contrasted with dispositions and mongrel categorical-hypothetical states. It should be noticed that the fact that one has in some sense "privileged access" to a state of oneself doesn't by itself imply that this state is a pure episode. Children can be trained to respond linguistically to short-term dispositional states of their organism, e.g. anger. Nor, as this point in turn suggests, need "privileged access" be construed in terms of classical theories of the given. The identity theory we are examining, however, is committed to the idea that raw feels are pure episodes and that raw-feel facts are "given" in something like the classical sense.

IV

28. Before taking the bull by the horns, a word or two about the other terms of the identities envisaged by the identity theory. It

[6] For an elaboration and defense of these distinctions, see Chapter II, sections 22 ff., and Chapter III, section VI of *Science, Perception and Reality;* also "Reply to Aune" in *Intentionality, Minds, and Perception*, a volume of essays edited by Hector Castañeda, published by the Wayne State University Press (1966).

will be remembered that according to the theory, raw feel universals are identical with certain brain state universals. Which brain state universals? Indeed, which brains?

29. For there is, in the first place, the brain as an empirical object to which empirical properties definable in observation terms can be ascribed. Can raw feel universals be identical with universals which characterize the empirical brain? They cannot, of course, be identical with any universals expressed by empirical predicates defined in terms of the publicly observable features of the brain, for raw feels are pure episodes which are public only in the sense that others can infer that which is given to oneself. (What authorizes the inference is, of course, a classic question.) Nevertheless it is important to see that there is a sense in which it is perfectly legitimate to suppose that raw feels *are identical with* certain states of the empirical brain. This, for the simple reason that it makes sense to suppose that they *are* states of the empirical brain. Imagine a person who has been defleshed and deboned, but whose nervous system is alive, intact and in functioning order. Imagine its sensory nerves hooked up with input devices and its motor nerves hooked up with an electronic system which enables it to communicate. Without expanding on this familiar science fiction, let me simply suggest that we think of what we ordinarily call a person as a nervous system clothed in flesh and bones. In view of what we know, it makes perfectly good sense to introduce the term "core person" for the empirical nervous system, and to introduce a way of talking according to which raw feels and, for that matter, thoughts are in the first instance states of "core persons" and only derivatively of the clothed person.

30. I submit that in this sense most scientifically oriented philosophers think of raw feels and thoughts as brain states. But while the thesis that raw feel universals *are*, in this sense, brain states and therefore trivially[7] identical with certain brain state universals is almost undoubtedly *true*, it is relatively non-controversial and unexciting. If the issue is put in these large scale terms, only those who demand really distinct logical subjects for the sense-impressions and the material states of persons—thus Cartesian dualists—would demur. Aristotelians and Strawsonians could take it in their stride.

31. For the claim that raw feels (or even thoughts) are in this

[7] Compare the trivial move from 'shapes are properties of physical objects' to 'shapes are identical with certain properties of physical objects.'

sense identical with brain states simply transfers the episodes and dispositions initially attributed to persons to the central nervous system, now conceived of as a core person. All of the important philosophical problems pertaining to the relation of mental states to physical states remain.

32. These considerations give proper perspective to the fact that according to the identity theory in the more challenging form in which it is currently defended, the brain state universals which are identical with raw feel universals, are universals which would be expressed by certain predicates of an as yet to be elaborated *theory* of brain activity. Thus, instead of making the relatively unexciting claim that raw feel universals are identical with certain brain state universals, where this reduces to the claim that raw feel universals *are* brain state universals (i.e., ascribable to brains as core persons) the identity theory in question claims that raw feel universals are not only brain state universals in this unexciting sense, but are identical with certain complex micro-physical universals to be 'discovered' in the course of developing a scientific theory of brains.

33. Thus the question arises, "Is it reasonable to suppose that the scientific study of brains will lead to the discovery of brain state universals which are identical with raw feel universals?" And to this question we are strongly tempted to answer 'no!' For interpreted along the lines sketched at the beginning of this paper it becomes, "Would an adequate theory of brains contain predicates which had the same use as raw feel predicates?" And the idea that this might be so has a most implausible ring. It will be useful to formulate some of the objections which this idea tends to arouse.

34. The first is that since predicates which would stand for the relevant brain state universals are *ex hypothesi* theoretical predicates, they would not have the avowal or reporting use which is characteristic of some, if not all, raw feel predicates. To this objection the identity theorist replies that once the theory was developed, people could be trained to respond to the brain states in question with the predicates of the theory—which would thus gain an avowal use.

35. The second objection is that raw-feel predicates do not have a theoretical use, or, to put it in the material mode, raw feels are not theoretical entities. Here the identity theorist might reply that the *other*-ascriptive use of raw-feel predicates is, in effect, a theoretical use. The force of this reply will be explored subsequently.

36. The third objection is the challenge "How can a predicate (e.g. 'having an impression of a red and triangular surface') which applies to a single logical subject (a person) have the same use as a predicate which applies to a multiplicity of scientific objects (micro-physical entities)?" The effect of this challenge is to make the point that the identity theory involves not only the identity of raw feel universals with certain brain state universals, but of persons with systems of scientific objects. The identity theorist can be expected to reply that it is enough for his purposes if raw feel universals which differ only in this categorical respect from the raw feel universals expressed by predicates which apply to persons as single logical subjects are identical with certain brain state universals. We shall leave this reply untouched, although we shall return to something like it at the end of our argument.

37. The fourth objection, however, is the most familiar and goes to the heart of the matter. "How," it asks, "can a property which is in the logical space of neurophysiological states be identical with a property which is not?" Otherwise put, "How could a predicate defined in terms of neurophysiological primitives have the same use as (be synonymous with) a predicate which is not?" To *this* question the inevitable answer is "It could not."

V

38. It might seem, as it has to many, that this is the end of the matter. The identity theory is absurd, and that is all there is to it. And, indeed, the identity theory as we have so far described it has no obvious defense against this standard objection. Yet it is not difficult to discern the fundamental strategy of the identity theorist in the fact of this objection. It consists in an appeal to a supposed analogy between the speculatively entertained identity of raw feel universals with brain state universals, and the once speculative but now established identity of chemical universals with certain micro-physical universals. The story is a familiar one, and I shall not bore you with the details.[8] The relevant points are quickly made. Suppose U_c is a certain universal which the predicate 'P_c' in the chemical theory current at time T stands for. And suppose that this chemical

[8] See my paper on "Theoretical Explanation" in B. Baumrin, ed., *Philosophy of Science* (New York: Wiley, 1963).

theory has a degree of sophistication essentially that of chemical theory today, but that micro-physics current at T is rudimentary. An 'identity theorist' puts forward at T the thesis that chemical universals will turn out to be identical with certain to-be-discovered micro-physical universals, i.e. universals which would be expressed by the predicates of a more sophisticated micro-physics. An opponent raises the following objections:

1. How can micro-physical predicates which are not tied to Chem Lab observables have the same use as chemical predicates which are?

The 'identity theorist' replies that once the theory is developed, these defined micro-physical predicates are given this new use, and therefore acquire a chemical-theoretical role.

2. How can the predicates of current chemical theory, which have no definitional tie to micro-physical primitives have the same use as any predicates of future micro-physical theory which will have such a tie?

This objection corresponds to the fourth and most telling objection to the mind-body identity theorist. And once again the objection is, in a certain sense, decisive. But here the 'identity theorist' has available to him a move which is, at first sight, not available in the raw feel, brain state case. He can argue that *both* of the universals involved in the identification are *to-be-discovered* universals, the chemical ones as well as the micro-physical ones. Roughly, the identity claim takes the form,

> The universals which will be expressed at T by the predicates of a more adequate theory of chemical processes are identical with the universals which would be expressed at T by the predicates of a more adequate micro-physical theory.

and while the universals which the predicates of chemical theory current at T express would not be identical with micro-physical universals, the universals which would be expressed by its more powerful successor might be.

39. For just as universals can be "discovered" and "given effective expression in our language" by our coming to use predicates in various ways, so universals can be "abandoned" by no longer finding expression in our language, and even lost. A chemical predicate which at T did not stand for a micro-physical universal may come to do

so at T. And the chemical universal for which it stood at T may be left in the lurch for a more sophisticated face.

40. The situation can be represented as one in which chemical theoretic predicates cease to stand for universals which are merely constantly co-exemplified with micro-physical universals ("bridge laws") and come to stand for micro-physical universals. The identification is *made* rather than *discovered*—though the possibility of identification is discovered.

VI

41. Is anything like this move possible in the raw feel, brain state case? Can the identity of raw feel universals with brain state universals be assimilated to the identity of chemical and micro-physical universals? Can raw feel predicates and brain state predicates be regarded as on the move towards a possible synonymity as was correctly predicted for the predicates of chemical and micro-physical theory? Summarily put, can raw feels be *reduced* to neurophysiological states?

42. This suggestion runs up against the obvious objection that according to typical identity theories, raw feel predicates, at least in their first person use, are as *untheoretical* as predicates can be. Unlike the predicates of chemical theory, they are not on the move towards a more adequate logical space which they might come to express. Like the Bostonian, they are *there*. This is often put by saying that they "label" directly given qualities and relations.

43. And even if the identity theorist were to hold that the *other*-ascriptive use of raw feel predicates is to be reconstructed as involving something like a common sense theory which postulates them as inner episodes to account for the perceptual behavior (including verbal behavior) of *others*, so that the identification of the raw feels of *others* with neurophysiological states would be immune to this objection, the latter would still apply to any attempt to identify the theoretical 'raw feels' of others with the (supposedly) radically *non-theoretical* raw feels of first person discourse. But no identity theorist worth his salt would restrict his thesis to the raw feels of others.

44. Suppose that at this point the identity theorist switches his tactics to conform to his reductionist strategy and abandons the thesis of givenness. In other words, he now argues that instead of the

use of raw-feel predicates being a confluence of two autonomous uses, a *self*-ascriptive use in which they "label given universals" and an *other*-ascriptive use in which they can be compared to theoretical predicates, there is one basic use in which they can be compared to predicates in a common sense theory of perceptual behavior; that is *anybody*-ascriptive use, and that such avowal or reporting use as raw feel predicates have is a dimension of use which is built on and presupposes this anybody-ascriptive common sense theoretical use. Would not this complete the parallel with the chemistry-physics model? For if both raw feel and brain state predicates are in a suitably broad sense *theoretical* predicates, can we not conceive of a reduction of raw feel theory to brain state theory?

45. If the concept of reduction is construed on the model of the physics-chemistry case, then, as I see it, the answer is "No." For reduction in this sense is a *special case* of the identification of universals located with respect to two theoretical structures which are expected to merge. A second alternative must be taken into account. Roughly, instead of the primitive predicates of the reduced theory ending up as *defined* predicates in the unified theory—which is the chemistry-physics case—these primitive predicates could perfectly well end up as *primitive* predicates once more in the unified theory. On this alternative, the *to-be-discovered* sense impression universals would be no more complex than the sense impression universals expressed by current sense impression predicates; they would have a different categorical framework, and be nomologically related to (but *not* analysable into) universals expressed by other primitive predicates in the to-be-achieved unified sense impression brain state theory. While all these predicates—including sense impression predicates—would be physicalistic in a broad sense ($physical_1$) as belonging to a spatio-temporal–nomological framework of scientific explanation, they would not be physicalistic in that narrower sense ($physical_2$) in which to be physicalistic is to belong to a set of predicates adequate to the theoretical description of non-living matter.[9] As I see it, then in the never-never land of ideal brain state theory the logical space of sense-

[9] For the distinction here drawn between '$physical_1$' and '$physical_2$' see "The Concept of Emergence" by Paul E. Meehl and Wilfrid Sellars in Vol. I of *Minnesota Studies in the Philosophy of Science*. According to the view I would defend, the to-be-discovered raw-feel universals are $physical_1$ but not $physical_2$. Feigl, on the other hand, is strongly inclined to argue that they are $physical_2$ and to make this claim essential to any identity theory worth the name.

impressions would, so to speak, be transposed into a new key and located in a new context. It would not, however, have become internally more complex in the way in which the logical space of chemical properties becomes internally more complex by virtue of their identification with micro-physical properties. That is to say, there would be no increase in complexity with respect to what might be called the factual content of sense impression universals: such increased complexity as occurred would be of a logical character. Roughly, the new sense impression universals would be exemplified not by single logical subjects (persons) but rather by manifold of logical subjects which might be called—borrowing a term without its philosophical commitments—sensa.[10]

46. But if sense-impression or raw-feel theory is to merge with brain-state theory, the latter phrase must be used in its proper sense of "theory adequate to explain the properties of empirical brains as 'core persons' " and freed from any commitment to the idea that neurophysiological theory is of necessity a theory the scientific objects of which are nerves which are reducible, along with their properties, to systems of micro-*physical* entities in a sense which implies that all the predicates of an ideal neurophysiology would be definable in terms of micro-physical primitives none of which apply *exclusively* to micro-physical systems which are the theoretical counterparts of brains.[11]

47. Thus, if the objects of brain state theory are conceived to be reducible to micro-physical objects (however un-thingish) by an adequate micro-physical theory, the latter phrase must connote *not* 'micro-theory adequate to the explanation of *inanimate* physical objects' (as it often tends to do), but rather 'micro-theory adequate to the explanation of any physical object, animate or inanimate.'

48. It is my conviction that a theory which is to explain the properties of core persons will involve a family of families of predicates which would be a categorial transformation, but not substantive reduction, of raw feel predicates, and which would apply only to systems of scientific objects which are the theoretical counterparts at the most fundamental level of empirical brains. In other words

[10] For a development of this point see *Science, Perception and Reality*, pp. 100–105; 190–96.

[11] Compare the distinction drawn above (45) between $physical_1$ and $physical_2$ primitives.

I accept the identity theory only in its *weak* form according to which raw feels or sense impressions are states of core persons, for as I see it, the logical space of raw feels will reappear transposed *but unreduced* in a theoretical framework adequate to the job of explaining what core persons can do. In my opinion such a theory is not yet even on the horizon.

49. The plausibility of the more radical interpretation of the reducibility of neurophysiology to micro-physics rests on the fact that if one thinks of 'sense impressions' or 'raw feels' as theoretical constructs introduced for the purpose of explaining simple 'discriminative behavior' such as is found in white rats, then one would indeed find no reason to suppose that the postulated states might not be conceived of as reducible along the lines described in 46. After all, we can conceive of—and even construct—machines which can perform these discriminations. It is therefore crucial to my thesis to emphasize that sense impressions or raw feels are common sense theoretical constructs introduced to explain the occurrence *not* of white rat type discriminative behavior, *but rather of perceptual propositional attitudes*, and are therefore bound up with the explanation of why human language contains families of predicates having the logical properties of words for perceptible qualities and relations. In this radically transformed sense, then, I would defend the thesis of concept empiricism according to which the content and structure of our *concepts* of the perceptible qualities of things is derived from the presence of this content and structure in the world—though I would reject the idea that the derivation involves an 'act of abstraction.' [12]

50. I shall conclude with a brief mention of other facets of the problem. Perhaps the most important of these is the fact that the logical space of the perceptible qualities and relations of physical things and processes on which that of the attributes and relations of raw feels is modeled, is, in an important sense, *closed*. Perceptible qualities and relations are, as the identity theory indirectly acknowledges, pure occurrent qualities and relations. They are neither dispositional nor mongrel states. To say of a physical object that it is

[12] For an elaboration of this point see section III of "Philosophy and the Scientific Image of Man" in Robert Colodny, ed., *Frontiers of Science and Philosophy* (Pittsburgh: University of Pittsburgh Press, 1962), reprinted as Chapter I in *Science, Perception and Reality*.

red and triangular is not to ascribe a power or disposition to it, though it is, in a very strong sense, to imply that it has certain powers and dispositions. Now it is not the "internal structure" of the families of occurrent perceptible qualities and relations which generate the demand for theoretical explanation, but rather the nomological structure of the changes and interactions of the physical things and processes to which these qualities and relations belong. Roughly, it is not such facts, expounded in a 'phenomenology' of sensible qualities and relations, as that to be orange is to be between red and yellow in color which demand scientific explanation, but rather such nomological facts as that black objects sink further into snow than white objects when the sun is shining.[13] And when physical theory explains the powers and dispositions of perceptible things and processes by "identifying" perceptible things and processes with systems of micro-physical objects, the "identification" is not to be construed as involving a *reduction* of perceptible qualities and relations to the qualities and relations of scientific objects, but rather as a *correlation* of these two sets of qualities and relations by means of "bridge laws." On the other hand, a realistic interpretation of theoretical entities—such as has been presupposed throughout the argument of this paper—requires that physical objects and processes be reducible to, i.e. *identifiable with* (rather than merely correlated with) systems of scientific objects.

51. But how can it be maintained that perceptible things *but not the perceptible qualities and relations in terms of which all their empirical properties are defined* are, in the strict sense reducible? The answer, surely, must be that once again the chemistry-physics paradigm is inadequate.

52. Scientific Realism maintains the *in principle* replaceability of the framework of perceptible things by a framework of scientific objects which contains highly derived counterparts of the inductively established *causal properties* of the former. But while Scientific Realism grants that the framework of scientific objects also contains highly derived counterparts of the *occurrent perceptible qualities* of perceptible things, it need not and, if my argument is correct, must not hold that these qualities are reducible to, i.e. replaceable by, their counterparts in micro-physical theory—as in the chemistry-physics case. The intrinsic structure of their "closed" logical space (50) re-

[13] Cf. William Kneale, *Probability and Induction* (Oxford, 1949), pp. 78 ff.

quires rather that they be *relocated.* This relocation involves a simultaneous move on the sense-impression front. For the qualities and relations which are irreducible to their counterparts in the microphysics of the objects of perception, *are* reducible, i.e. identifiable with, the qualities and relations which, I have contended (45–48), must be postulated in an adequate theoretical explanation of the nature and function of sense impressions or "raw feels." [14]

[14] I have explored the conceptual problems involved in this "relocation" of the perceptible qualities of common sense things in a number of places, most recently in the essay referred to in footnote 12. See also the concluding sections of Chapter III ("Phenomenalism") in *Science, Perception and Reality.*

9 *Richard Rorty*

Mind-Body Identity, Privacy, and Categories

Richard Rorty was born on October 4, 1931, in New York City. He was educated at the University of Chicago and Yale, and is now Associate Professor of Philosophy at Princeton. He specializes in metaphysics and the history of philosophy, and he is the editor of *The Linguistic Turn: Recent Essays in Philosophic Method.*

INTRODUCTORY

Current controversies about the Mind-Body Identity Theory form a case-study for the investigation of the methods practised by linguistic philosophers. Recent criticisms of these methods question that philosophers can discern lines of demarcation between "categories" of entities, and thereby diagnose "conceptual confusions" in "reductionist" philosophical theories. Such doubts arise once we see that it is very difficult, and perhaps impossible, to draw a firm line between the "conceptual" and the "empirical," and thus to differentiate between a statement embodying a conceptual confusion and one that expresses a surprising empirical result. The proponent of the Identity Theory (by which I mean one who thinks it sensible to assert that empirical inquiry will discover that *sensations* (not thoughts) are identical with certain brain-processes[1]) holds that his

FROM *The Review of Metaphysics,* XIX (1965), pp. 24–54. Reprinted by permission of the author and the editors.

[1] A proponent of the Identity Theory is usually thought of as one who predicts that empirical inquiry *will* reach this result—but few philosophers in fact stick their necks out in this way. The issue is not the truth of the prediction, but

opponents' arguments to the effect that empirical inquiry *could* not identify brain-processes and sensations are admirable illustrations of this difficulty. For, he argues, the classifications of linguistic expressions that are the ground of his opponents' criticism are classifications of a language which is as it is because it is the language spoken at a given stage of empirical inquiry. But the sort of empirical results that would show brain processes and sensations to be identical would also bring about changes in our ways of speaking. These changes would make these classifications out of date. To argue against the Identity Theory on the basis of the way we talk now is like arguing against an assertion that supernatural phenomena are identical with certain natural phenomena on the basis of the way in which superstitious people talk. There is simply no such thing as a method of classifying linguistic expressions that has results guaranteed to remain intact despite the results of future empirical inquiry. Thus in this area (and perhaps in all areas) there is no method which will have the sort of magisterial neutrality of which linguistic philosophers fondly dream.

In this paper I wish to support this general line of argument. I shall begin by pressing the claims of the analogy between mental events and supernatural events. Then I shall try to rebut the objection which seems generally regarded as fatal to the claims of the Identity Theory—the objection that "privacy" is of the essence of mental events, and thus that a theory which holds that mental events might *not* be "private" is *ipso facto* confused. I shall conclude with some brief remarks on the implications of my arguments for the more general metaphilosophical issues at stake.

THE TWO FORMS OF THE IDENTITY THEORY

The obvious objection to the identity theory is that "identical" either means a relation such that

$$(x)\ (y)\ [(x = y)\ \supset\ (F)\ (Fx \equiv Fy)]$$

---

whether such a prediction makes sense. Consequently, by "Identity Theory" I shall mean the assertion that it does make sense.

I include only sensations within the scope of the theory because the inclusion of thoughts would raise a host of separate problems (about the reducibility of intentional and semantic discourse to statements about linguistic behavior), and because the form of the Identity Theory which has been most discussed in the recent literature restricts itself to a consideration of sensations.

(the relation of "strict identity") or it does not. If it does, then we find ourselves forced into

> saying truthfully that physical processes such as brain processes are dim or fading or nagging or false, and that mental phenomena such as after-images are publicly observable or physical or spatially located or swift.[2]

and thus into using meaningless expressions, for

> we may say that the above expressions are meaningless in the sense that they commit a category mistake; i.e., in forming these expressions we have predicated predicates, appropriate to one logical category, of expressions that belong to a different logical category. This is surely a conceptual mistake.[3]

But if by "identical" the Identity Theory does *not* mean a relation of strict identity, then what relation *is* intended? How does it differ from the mere relation of "correlation" which, it is admitted on all sides, might without confusion be said to hold between sensations and brain processes?

Given this dilemma, two forms of the identity theory may be distinguished. The first, which I shall call the *translation* form, grasps the first horn, and attempts to show that the odd-sounding expressions mentioned above do not involve category mistakes, and that this can be shown by suitable translations into "topic-neutral" language of the sentences in which these terms are originally used.[4] The second, which I shall call the *disappearance* form, grasps the second horn, and holds that the relation in question is not strict identity, but rather the sort of relation which obtains between, to put it crudely, existent entities and non-existent entities when refer-

[2] James Cornman, "The Identity of Mind and Body," *Journal of Philosophy*, LIX (1962), p. 490.

[3] Cornman, p. 491.

[4] Cf. J. J. C. Smart, "Sensations and Brain Processes," reprinted in this volume, pp. 32–47 (subsequent page references to Smart's article are to the reprint in this volume), esp. pp. 39–43, and especially the claim that "When a person says 'I see a yellowish-orange after-image' he is saying something like this: 'There is something going on which is like what is going on when I have my eyes open, am awake, and there is an orange illuminated in good light in front of me, that is, when I really see an orange,' " (p. 41). For criticisms of Smart's program of translation, see Cornman, *op. cit.*; Jerome Shaffer, "Could Mental States Be Brain Processes?," *Journal of Philosophy*, LVIII (1961), pp. 812–22; Shaffer, "Mental Events and the Brain," *Journal of Philosophy*, LX (1963), pp. 160–66. See also the articles cited in the first footnote to Smart's own article.

ence to the latter once served (some of) the purposes presently served by reference to the former—the sort of relation that holds, e.g., between "quantity of caloric fluid" and "mean kinetic energy of molecules." There is an obvious sense of "same" in which what used to be called "a quantity of caloric fluid" is *the same thing* as what is now called a certain mean kinetic energy of molecules, but there is no reason to think that all features truly predicated of the one may be sensibly predicated of the other.[5] The translation form of the theory holds that if we really understood what we were saying when we said things like "I am having a stabbing pain" we should see that since we are talking about "topic-neutral" matters, we might, for all we know, be talking about brain-processes. The disappearance form holds that it is unnecessary to show that suitable translations (into "topic-neutral" language) of our talk about sensations can be given—as unnecessary as to show that statements about quantities of caloric fluid, when properly understood, may be seen to be topic-neutral statements.[6]

From the point of view of this second form of the theory, it is a mistake to assume that "X's are nothing but Y's" entails "All attributes meaningfully predicable of X's are meaningfully predicated of Y's," for this assumption would forbid us ever to express the results of scientific inquiry in terms of (in Cornman's useful phrase) "cross-category identity." [7] It would seem that the verb in such statements as "Zeus's thunderbolts are discharges of static electricity" and "Demoniacal possession is a form of hallucinatory psychosis" is the "is" of identity, yet it can hardly express *strict* identity. The disappear-

[5] No statement of the disappearance form of the theory with which I am acquainted is as clear and explicit as Smart's statement of the translation form. See, however, Feyerabend, "Mental Events and the Brain," *Journal of Philosophy*, LX (1963), pp. 295–96, and "Materialism and the Mind-Body Problem," *The Review of Metaphysics*, XVII (1963), pp. 49–66; reprinted in this volume, pp. 82–98. See also Wilfrid Sellars, "The Identity Approach to the Mind-Body Problem," reprinted in this volume, pp. 124–44. My indebtedness to this and other writings of Sellars will be obvious in what follows.

[6] Both forms agree, however, on the requirements which would have to be satisfied if we are to claim that the empirical discovery in question has been made. Roughly, they are (1) that one-one or one-many correlations could be established between every type of sensation and some clearly demarcated kind(s) of brain-processes; (2) that every known law which refers to sensations would be subsumed under laws about brain-processes; (3) that new laws about sensations be discovered by deduction from laws about brain-processes.

[7] Cornman, p. 492.

ance form of the Identity Theory suggests that we view such statements as elliptical for e.g., "What people used to call 'demoniacal possession' is a form of hallucinatory psychosis," where the relation in question *is* strict identity. Since there is no reason why "what people call 'X' " should be in the same "category" (in the Rylean sense) as "X," there is no need to claim, as the translation form of the theory must, that topic-neutral translations of statements using "X" are possible.

In what follows, I shall confine myself to a discussion and defense of the disappearance form of the theory. My first reason for this is that I believe that the analysis of "Sensations are identical with certain brain-processes" proposed by the disappearance form (viz., "What people now call 'sensations' are identical with certain brain-processes") accomplishes the same end as the translation form's program of topic-neutral translation—namely, avoiding the charge of "category-mistake!" while preserving the full force of the traditional materialist position. My second reason is that I believe that an attempt to defend the translation form will inevitably get bogged down in controversy about the adequacy of proposed topic-neutral translations of statements about sensations. There is obviously a sense of "adequate translation" in which the topic-neutrality of the purported translations *ipso facto* makes them inadequate. So the proponent of the translation form of the theory will have to fall back on a weaker sense of "adequate translation." But the weaker this sense becomes, the less impressive is the claim being made, and the less difference between the Identity Theory and the non-controversial thesis that certain brain-processes may be constantly correlated with certain sensations.

THE ANALOGY BETWEEN DEMONS AND SENSATIONS

At first glance, there seems to be a fatal weakness in the disappearance form of the Identity Theory. For normally when we say "What people call 'X's' are nothing but Y's" we are prepared to add that "There are no X's." Thus when, e.g., we say that "What people call 'caloric fluid' is nothing but the motion of molecules" or "What people call 'witches' are nothing but psychotic women" we are prepared to say that there are no witches, and no such thing as caloric fluid. But it seems absurd to say that there might turn out to be no such things as sensations.

To see that this disanalogy is not fatal to the Identity Theory, let us consider the following situation. A certain primitive tribe holds the view that illnesses are caused by demons—a different demon for each sort of illness. When asked what more is known about these demons than that they cause illness, they reply that certain members of the tribe—the witch-doctors—can see, after a meal of sacred mushrooms, various (intangible) humanoid forms on or near the bodies of patients. The witch-doctors have noted, for example, that a blue demon with a long nose accompanies epileptics, a fat red one accompanies sufferers from pneumonia, etc. They know such further facts as that the fat red demon dislikes a certain sort of mold which the witch-doctors give people who have pneumonia. (There are various competing theories about what demons do when not causing diseases, but serious witch-doctors regard such speculations as unverifiable and profitless.)

If we encountered such a tribe, we would be inclined to tell them that there are no demons. We would tell them that diseases were caused by germs, viruses, and the like. We would add that the witch-doctors were not seeing demons, but merely having hallucinations. We would be quite right, but would we be right on *empirical* grounds? What empirical criteria, built into the demon-talk of the tribe, go unsatisfied? What predictions which the tribesmen make fail to come true? If there are none, a sophisticated witch-doctor may reply that all modern science can do is to show (1) that the presence of demons is constantly correlated with that of germs, viruses, and the like, and (2) that eating certain mushrooms sometimes makes people think they see things that aren't really there. This is hardly sufficient to show that there are no demons. At best, it shows that if we forget about demons, then (a) a simpler account of the cause and cure of disease and (b) a simpler account of why people make the perceptual reports they do, may be given.

What do we reply to such a sophisticated witch-doctor? I think that all that we would have left to say is that the simplicity of the accounts which can be offered if we forget about demons *is* an excellent reason for saying that there are no demons. Demon-discourse is one way of describing and predicting phenomena, but there are better ways. We *could* (as the witch-doctor urges) tack demon-discourse on to modern science by saying, first, that diseases are caused by the compresence of demons and germs (each being a necessary, but neither a sufficient, condition) and, second, that the witch-doctors (unlike drunkards and psychotics) really do see intangible beings (about whom, alas, nothing is known save their visual appearances). If we did so, we would retain all the predictive and explanatory advantages of modern science. We could know as much about the cause and cure of disease, and about hallucinations, as we did before. We would, however, be burdened with problems which we did not have before: the problem of why demons are visible only to witch-doctors, and the problem of why germs cannot cause diseases all by themselves. We avoid both problems by saying that demons do not exist. The witch-doctor may remark that this use of Occam's Razor has the same advantage as that of theft over honest toil. To such a remark, the only reply could be an account of the practical advantages gained by the use of the Razor in the past.

Now the Identity Theorist's claim is that sensations may be to the future progress of psycho-physiology as demons are to modern science. Just as we now want to deny that there are demons, future science may want to deny that there are sensations. The only obstacle to replacing sensations discourse with brain-discourse seems to be that sensation-statements have a reporting as well as an explanatory function. But the demon case makes clear that the discovery of a new way of explaining the phenomena previously explained by reference to a certain sort of entity, *combined with a new account of what is being reported by observation-statements about that sort of entity*, may give good reason for saying that there are no entities of that sort. The absurdity of saying "Nobody has ever felt a pain" is no greater than that of saying "Nobody has ever seen a demon," *if* we have a suitable answer to the question "What *was* I reporting when I said I felt a pain?" To this question, the science of the future may reply "You were reporting the occurrence of a certain brain-process, and it would make life simpler for us if you would, in the future, *say* 'My C-fibers are firing' instead of saying 'I'm in pain.'" In so saying, he has as good a *prima facie* case as the scientist who answers the witch-doctor's question "What *was* I reporting when I reported a demon?" by saying "You were reporting the content of your hallucination, and it would make life simpler if, in the future, you would describe your experiences in those terms."

Given this *prima facie* analogy between demons and sensations, we can now attend to some disanalogies. We may note, first, that there is no simple way of filling in the blank in "What people called 'demons' are nothing but ———." For neither "hallucinatory contents" nor "germs" will do. The observational and the explanatory roles of "demon" must be distinguished. We need to say something like "What people who reported seeing demons were reporting was simply the content of their hallucinations," and *also* something like "What people explained by reference to demons can be explained better by reference to germs, viruses, etc." Because of the need for a relatively complex account of how we are to get along without reference to demons, we cannot *identify* "What we called 'demons' " with anything. So, instead, we simply deny their existence. In the case of sensations, however, we can give a relatively simple account of how to get along in the future. Both the explanatory *and* the reporting functions of statements about sensations can be taken over by statements about brain-processes. Therefore we are prepared to identify "What we called 'sensations' " with brain-processes, and to say "What we called 'sensations' turn out to be nothing but brain-processes."

Thus this disanalogy does not have the importance which it appears to have at first. In both the demon case and the sensation case, the proposed reduction has the same pragmatic consequences: namely, that we should stop asking questions about the causal and/or spatio-temporal relationships holding between the "reduced" entities (demons, sensations) and the rest of the universe, and replace these with questions about the relationships holding between certain other entities (germs, hallucinatory experiences, brain-processes) and the rest of the universe. It happens, for the reasons just sketched, that the proposed reduction is put in the form of a denial of existence in one case, and of an identification in another case. But "There are no demons" and "What people call 'sensations' are nothing but brain processes" can both equally well be paraphrased as "Elimination of the referring use of the expression in question ('demon,' 'sensation') from our language would leave our ability to describe and predict undiminished."

Nevertheless, the claim that there might turn out to be no such thing as a "sensation" seems scandalous. The fact that a witch-doctor might be scandalized by a similar claim about demons does not, in itself, do much to diminish our sense of shock. In what follows, I wish to account for this intuitive implausibility. I shall argue that it rests *solely* upon the fact that elimination of the referring use of "sensation" from our language would be in the highest degree *impractical*. If this can be shown, then I think that the Identity Theorist will be cleared of the charge of "conceptual confusion" usually leveled against him. Rather than proceeding directly to this argument, however, I shall first consider a line of argument which has often been used to show that he *is* guilty of this charge. Examining this line of argument will permit me to sketch in greater detail what the Identity Theorist is and is not saying.

THE ELIMINABILITY OF OBSERVATION TERMS

The usual move made by the opponents of the Identity Theory is to compare suggested reduction of sensations to brain-processes to certain other cases in which we say that "X's turn out to be nothing but Y's." There are two significantly different classes of cases and it might seem that the Identity Theorist confuses them. First, there is the sort of case in which both "X" and "Y" are used to refer to observable entities, and the claim that "What people called 'X's' are nothing but Y's" is backed up by pointing out that the statement "This is an X" commits one to an empirically false proposition. For example, we say that "What people called 'unicorn horns' are nothing but narwhal horns," and urge that we cease to respond to a perceptual situation with "This is a unicorn horn." We do this because "This is a unicorn horn" commits one to the existence of unicorns, and there are, it turns out, no unicorns. Let us call this sort of case *identification of observables with other observables.* Second, there is the sort of case in which "X" is used to refer to an observable entity and "Y" is used to refer to an unobservable entity. Here we do not (typically) back up the claim that "What people called 'X's' are nothing but Y's" by citing an empirically false proposition presupposed by "This is an X." For example, the statement that "What people call 'tables' are nothing but clouds of molecules" does not suggest, or require as a ground, that people who say "This is a table" hold false beliefs. Rather, we are suggesting that something *more* has been found out about the sort of situation reported by "This is a table." Let us call this second sort of case *identification of observables with theoretical entities.*

It seems that we cannot assimilate the identification of sensations with brain-processes to either of these cases. For, unlike the typical case of identification of observables with other observables, we do not wish to say that people who have reported sensations in the past have (necessarily) any empirically disconfirmed beliefs. People are not wrong about sensations in the way in which they were wrong about "unicorn horns." Again, unlike the typical case of the identification of observables with theoretical entities, we do not want to say that brain-processes are "theoretical" or unobservable. Furthermore, in cases in which we identify an observable X with an unobservable Y, we are usually willing to accept the remark that "That does not show that there are no X's." The existence of tables is not (it would seem) impugned by their identification with clouds of electrons, as the existence of unicorn horns is impugned by their identification with narwhal horns. But a defender of the Disappearance Form of the Identity Theory *does* want to impugn the existence of sensations.

Because the claim that "What people call 'sensations' may turn out to be nothing but brain-processes" cannot be assimilated to either of these cases, it has been attacked as trivial or incoherent. The following dilemma is posed by those who attack it: either the Identity Theorist claims that talk about sensations presupposes some empirically disconfirmed belief (and what could it be?) or the "identity" which he has in mind is the uninteresting sort of identity which holds between tables and clouds of molecules (mere "theoretical replaceability").

The point at which the Identity Theorist should attack this dilemma is the premise invoked in stating the second horn—the premise that the identification of tables with clouds of molecules does not permit us to infer to the non-existence of tables. This premise is true, but *why* is it true? That there is room for reflection here is apparent when we place the case of tables side-by-side with the case of demons. If there is any point to saying that tables are nothing but clouds of molecules it is presumably to say that, in principle, we could stop making a referring use of "table," and of any extensionally equivalent term, and still leave our ability to describe and predict undiminished. But this would seem just the point of (and the justification for) saying that there are no demons. Why does the realization that nothing would be lost by the dropping of "table" from our vocabulary still leave us with the conviction that there are tables, whereas the same realization about demons leaves us with the conviction that there are no demons? I suggest that the only answer to this question which will stand examination is that although we could *in principle* drop "table," it would be monstrously inconvenient to do so, whereas it is both possible in principle and convenient in practice to drop "demon." The reason "But there still are tables" sounds so plausible is that nobody would dream of suggesting that we stop reporting our experiences in table-talk and start reporting them in molecule-talk. The reason "There are no demons" sounds so plausible is that we are quite willing to suggest that the witch-doctors stop reporting their experiences in demon-talk and start reporting them in hallucination-talk.

A conclusive argument that this practical difference is the *only* relevant difference would, obviously, canvass all the other differences which might be noted. I shall not attempt this. Instead, I shall try to make my claim plausible by sketching a general theory of the conditions under which a term may cease to have a referring use without those who made such a use being convicted of having held false beliefs.

Given the same sorts of correlations between X's and Y's, we are more likely to say "X's are nothing but Y's" when reference to X's is habitually made in non-inferential reports, and more likely to say "There are no 'X's' when such reference is never or rarely made. (By "non-inferential report" I mean a statement in response to which questions like "How did you know?" "On what evidence do you say . . . ?" and "What leads you to think . . . ?" are normally considered misplaced and unanswerable, but which is nonetheless capable of empirical confirmation.) Thus we do not say that the identification of temperature with the kinetic energy of molecules shows that there is no such thing as temperature, since "temperature" originally (i.e., before the invention of thermometers) stood for something which was always reported non-inferentially, and still is frequently so reported. Similarly for all identifications of familiar macro-objects with unfamiliar micro-objects. But since in our culture-circle we do not *habitually* report non-inferentially the presence of caloric fluid, demons, etc., we do not feel unhappy at the bald suggestion that there are no such things.

Roughly speaking, then, the more accustomed we are to "X" serving as an observation-term (by which I mean a term habitually used in non-inferential reports) the more we prefer, when enquiry shows the possibility of accounting for the phenomena explained by reference to X's without such reference, to "identify" X's with some sort of Y's, rather than to deny existence to X's *tout court. But the more grounds we have for such identification, the more chance there is that we shall stop using* "X" *in non-inferential reports,* and thus the greater chance of our eventually coming to accept the claim that "there are no X's" with equanimity. This is why we find borderline cases, and gradual shifts from assimilations of X's to Y's to an assertion that X's do not exist. For example, most people do not report the presence of pink rats non-inferentially (nor inferentially, for that matter), but some do. The recognition that they are in the minority helps those who do so to admit that there are no pink rats. But suppose that the vast majority of us had always seen (intangible and uncatchable) pink rats; would it not then be likely that we should resist the bald assertion that there are no pink rats and insist on something of the form "pink rats are nothing but . . . ?" It might be a very long time before we came to drop the habit of reporting pink rats and begin reporting hallucinations instead.

The typical case-history of an observation-term ceasing to have a referring use runs the following course: (1) X's are the subjects of both inferential and non-inferential reports;[8] (2) empirical discoveries are made which enable us to subsume X-laws under Y-laws and to produce new X-laws by studying Y's; (3) inferential reports of X's cease to be made; (4) non-inferential reports of X's are reinterpreted either (4a) as reports of Y's, *or* (4b) as reports of mental entities (thoughts that one is seeing an X, hallucinatory images, etc.); (5) non-inferential reports of X's cease to be made (because their place is taken by non-inferential reports either of Y's or of

[8] Note that if X's are *only* referred to in inferential reports—as in the case of "neutrons" and "epicycles," no philosophically interesting reduction takes place. For in such cases there is no hope of getting rid of an explanandum; all we get rid of is a putative explanation.

thoughts, hallucinatory images, etc.); (6) we conclude that there simply are no such things as X's.

This breakdown of stages lets us pick out two crucial conditions that must be satisfied if we are to move from "X's are nothing but Y's" (stage 2) to "there are no X's" (stage 6). These conditions are:

A. The Y-laws must be *better* at explaining the kinds of phenomena explained by the X-laws (not just equally good). Indeed, they must be sufficiently better so that *the inconvenience of changing one's linguistic habits by ceasing to make inferential reports about X's is less than the inconvenience of going through the routine of translating one's X-reports into Y-reports in order to get satisfactory explanations of the phenomena in question.* If this condition is not satisfied, the move from stage (2) to stage (3) will not be made, and thus no later move will be made.

B. Either Y-reports may themselves be made non-inferentially, or X-reports may be treated as reports of mental entities. For we must be able to have some answer to the question "What *am* I reporting when I non-inferentially report about an X?," and the only answers available are "you're reporting on a Y" or "you're reporting on some merely mental entity." If neither answer is available, we can move neither to (4a) nor to (4b), nor, therefore, on to (5) and (6).

Now the reason we move from stage (2) to stage (3) in the case of demons is that A is obviously satisfied. The phenomena which we explained by reference to the activity of demons are so much better explained in other ways that it is simpler to stop inferring to the existence of demons altogether than to continue making such inferences, and then turning to laws about germs and the like for an explanation of the behavior of the demons. The reason why we do *not* move from (2) to (3) (much less to (6)) in the case of temperature or tables is that explanations formulated in terms of temperatures are so good, on the ground which they were originally intended to cover, that we feel no temptation to stop talking about temperatures and tables merely because we can, in some cases, get more precise predictions by going up a level to laws about molecules. The reason why we move on from (3) to (4) in the case of demons is that the alternative labeled (4b) is readily available—we can easily consign experiences of demons to that great dumping-ground of out-dated entities, the Mind. There were no experiences of demons, we say, but only experiences of mental images.

Now it seems obvious that, in the case of sensations, A will not be satisfied. The inconvenience of ceasing to talk about sensations would be so great that only a fanatical materialist would think it worth the trouble to cease referring to sensations. If the Identity Theorist is taken to be predicting that some day "sensation," "pain," "mental image," and the like will drop out of our vocabulary, he is almost certainly wrong. But if he is saying simply that, at no greater cost than an inconvenient linguistic reform, we *could* drop such terms, he is entirely justified. And I take this latter claim to be all that traditional materialism has ever desired.

Before leaving the analogy between demons and sensations, I wish to note one further disanalogy which an opponent of the Identity Theory might pounce upon. Even if we set aside the fact that A would not be satisfied in the case of sensations, such an opponent might say, we should note the difficulty in satisfying B. It would seem that there is no satisfactory answer to the question "What *was* I non-inferentially reporting when I reported on my sensations?" For neither (4a) nor (4b) seems an available option. The first does not seem to be available because it is counter-intuitive to think of, e.g., "I am having my C-fibers stimulated," as capable of being used to make a non-inferential report. The second alternative is simply silly—there is no point in saying that when we report a sensation we are reporting some "merely mental" event. For sensations are *already* mental events. The last point is important for an understanding of the *prima facie* absurdity of the disappearance form of the Identity Theory. The reason why most statements of the form "there might turn out to be no X's at all" can be accepted with more or less equanimity in the context of forecasts of scientific results is that we are confident we shall always be able to "save the phenomena" by answering the question "But what about all those X's we've been accustomed to observe?" with some reference to thoughts-of-X's, images-of-X's, and the like. Reference to mental entities provides non-inferential reports of X's with something to have been about. But when we want to say "There might turn out to be no mental entities at all," we cannot use this device. This result makes clear that if the analogy between the past disappearance of supernatural beings and the possible future disappearance of sensations is to be pressed, we must claim that alternative (4a) is, appearances to the contrary, still open. That is, we must hold that the question "What *was* I non-inferentially reporting when I non-inferentially reported a stabbing pain?" can be sensibly answered "You were reporting a stimulation of your C-fibers."

Now why should this *not* be a sensible answer? Let us begin by getting a bad objection to it out of the way. One can imagine someone arguing that this answer can only be given if a stimulation of C-fibers is strictly identical with a stabbing pain, and that such strict identification involves category-mistakes. But this objection presupposes that "A report of an X is a report of a Y" entails that "X's are Y's." If we grant this presupposition we shall not be able to say that the question "What was I reporting when I reported a demon?" is properly answered by "You were reporting the content of an hallucination which you were having." However, if we ask why this objection is plausible, we can see the grain of truth which it embodies and conceals. We are usually unwilling to accept "You were reporting a Y" as an answer to the question "What *was* I non-inferentially reporting when I non-inferentially reported an X?" unless (a) Y's are themselves the kind of thing we habitually report on non-inferentially, and (b) there does not exist already an habitual practice of reporting Y's non-inferentially. Thus we accept "the content of an hallucination" as a sensible answer because we know that such contents, being "mental images," are just the sort of thing which does get non-inferentially reported (once it is recognized for what it is) and because we are not accustomed to making non-inferential reports in the form "I am having an hallucinatory image of . . ."[9] To take an example of answers to this sort of question that are *not* sensible, we reject the claim that when we report on a table we are reporting on a mass of whirling particles, for either we think we know under what circumstances we should make such a report, and know that these circumstances do not obtain, or we believe that the presence of such particles can only be inferred and never observed.

[9] Note that people who *become* accustomed to making the latter sort of reports may no longer accept explanations of their erroneous non-inferential reports by reference to hallucinations. For they know what mental images are like, and they know that *this* pink rat was not an hallucinatory content. The more frequent case, fortunately, is that they just cease to report pink rats and begin reporting hallucinations, for their hallucinations no longer deceive them.

The oddity of saying that when I think I am reporting on a stabbing pain I am actually reporting on a stimulation of my C-fibers is similar to these last two cases. We either imagine a situation in which we can envisage ourselves non-inferentially reporting such stimulation (periscope hitched up to a microscope so as to give us a view of our trepanned skull, overlying fibers folded out of the way, stimulation evident by change in color, etc.), or else we regard "stimulation of C-fibers" as not the sort of thing which *could* be the subject of a non-inferential report (but inherently a "theoretical" state of affairs whose existence can only be inferred, and not observed). In either case, the assertion that we have been non-inferentially reporting on a brain-process all our lives seems absurd. So the proponent of the disappearance form of the Identity Theory must show that reports of brain-processes are neither incapable of being non-inferential nor, if non-inferential, necessarily made in the way just imagined (with the periscope-microscope gadget) or in some other peculiar way. But now we must ask who bears the burden of proof. Why, after all, should we think that brain-processes are *not* a fit subject-matter for non-inferential reports? And why should it not be the case that the circumstances in which we make non-inferential reports about brain-processes are just those circumstances in which we make non-inferential reports about sensations? For this will in fact be the case if, when we were trained to say, e.g., "I'm in pain" we were in fact being trained to respond to the occurrence within ourselves of a stimulation of C-fibers. If this is the case, the situation will be perfectly parallel to the case of demons and hallucinations. We *will*, indeed, have been making non-inferential reports about brain-processes all our lives *sans le savoir*.

This latter suggestion can hardly be rejected *a priori*, unless we hold that we can only be taught to respond to the occurrence of A's with the utterance "A!" if we were able, prior to this teaching, to be aware, when an A was present, that it was present. But this latter claim is plausible only if we assume that there is an activity which can reasonably be called "awareness" prior to the learning of language. I do not wish to fight once again the battle which has been fought by Wittgenstein and many of his followers against such a notion of awareness. I wish rather to take it as having been won, and to take for granted that there is no *a priori* reason why a brain-process is inherently unsuited to be the subject of a non-inferential report. The distinction between observation-terms and non-observation-terms is relative to linguistic practices (practices which may change as inquiry progresses), rather than capable of being marked out once and for all by distinguishing between the "found" and the "made" elements in our experience. I think that the recognition of this relativity is the first of the steps necessary for a proper appreciation of the claims of the Identity Theory. In what follows, I want to show that this first step leads naturally to a second: the recognition that the distinction between *private* and *public* subject-matters is as relative as that between items signified by observation-terms and items not so signified.

The importance of this second step is clear. For even if we grant that reports of brain-processes may be non-inferential, we still need to get around the facts that reports of sensations have an epistemological peculiarity that leads us to call them reports of *private* entities, and that brain-processes are intrinsically *public* entities. Unless we can overcome our intuitive conviction that a report of a private matter (with its attendant infallibility) cannot be identified with a report of a public matter (with its attendant fallibility), we shall not be able to take seriously the claim of the proponents of the Disappearance Form of the Identity Theory that alternative (4a) is open, and hence that nothing prevents sensations from disappearing from discourse in the same manner, and for the same reasons, as supernatural beings have disappeared from discourse. So far in this paper I have deliberately avoided the problem of the "privacy" of sensations, because I wished to show that if this problem *can* be surmounted, the Identity Theorist may fairly throw the burden of proof onto his opponent by asking whether a criterion can be produced which would show that the identification of sensations and brain-processes involves a conceptual confusion, while absolving the claim that demons do not exist of such a confusion. Since I doubt that such a criterion *can* be produced, I am inclined to say that if the problem about "privacy" is overcome, then the Identity Theorist has made out his case.

THE "PRIVACY" OBJECTION

The problem that the privacy of first-person sensation reports presents for the Identity Theory has recently been formulated in considerable detail by Baier.[10] In this section, I shall confine myself to a discussion of his criticism of Smart's initial reply to this argument. Smart holds that the fact that "the language of introspective reports has a different logic from the logic of material processes" is no objection to the Identity Theory, since we may expect that empirical inquiry can and will change this logic:

> It is obvious that until the brain-process theory is much improved and widely accepted there will be no *criteria* for saying "Smith has an experience of such-and-such a sort" except Smith's introspective reports. So we have adopted a rule of language that (normally) what Smith says goes.[11]

Baier thinks that this reply "is simply a confusion of the privacy of the subject-matter and the availability of external evidence." [12] Baier's intuition is that the difference between a language-stratum in which the fact that a report is sincerely made is sufficient warrant for its truth, and one in which this situation does not obtain, seems so great as to call for an explanation—and that the only explanation is that the two strata concern different subject-matters. Indeed Baier is content to let the mental-physical distinction stand or fall with the distinction between "private" subject-matters and "public" subject-matters, and he therefore assumes that to show that "introspective reports are necessarily about something private, and that being about something private is *incompatible with being* about something public" [13] is to show, once and for all, that the Identity Theory involves a conceptual confusion. Baier, in short, is undertaking to show that "once private, always private."

He argues for his view as follows:

> To say that one day our physiological knowledge will increase to such an extent that we shall be able to make absolutely reliable encephalograph-based claims about people's experiences, is only to say that, if carefully checked, our encephalograph-based claims about 'experiences' will always be *correct*, i.e. will make the *same claims* as a *truthful* introspective report. If correct encephalograph-based claims about Smith's experiences contradict Smith's introspective reports, we shall be entitled to infer that he is *lying*. In that sense,

[10] Kurt Baier, "Smart on Sensations," *Australasian Journal of Philosophy*, XL (1962), pp. 57–68.
[11] Smart, "Sensations and Brain Processes," pp. 43–44.
[12] Baier, p. 63.
[13] Baier, p. 59.

> what Smith says will no longer go. But we cannot of course infer that he is making a mistake, for that is nonsense. . . . *However good the evidence may be, such a physiological theory can never be used to show to the sufferer that he was mistaken in thinking that he had a pain, for such a mistake is inconceivable.* The sufferer's epistemological authority must therefore be better than the best physiological theory can ever be. Physiology can therefore never provide a person with more than *evidence* that someone else is having an experience of one sort or another. It can never lay down *criteria* for saying that someone is having an experience of a certain sort. Talk about brain-processes therefore must be about something other than talk about experiences. Hence, introspective reports and brain-process talk cannot be merely different ways of talking about the same thing.[14]

Smart's own reply to this line of argument is to admit that

> No physiological evidence, say from a gadget attached to my skull, could make me withdraw the statement that I have a pain when as a matter of fact I feel a pain. For example, the gadget might show no suitable similarities of cerebral processes on the various occasions on which I felt pain. . . . I must, I think, agree with Baier that if the sort of situation which we have just envisaged did in fact come about, then I should have to reject the brain-process thesis, and would perhaps espouse dualism.[15]

But this is not the interesting case. The interesting case is the one in which suitable similarities are in fact found to occur—the same similarities in all subjects—until one day (long after all empirical generalizations about sensations *qua* sensations have been subsumed under physiological laws, and long after direct manipulation of the brain has become the exclusive method of relieving pain) somebody (call him Jones) thinks he has no pain, but the encephalograph says that the brain-process correlated with pain did occur. (Let us imagine that Jones himself is observing the gadget, and that the problem about whether he might have made a mistake is a problem for Jones; this eliminates the possibility of lying.) Now in most cases in which one's observation throws doubt on a correlation which is so central to current scientific explanations, one tries to eliminate the possibility of observational error. But in Baier's view it would be absurd for Jones to do this, for "a mistake is inconceivable." Actually, however, it is fairly clear what Jones' first move would be—he will

[14] Baier, pp. 64–65; italics added.
[15] Smart, "Brain Processes and Incorrigibility—a Reply to Professor Baier," *Australasian Journal of Philosophy*, XL (1962), p. 68.

begin to suspect that he does not know what pain is—i.e., that he is not using the word "pain" in the way in which his fellows use it.[16]

So now Jones looks about for independent verification of the hypothesis that he does not use "I am in pain" incorrectly. But here he runs up against the familiar difficulty about the vocabulary used in making introspective reports—the difficulty of distinguishing between "misuse of language" and "mistake in judgment"—between (a) recognizing the state of affairs which obtains for what it is, but describing it wrongly because the words used in the description are not the right words, and (b) being able to describe it rightly once it is recognized for what it is, but not in fact recognizing it for what it is (in the way in which one deceived by an illusion does not recognize the situation for what it is). If we do not have a way of determining which of these situations obtains, we do not have a genuine contrast between misnaming and misjudging. To see that there is no genuine contrast in this case, suppose that Jones was not burned prior to the time that he hitches on the encephalograph, but now he is. When he is, the encephalograph says that the brain-process constantly correlated with pain-reports occurs in Jones' brain. However, although he exhibits pain-behavior, Jones thinks that he does not feel pain. (But, now as in the past, he both exhibits pain-behavior and thinks that he feels pain when he is frozen, stuck, struck, racked, etc.) Now is it that he does not know that *pain* covers what you feel when you are burned as well as what you feel when you are stuck, struck, etc.? Or is it that he really does not feel pain when he is burned? Suppose we tell Jones that what he feels when he is burned is *also* called "pain." Suppose he then admits that he does feel *something,* but insists that what he feels is quite *different* from what he feels when he is stuck, struck, etc. Where does Jones go from here? Has he failed to learn the language properly, or is he correctly (indeed infallibly) reporting that he has different sensations than those normally had in the situation in question? (Compare the parallel question in the case of a man who uses "blue" in all the usual ways except that he refuses to grant that blue is a color—on the ground that it is so different from red, yellow, orange, violet, etc.)

The only device which would decide this question would be to

[16] This problem will remain, of course, even if Jones merely *thinks* about whether he is in pain, but does not say anything.

establish a convention that anyone who sincerely denied that he felt a pain while exhibiting pain-behavior and being burned *ipso facto* did not understand how to use "pain." This denial would *prove* that he lacked such an understanding. But this would be a dangerous path to follow. For not to understand when to use the word "pain" in non-inferential reports is presumably to be unable to know which of one's sensations to call a "pain." And the denial that one felt pain in the circumstances mentioned would only prove such inability if one indeed *had* the sensation normally called a pain. So now we would have a public criterion, satisfaction of which would count as showing that the subject had such a sensation—i.e., that he felt a pain even though he did not think that he did. But if such a criterion exists, its application overrides any contradictory report that he may make—for such a report will be automatically disallowed by the fact that it constitutes a demonstration that he does not know what he is talking about. The dilemma is that either a report about one's sensations which violates a certain public criterion is a sufficient condition for saying that the reporter does not know how to use "pain" in the correct way, or there is no such criterion. If there is, the fact that one cannot be mistaken about pains does not entail that sincere reports of pain cannot be over-ridden. If there is not, then there is no way to answer the question formulated at the end of the last paragraph, and hence no way to eliminate the possibility that Jones may not know what pain is. Now since the *a priori* probability that he does not is a good deal higher than the *a priori* probability that the psychophysiological theory of Jones' era is mistaken, this theory has little to fear from Jones. (Although it would have a great deal to fear from a sizable accumulation of cases like Jones'.)

To sum up this point, we may look back at the italicized sentence in the above quotation from Baier. We now see that the claim that "such a mistake is inconceivable" is an ellipsis for the claim that a mistake, made *by one who knows what pain is,* is inconceivable, for only this expanded form will entail that when Jones and the encephalograph disagree, Jones is always right. But when formulated in this way our infallibility about our pains can be seen to be empty. Being infallible about something would be useful only if we could draw the usual distinction between misnaming and misjudging, and, having ascertained that we were not misnaming, know that we were not misjudging. But where there are no criteria for misjudging (or to put it more accurately, where in the crucial cases the criteria for misjudging turn out to be the same as the criteria for misnaming), then to say that we are infallible is to pay ourselves an empty compliment. Our neighbors will not hesitate to ride roughshod over our reports of our sensations unless they are assured that we know our way around among them, and we cannot satisfy them on this point unless, up to a certain point, we tell the same sort of story about them as they do. The limits of permissible stories are flexible enough for us to be able to convince them occasionally that we have odd sensations, but not flexible enough for us to use these surprising sensations to break down, at one blow, well-confirmed scientific theories. As in the case of other infallible pronouncements, the price of retaining one's epistemological authority is a decent respect for the opinions of mankind.

Thus the common-sense remark that first-person reports always will be a better source of information about the occurrence of pains than any other source borrows its plausibility from the fact that we normally do not raise questions about a man's ability to use the word "pain" correctly. Once we *do* raise such questions seriously (as in the case of Jones), we realize that the question (1) "Does he know which sensations are called 'pains'?" and (2) "Is he a good judge of whether he is in pain or not?" are simply two ways of asking the same question—viz., "Can we fit his pain-reports into our scheme for explaining and predicting pains?" or, more bluntly, "Shall we disregard his pain-reports or not?" And once we see this we realize that if "always be a better source of information" means "will never be over-ridden on the sort of grounds on which presumed observational errors are over-ridden elsewhere in science," then our common-sensical remark is probably false. If "always be a better source of information" means merely "can only be overridden on the basis of a charge of misnaming, and never on the basis of a charge of misjudging," then our common-sensical remark turns out to depend upon a distinction that is not there.

This Wittgensteinian point that sensation-reports must conform to public criteria or else be disallowed may also be brought out in the following way. We determine whether to take a surprising first-person report of pain or its absence seriously (that is, whether to say that the sensation reported is something that science must try to explain) by seeing whether the reporter's over-all pattern of pain-reporting is, by the usual behavioral and environmental criteria, normal. Now suppose that these public criteria (for "knowing how to use 'pain' ") change as physiology and technology progress. Suppose, in particular, that we find it convenient to speed up the learning of contrastive observation predicates (such as "painful," "tickling," etc.) by supplying children with portable encephalographs-cum-teaching-machines which, whenever the appropriate brain-process occurs, murmur the appropriate term in their ears. Now "appropriate brain-process" will start out by meaning "brain-process constantly correlated with sincere utterances of 'I'm in pain' by people taught the use of 'pain' in the old rough-and-ready way." But soon it will come to mean, "the brain-process which we have always programmed the machine to respond to with a murmur of 'pain.' " (A meter is (now, but was not always) what matches the Standard Meter; intelligence is (now, but was not always) what intelligence tests test; pains will be (but are not now) what the Standard "Pain"-Training Program calls "pain.") Given this situation, it would make sense to say things like "You say you are in pain, and I'm sure you are sincere, but you can see for yourself that your brain is not in the state to which you were trained to respond to with "Pain," so apparently the training did not work, and you do not yet understand what pain is." In such a situation, our "inability to be mistaken" about our pains would remain, but our "final epistemological authority" on the subject would be gone, for there would be a standard procedure for over-riding our reports. Our inability to be mistaken is, after all, no more than our ability to have such hypothetical statements as "If you admit that I'm sincere and that I know the language, you have to accept what I say" accepted by our fellows. But this asset can only be converted into final epistemological authority if we can secure both admissions. Where a clear-cut public criterion *does* exist for "knowing the language," inability to be mistaken does not entail inability to be over-ridden.

Now Baier might say that if such criteria did exist, then we should no longer be talking about what we presently mean by "pains." I do not think that this needs to be conceded,[17] but suppose that it

[17] My reasons for thinking this concession unnecessary are the same as those presented in some recent articles by Hilary Putnam: cf. "Minds and Machines," S. Hook, ed., *Dimensions of Mind* (New York: New York University Press, 1960),

is. Would this mean that there was now a subject-matter which was not being discussed—viz., the private subject-matter the existence of which Baier's argument was intended to demonstrate? That we once had contact with such a subject-matter, but lost it? These rhetorical questions are meant to suggest that Baier's explanation of the final epistemological authority of first-person reports of pains by the fact that this "logic" is "a function of this type of subject-matter" rather than, as Smart thinks, a convention is an explanation of the obscure by the more obscure. More precisely, it will not be an explanation of the epistemological authority in question—but only an unenlightening redescription of it—unless Baier can give a meaning to the term "private subject-matter" other than "kind of thing which is reported in reports which cannot be over-ridden." These considerations show the need for stepping back from Baier's argument and considering the criteria which he is using to demarcate distinct subject-matters.

"PRIVACY" AS A CRITERION OF CATEGORIAL DEMARCATION

The closest Baier comes to giving a definition of "private subject-matter" is to say that:

> We must say that "I have a pain" is about "something private," because in making this remark we report something which is (1) *necessarily owned* . . . is (2) *necessarily exclusive and unsharable* . . . (3) *necessarily imperceptible by the senses* . . . (4) *necessarily asymmetrical*, for whereas it makes no sense to say "I could see (or hear) that I had a pain," it makes quite good sense to say "I could see (or hear) that *he* had a pain"; (5) something about the possession of which the person who claims to possess it could not possibly examine, consider, or weigh any evidence, although other people could . . . and lastly (6) it is something about which the person whose private state it is has final epistemological authority, for it does not make sense to say "I have a pain unless I am mistaken." [18]

pp. 138–61, esp. pp. 153–60; "The Analytic and the Synthetic," *Minnesota Studies in the Philosophy of Science*, III, pp. 358–97; "Brains and Behavior," in *Analytic Philosophy*, II, ed. R. J. Butler (Oxford: Blackwell, 1965).

[18] Baier, "Smart on Sensations," p. 60. The numbers in parentheses have been added.

Now this definition of "something private" entails that nothing could be private except a state of a person, and is constructed to delimit all and only those states of a person which we call his "mental" states. To say that mental states are private is to say simply that mental states are described in the way in which mental states are described. But it is not hard to take *any* Rylean category of terms (call it C), list all the types of sentence-frames which do and do not make sense when their gaps are filled with terms belonging to this category, and say that "something C" is distinguished by the fact that it is "necessarily X," "necessarily Y," etc., where "X" and "Y" are labels for the fact that certain sentence-frames will or will not receive these terms as gap-fillers. For example, consider the thesis that:

> We must say that "The devil is in that corner" is about "something supernatural" because in making this report we report something which is *necessarily intangible,* since it makes no sense to ask about the texture of his skin, not *necessarily simply located,* since it does not follow from the fact that a supernatural being is in the corner that the same supernatural being is not simultaneously at the other side of the globe, *necessarily immortal,* since it does not make sense to say that a supernatural being has died, *necessarily perceptible to exorcists,* since it would not make sense to say that a man was an exorcist and did not perceive the devil when he was present. . . .

Are devils hallucinations? No, because when one reports an hallucination one reports something which, though intangible, is simply-located, is neither mortal nor immortal, and is not always perceptible to exorcists. Are reports of devils reports of hallucinations? No, because reports of devils are reports of something supernatural, and reports of hallucinations are reports of something private. Is it simply because we lack further information about devils that we take exorcists' sincere reports as the best possible source for information about them? No, for this suggestion confuses the supernatural character of the subject-matter with the availability of external evidence. Those without the supernatural powers with which the exorcist is gifted may find ways of gathering *evidence* for the presence of supernatural beings, but they can never formulate an overriding and independent *criterion* for saying that such a being is present. Their theories might become so good that we might sometimes say that a given exorcist was *lying,* but we could never say that he was *mistaken.*

If this pastiche of Baier's argument seems beside the point, it is presumably either (1) because the language-game I have described is not in fact played, or else (2) because "necessarily intangible, not necessarily simply-located, necessarily immortal, and necessarily perceptible to exorcists" does not delimit a subject-matter in the way in which "necessarily owned, exclusive, imperceptible by the senses, asymmetrical, etc., etc.," does. In (1) one has to ask "what if it *had* been played?" After all, if the technique of detecting distinct subject-matters which Baier uses is a generally applicable technique, and not just constructed *ad hoc* to suit our Cartesian intuitions, then it ought to work on imaginary as well as real language games. But if it is, we ought to be able to formulate rules for applying it which would tell us *why* (2) is the case. For if we cannot, and if the language-game described once was played, then Baier's objection to the Identity Theory is an objection to the theory that reports of visible supernatural beings are reports of hallucinations. Baier gives no more help in seeing what these rules would be. But I think that the root of Baier's conviction that "something private" is a suitable candidate for being a "distinct subject-matter" is the thesis that certain terms are *intrinsically* observation predicates, and signify, so to speak, "natural explananda." When in quest of such predicates we look to the "foundations" of empirical knowledge, we tend to rapidly identify "observation predicate" with "predicate occurring in report having final epistemological authority" with "predicate occurring in report about something private." This chain of identifications leaves us with the suspicion that if there were no longer a private subject-matter to be infallible about, the whole fabric of empirical inquiry about public matters would be left up in the air, unsupported by any absolute epistemological authority. The suggestion that the distinction between items reportable in infallible reports and items not so reportable is "ultimate," or "irreducible," or "categorical," owes its intuitive force to the difficulty of imagining a stage in the progress of inquiry in which there was not *some* situation in which absolute epistemological authority about *something* would be granted to *somebody*.

There probably, indeed, could *not* be such a stage, for inquiry cannot proceed if everything is to be doubted at once, and if inquiry is even to get off the ground we need to get straight about what is to be questioned and what not. These practical dictates show the kernel of truth in the notion that inquiry cannot proceed without a foundation. Where we slide from truth into error is in assuming that certain items are *naturally* reportable in infallible reports, and thus assume that the items presently so reportable always were and always will be reportable (and conversely for items not presently so reportable). A pain looks like the paradigm of such an item, with the situation described by "seems to me as if I were seeing something red" almost as well-qualified. But in both cases, we can imagine situations in which we should feel justified in over-riding sincere reports using these predicates. More important, we see that the device which we should use to justify ourselves in such situations—viz., "The reporter may not know how to use the word . . ."—is one which can apply in *all* proposed cases. Because this escape-hatch is always available, and because the question of whether the reporter does know how to use the word or does not is probably not itself a question which could ever be settled by recourse to any absolute epistemological authority, the situation envisaged by Baier—namely, the body of current scientific theory foundering upon the rock of a single over-riding report—can probably never arise. Baier sees a difference in kind between the weight of *evidence* produced by such a theory and the single, authoritative, *criterion* provided by such a report. But since there can be no over-riding report until the ability of the speaker to use the words used in the report is established, and since this is to be established only by the weight of the evidence and not by recourse to any single criterion, this difference in kind (even though it may indeed be "firmly embedded in the way we talk" for millennia) is always capable of being softened into a difference of degree by further empirical inquiry.

REDUCTIONIST PHILOSOPHICAL THEORIES AND CATEGORIAL DISTINCTIONS

In the preceding sections of this paper I have constantly invoked the fact that language changes as empirical discoveries are made, in order to argue that the thesis that "what people now call 'sensations' might be discovered to be brain-processes" is sensible and unconfused. The "deviance" of a statement of this thesis should not, I have been urging, blind us to the facts that (a) entities referred to by expressions in one Rylean category may also be referred to by expressions in another, (b) expressions in the first category may drop out of the language once this identity of reference is realized, and (c) the thesis in question is a natural way of expressing the result of this realization in the case of "sensation" and "brain-process." Now a critic might object that this strategy is subject to a *reductio ad absurdum.* For the same fact about linguistic change would seem to justify the claim that *any* statement of the form (S) "What people call 'X's' may be discovered to be Y's" is *always* sensible and unconfused. Yet this seems paradoxical, for consider the result of substituting, say "neutrino" for "X" and "mushroom" for "Y." If the resulting statement is not conceptually confused, what statement is?

In answer to this objection, I should argue that it is a mistake to attribute "conceptual confusions" to *statements.* No statement can be known to express a conceptual confusion simply by virtue of an acquaintance with the meanings of its component terms. Confusion is a property of people. Deviance is a property of utterances. Deviant utterances made by using sentences of the form (S) *may* be token confusion on the part of the speaker about the meanings of words, but it may simply indicate a vivid (but unconfused) imagination, or perhaps (as in the neutrino-mushroom case) merely idle fancy. Although the making of such statements may be *prima facie* evidence of conceptual confusion—i.e., of the fact that the speaker is insufficiently familiar with the language to find a non-deviant way of making his point—this evidence is only *prima facie,* and questioning may bring out evidence pointing the other way. Such questioning may show that the speaker actually has some detailed suggestions about possible empirical results which would point to the discovery in question, or that he has no such suggestions, but is nevertheless not inclined to use the relevant words in any *other* deviant utterances, and to cheerfully admit the deviance of his original utterance. The possibility of such evidence, pointing to imagination or to fancy rather than to confusion, shows that from the fact that certain questions are typically asked, and certain statements typically made, by victims of conceptual confusion, it does not follow that all those who use the sentences used to ask these questions or to make these statements are thus victimized.

This confusion about confusion is due to the fact that philosophers who propound "reductionist" theories (such as "There is no insensate matter," "There are no minds," "There are no physical objects," etc.) often *have* been conceptually confused. Such theories are often advocated as solutions to pseudo-problems whose very formulation involves deviant uses of words—uses which in fact result from a confusion between the uses of two or more senses of the same term, or between two or more related terms (e.g., "name" and "word") or between the kind of questions appropriately asked of entities referred to by one set of terms and the kind appropriately asked of entities referred to by another. (That these deviant uses *are* the result of such confusion, it should be noticed, is only capable of being determined by questioning of those who use them—and we only feel *completely* safe in making this diagnosis when the original user has, in the light of the linguistic facts drawn to his attention, admitted that his putative "problem" has been dissolved.) Because reductionist theories may often be choked off at the source by an examination of uses of language, antireductionist philosophers have lately become prone to use "conceptual confusion" or "category mistake" as an all-purpose diagnosis for any deviant utterance in the mouth of a philosopher. But this is a mistake. Predictions of the sort illustrated by (S) may be turned to confused purposes, and they may be made by confused people. But we could only infer with certainty from the deviance of the utterance of a sentence of the form (S) to the conceptual confusion of the speaker if we had a map of the categories which are exhibited in all possible languages, and were thus in a position to say that the cross-category identification envisaged by the statement was eternally impossible. In other words, we should only be in a position to make this inference with certainty if we knew that empirical inquiry could *never* bring about the sort of linguistic change which permits the non-deviant use of "There are no X's" in the case of the "X's" to which the statement in question refers. But philosophers are in no position to say that such change is impossible. The hunt for categorial confusions at the source of reductionist philosophical theories is an extremely valuable enterprise. But their successes in this enterprise should not lead linguistic philosophers to think that they can do better what metaphysicians did badly—namely, prove the irreducibility of entities. Traditional materialism embodied many confusions, but at its heart was the unconfused prediction about future empirical inquiry which is the Identity Theory. The confusions may be eradicated without affecting the plausibility or interest of the prediction.[19]

[19] I have been greatly helped in preparing this paper by the comments of Richard Bernstein, Keith Gunderson, Amélie Rorty, and Richard Schmitt.

10 James Cornman

On the Elimination of 'Sensations' and Sensations

⁂ James Cornman was born in Philadelphia, Pennsylvania, on August 16, 1927, and was educated at Dartmouth College and Brown University. He is now Associate Professor of Philosophy at the University of Pennsylvania and works primarily in the philosophy of language and the philosophy of mind. He is the author of *Metaphysics, Reference, and Language*, and his articles have appeared in important journals. ⁂

The metaphysical doctrine of materialism is attractive to many philosophers, especially those impressed with the physical sciences and the obvious advances in knowledge resulting from them. It often seems to such philosophers that science is advancing towards a state where physics will be not only the basic science upon which all other sciences are erected, but also the one science to which all other sciences are reducible. This is the view, then, that in the millennium physics will be sufficient for the purposes of explaining and predicting the behavior of everything including persons. The contemplation of this "future" state has led many philosophers to materialism.

Nevertheless, despite whatever optimism about the future unification of sciences is justified, there are now, as there have been for centuries, difficult problems confronting the materialist. Perhaps the crucial problem concerns the status of sensations, a problem clearly evident as far back as Hobbes, who said that sense is "some internal motion in the sentient, generated by some internal motion, of the parts of the object, and propagated through all the media to the

FROM *The Review of Metaphysics*, XXII (1968), pp. 15–35. Reprinted by permission of the author and the editors.

innermost part of the organ." [1] Here Hobbes reduces sense to physical motion. But he is also found to say that sense is not motion, but "in all cases, is nothing else but original fancy," or, he says elsewhere, "phantasms" caused by internal motions.[2] He is then directly faced with the problem of reconciling appearances and sensations with his avowed materialism. Neither Hobbes nor any one else has solved this problem, although there have recently been some novel and instructive attempts to do so.

TWO MATERIALISTIC THEORIES: THE IDENTITY THEORY AND THE POSTULATION ELIMINATION THEORY

The most widely discussed recent attempt tries to justify the claim that each sensation is identical with some physical phenomenon, presumably, a brain process. Thus pains have been claimed to be identical with stimulations of the C-fibers of certain kinds of brains. Such a mind-body identity theory can be called a *reductive materialism*, because while admitting that there are mental phenomena such as sensations, it states they are identical with and thus reducible to brain processes.[3] Another recent attempt tries to justify the claim that there are no mental phenomena such as sensations, because such phenomena, like electrons, are theoretical entities postulated by scientific theories to explain observable behavior, but, unlike electrons, are unnecessary for such explanations.[4] As Quine says, "But if a certain organization of theory is achieved by thus positing distinctive mental states and events behind physical behavior, surely as much organization could be achieved by positing merely certain correlative physiological states and events instead. . . . The bodily states exist

[1] F. J. E. Woodbridge, ed., *Hobbes Selections* (New York: Scribner's, 1930), p. 139.

[2] *Ibid.*, p. 140.

[3] For examples of this position, see J. J. C. Smart, "Sensations and Brain Processes," *The Philosophical Review* (1959), pp. 141–56; reprinted in this volume, pp. 32–47. Subsequent references to Smart's article are to the reprint in this volume); see also H. Putnam, "Minds and Machines," S. Hook, ed., *Dimensions of Mind* (New York: New York University Press, 1960), p. 38.

[4] Cf. W. V. O. Quine, *Word and Object* (Cambridge, Mass.: M.I.T. Press, 1960), pp. 264–66. Quine, however, although he construes sensations as unnecessary postulated entities does not opt for either an eliminative or a reductive position. A similar view is expressed in D. K. Lewis, "An Argument for the Identity Theory," *The Journal of Philosophy* (1966), pp. 17–25.

anyway, why add the others?"[5] This second attempt to justify materialism can be called an *eliminative materialism,* because it attempts to eliminate mental phenomena rather than reduce them to something physical. Let us call this particular version of eliminative materialism the postulation-elimination theory.

Both the identity theory and the postulation-elimination theory face obvious objections which so far have not been countered. It seems that sensations are not identical with brain processes because they have properties no brain processes have.[6] And it seems sensations cannot be eliminated by construing them as unneeded postulated theoretical entities, because we directly experience them, and so they are not postulated.[7] Recently, however, Richard Rorty has made a new attempt to solve the materialist's problem with sensations in a way that avoids both of these objections.[8] Although Rorty claims his theory is a version of the identity theory, he does not construe the relation between brain processes and sensations to be "strict identity but rather the sort of relation which obtains between, to put it crudely, existent entities and non-existent entities. . . ."[9] His theory can, I think, best be explicated as a subtle kind of eliminative materialism that does not construe sensations as postulated. On this interpretation the theory avoids the objection to the postulation-elimination theory. And, not claiming sensations are strictly identical with brain processes, it avoids the property objection to the identity theory. It is, consequently, a position deserving close scrutiny.

A THIRD MATERIALISTIC THEORY: THE 'SENSATION'-ELIMINATION THEORY

To characterize this third theory, let me contrast it with the two previously discussed theories. This can best be done, I think, by construing all three theories to be about the reference of sensation-terms.

[5] W. Quine, p. 264.

[6] Cf. J. J. C. Smart, pp. 39–41; J. R. Stevenson, "Sensations and Brain Processes: A Reply to J. J. C. Smart," *The Philosophical Review* (1960), pp. 505–10; J. Cornman, "The Identity of Mind and Body," *The Journal of Philosophy* (1962), pp. 486–92.

[7] I have discussed this point in more detail in "Mental Terms, Theoretical Terms, and Materialism," *Philosophy of Science* (1968).

[8] R. Rorty, "Mind-Body Identity, Privacy, Categories," *The Review of Metaphysics* (1956–66), pp. 24–54; reprinted in this volume, pp. 145–74. Subsequent page references to Rorty's article are to the reprint in this volume.

[9] Rorty, p. 147.

All three theories, as I shall construe them, agree that sensation-terms are referring terms, but they disagree about whether they denote, that is, whether there exists anything which they refer to. In this regard all three theories disagree with certain versions of eliminative materialism we shall not examine here. According to the latter theories, psychological terms are not referring terms. For example, there is a form of logical behaviorism which states that psychological terms are incomplete symbols and therefore are not referring terms.[10] There is also a Rylean position that takes an instrumentalist or inference ticket view of psychological terms, that is, the view that they are merely non-denoting symbolic inference devices, and thus function solely to warrant inferences among observation claims.[11]

Whereas the postulation-elimination theory asserts that sensation terms do not denote anything at all, both the identity theory and the 'sensation'-elimination theory agree that sensation-terms denote certain phenomena, indeed phenomena we experience. The latter two theories further agree that what sensation-terms such as 'pain' denote is exactly what is denoted by certain physicalistic expressions such as 'stimulation of C-fibers', but they disagree about whether sensations are to be considered identical with anything physical. Both theories agree that what we denote when using sensation-terms are nothing but certain brain events, and thus that these brain processes exist. But while the identity theory agrees that there are sensations because they are identical with such brain processes, the 'sensation'-elimination theory denies there are sensations and thereby denies the identity claim.

OBJECTION TO THE 'SENSATION'-ELIMINATION THEORY: IT IS INCONSISTENT

At this point an objection might be raised against the 'sensation'-elimination theory. Surely, according to this objection, for any term

[10] For an example of logical behaviorism, see C. Hempel, "The Logical Analysis of Psychology" in H. Feigl and W. Sellars, eds., *Readings in Philosophical Analysis* (New York: Appleton-Century-Crofts, 1949), pp. 373–84. I have discussed this problem in *Metaphysics, Reference, and Language* (New Haven: Yale University Press, 1966), pp. 17–25.

[11] This view derives from Gilbert Ryle's discussion of psychological sentences as law-like and, thereby, as inference tickets, in *The Concept of Mind* (New York: Barnes & Noble, 1949), esp. chs. 1 and 5. I have discussed Ryle on this point in *Metaphysics, Reference, and Language*, pp. 63–70, 236–38.

'p', if what is denoted by 'p' is nothing but what is denoted by 'q', and what 'q' denotes, namely q, exists, then p exists, for it follows that p is identical with q. For example, if what is denoted by 'LBJ' is what 'the president of the U.S.A. in 1967' denotes, and the president exists in 1967, then it follows that LBJ is identical with the president in 1967, and that LBJ exists in 1967. Another way to put this objection is that if it is granted, as is done by a 'sensation'-elimination theorist, that the referents of sensation-terms and certain physicalistic terms are identical, and that these physicalistic terms denote brain processes, then the identity claim of the identity theory and with it the existence of sensations are entailed. The 'sensation'-elimination theory, according to this objection, is inconsistent.

This objection can be refuted. It states that two of the claims of the 'sensation'-elimination theory:

(a) What is denoted by 'sensation' is nothing but what is denoted by 'brain process'
(b) What is denoted by 'brain process' are brain processes

together entail:

(c) Sensations are identical with brain processes.

But because the 'sensation'-elimination theory denies (c), it is inconsistent.

It is true that (a) and (b) entail:

(d) There are brain processes

and also:

(e) What is denoted by 'sensation' exists.

But (a), (b), (d), and (e) do not entail (c). To show that they do not, I shall list seven cases in which statements of the same form as (a) and (b) are true and then point out that in some of the cases the corresponding claim of the same form as (c) is false. From this we can conclude that sentences of the same form as (a) and (b) do not entail (c). Thus (a) and (b) do not entail (c) and the objection fails.

(1) What is denoted by 'the morning star' is nothing but what is denoted by 'Venus', and that is Venus.
(2) What is denoted by 'unicorn horn' is nothing but what is denoted by 'narwhal horn', and they are narwhal horns.
(3) What is denoted by 'water' is nothing but what is denoted by

'conglomeration of H_2O molecules', and they are conglomerations of H_2O molecules.

(4) What is denoted by 'lightning flash' is nothing but what is denoted by 'electrical flash', and they are electrical flashes.

(5) What is denoted by 'Zeus' thunderbolt' is nothing but what is denoted by 'flash of electrical charges', and they are flashes of electrical charges.

(6) What is denoted by 'Zeus, the thrower of thunderbolts' is nothing but what is denoted by 'discharge of static electricity', and they are discharges of electricity.

(7) What is denoted by 'pink rat' is nothing but what is denoted by 'pink-rat-appearance', and they are pink-rat-appearances.[12]

The examples relevant to rebutting the objection mentioned above are (2), (5), (6), and (7). In each of the other three cases it is generally agreed that claims of the form of (a) and (b) are true and that the corresponding identity claims of the form of (c) are also true, whether or not the first two entail the third. The morning star is identical with Venus, water is identical with certain conglomerations of H_2O molecules, and flashes of lightning with electrical flashes. And, of course, in each case we would agree that these entities so "reduced" exist. But we would think differently in the other four examples. Surely there are narwhal horns, electrical flashes, discharges of static electricity, and pink-rat-hallucinations, but there is no reason to think there are unicorn horns, Zeus' thunderbolts, Zeus, and pink rats. In each of these cases, then, we should reject the identity claim, but at the same time accept the corresponding denotation claims. We can conclude from this that a conjunction of statements of the form of (a) and (b) do not entail identity claims of the form of (c), and therefore this objection to the 'sensation'-elimination theory fails. There is no reason to doubt that the theory is consistent. But is it plausible?

AN ATTEMPT TO JUSTIFY THE 'SENSATION'-ELIMINATION THEORY BY ANALOGY

An obvious way to try to justify the 'sensation'-elimination theory is to show its claim, i.e., what is denoted by sensation-terms is nothing but what is denoted by 'brain process,' is relevantly analogous to one

[12] Several of these examples and the subsequent discussions of them are derived from R. Rorty, pp. 149–58.

of the above-mentioned examples where we are justified in making the two claims about denotation, and also justified in denying the corresponding identity claim. Let us, therefore, compare it with each example.

Consider the second example about 'unicorn horn.' Here we have a claim about the common referents of two different observation terms when, for example, people have pointed to a narwhal horn and called it a unicorn horn. Such people have made a straightforward empirical mistake. This can be shown by gathering evidence to show that there are no unicorns and thus no unicorn horns, or by tracing the history of the particular horn in question. But in many cases of using sensation-terms to talk about something, no mistake can be shown by piling up this kind of nontheoretical, empirical evidence in these ways. In such cases a claim that someone is having a sensation does not entail any nontheoretical, empirical falsehood. We cannot, therefore, justify the claim of the 'sensation'-elimination theory by likening sensation-terms to 'unicorn horn'.

The fifth example about 'Zeus' thunderbolt' concerns two terms that, although they are observation terms, are not "pure" observation terms. That is, both terms, in the fifth example, unlike those in the second example, are theory-laden observation terms, in the sense that, although they are used to report what is observed, a report using them entails that there is some postulated theoretical entity, e.g., Zeus or an electrical charge. Here again we would agree that there are phenomena denoted by 'Zeus' thunderbolt' but deny the corresponding identity claim that these phenomena are identical with thunderbolts thrown by Zeus, because there is no being named 'Zeus'. In this case we deny that Zeus' thunderbolts exist because their existence entails that Zeus exists and we reject the latter claim for reasons quite different from the nontheoretical empirical grounds used in example (2). The statement 'Zeus exists' is not a false observation statement nor does it entail one. It is, let us say for our purposes here, a theoretical statement about the unobserved cause of lightning flashes. It, then, competes with the "more scientific" theoretical explanations of lightning and is rejected because, roughly, some scientific theory that competes with it has more explanatory and predictive power. It might be noted in passing, however, that one could consistently maintain that lightning is caused by Zeus, while accepting all available empirical evidence and also the justification of a competing scientific explanation of lightning, if he were to subscribe to an instrumentalist view of scientific theoretical terms.[13]

Can we liken sensation-terms to 'Zeus' thunderbolt'? One difference is that 'Zeus' thunderbolt' is used to report something perceivable, but sensation-terms are not. This is not a vital difference, however, because both terms are reporting terms, in the sense that both are used to refer to phenomena that we experience, in the one case via perception, in the other not. But there is an important difference. The term 'Zeus' thunderbolt' is theory laden because its use in a report entails that there is a postulated theoretical entity, Zeus. But not all sensation-terms are theory laden in this way, unless whatever they are used to refer to are themselves postulated theoretical entities, because many reports using sensation-terms do not entail that there is any other postulated theoretical entity.

The question at this point is whether what sensation-terms are used to refer to are postulated theoretical entities. Because something is such an entity only if we do not experience it, we can conclude that what sensation-terms refer to are postulated theoretical entities only if we do not experience the entities referred to. Consequently we can use the fifth example to justify the elimination of sensations only if sensation-terms are nonreporting, or pure, theoretical terms. But the 'sensation'-elimination theory cannot take this tack, because it construes sensation-terms as reporting terms. Furthermore, the theory is certainly correct in this; sensation-terms are clear cases of terms used to report what we experience.[14] Consequently the fifth example cannot help the justification of the elimination of sensation-terms and sensations.

The sixth example differs from the two previously discussed because it concerns two terms neither of which, for our purposes, are observation terms, either pure or theory laden. It is like the fifth example, however, in that we justify the denial of the existence of Zeus, and thereby the denial of the corresponding identity claim about Zeus and electrical discharges, on theoretical grounds. Indeed both

[13] This, in effect, is what Berkeley does in combining his instrumentalist view of scientific theoretical terms with his claim that God is the cause of the sensory ideas that make up the world. I have discussed this in "Theoretical Terms, Berkeleian Notions, and Minds," forthcoming in a book tentatively titled *Berkeley: Principles of Human Knowledge: Text and Commentaries,* ed. by C. M. Turbayne (Indianapolis: Bobbs-Merrill).

[14] I have discussed this in more detail in "Mental Terms, Theoretical Terms and Materialism."

terms of the sixth example are pure theoretical terms, because they are neither observation terms, nor definable by observation terms, nor reporting terms. It is examples such as this that the postulation-elimination theory uses to justify its position. It is claimed that sensation-terms are, in principle, like 'Zeus' in that their scientific explanatory role can be taken over by physiological terms, and thus sensation-terms are unnecessary for explanation and prediction. But we have already noted the problem facing this position. Sensation-terms are used to report phenomena we experience whether or not they have any explanatory function, and therefore we cannot justify their eliminability merely by eliminating their explanatory functions so long as they have a reporting function. Example (6) fails to help justify the elimination of sensations.

It is clear that example (7) cannot help, because the elimination of pink rats results from construing the reference of 'pink rat' to be sensations rather than physical objects. As Rorty notes, we cannot eliminate sensations by construing them as the referents of sensation-terms.[15] This leads us to the conclusion that none of the four examples of justified elimination of entities can be used to provide justification for eliminating sensations. If an eliminative materialist is to justify his position he must take a different line altogether.

ANOTHER ATTEMPT TO JUSTIFY THE 'SENSATION'-ELIMINATION THEORY: NO NEED FOR SENSATION-TERMS

Rorty's approach to the justification of what I have explicated as the 'sensation'-elimination theory is such a new line. Although he begins by likening the case of sensations to an hallucination example about demons, he ends by likening it to a physical object example about tables. What he does is liken claims such as: what is denoted by 'sensation' is nothing but what is denoted by 'brain process', to a claim such as: what is denoted by 'table' is nothing but what is denoted by 'conglomeration of molecules'. At first glance this move seems self-defeating, because the table case is like example (4) with 'water' where we do not conclude there is no water. But while admitting this, Rorty seeks to explain this conclusion about tables in such a way that it will aid the 'sensation'-elimination theory. He says,

[15] See Rorty, pp. 158–59.

> If there is any point to saying that tables are nothing but clouds of molecules it is presumably to say that, in principle, we could stop making a referring use of "table," and of any extensionally equivalent term, and still leave our ability to describe and predict undiminished. But this would seem just the point of (and the justification for) saying that there are no demons. Why does the realization that nothing would be lost by the dropping of "table" from our vocabulary still leave us with the conviction that there are tables, whereas the same realization about demons leaves us with the conviction that there are no demons? I suggest that the only answer to this question which will stand examination is that although we could *in principle* drop "table," it would be monstrously inconvenient to do so, whereas it is both possible in principle and convenient in practice to drop "demon." [16]

If Rorty is right, then the only relevant difference between hallucination examples such as cases of demons and pink rats, and physical object examples such as cases of tables and water, is that it is very inconvenient to give up table-talk for molecule-talk but not inconvenient to give up demon-talk for hallucination-talk. And if this is so, then, although as in example (4) we do not in practice say that there are no tables, we are nevertheless justified in concluding that there are none. This is because if the only thing that keeps us from drawing this conclusion is linguistic convenience, something of no ontological relevance, then the conclusion is justified for purposes of ontology. Rorty's point, then, is that for the purposes of justifying an ontological position, the 'sensation' case is relevantly like the 'table' case which is relevantly like the hallucination case after all. Our task in evaluating Rorty's claim, therefore, is to see whether there are any differences among these three cases sufficient to destroy his justification of the elimination of sensations.

Let us grant that if sensation-terms are not needed for correctly explaining, predicting, reporting, and describing, then Rorty has made his point that we are justified in eliminating sensations, while at the same time we are justified in using the terms to avoid inconvenience. Let us also grant, what is surely more debatable, that neither terms such as 'table' and 'water' nor sensation-terms are needed for either explanation or prediction. The question, then, is whether our ability to report and describe would remain undiminished if these terms were eliminated from language.

[16] *Ibid.*, pp. 154–55.

The crux of Rorty's case that sensation-terms are unnecessary for the purpose of correctly reporting and describing lies in the following passage:

> And why should it not be the case that the circumstances in which we make non-inferential reports about brain-processes are just those circumstances in which we make non-inferential reports about sensations? For this will in fact be the case if, when we were trained to say, e.g., "I'm in pain" we were in fact being trained to respond to the occurrence within ourselves of a stimulation of C-fibers. If this is the case, the situation will be perfectly parallel to the case of demons and hallucinations. We *will*, indeed, have been making non-inferential reports about brain-processes all our lives *sans le savoir*.[17]

Rorty is claiming here that there is no reason why we should deny an exact parallel between demon-reports or pink-rat-reports, and pain-reports. And he might add that the parallel should extend to water-reports. There certainly is at least one parallel here. We can use 'There's H_2O here' instead of 'There's water here', and it would seem we would be making more accurate reports in so doing. If we can also use some physicalistic expression such as, 'My C-fibers are stimulated' to report the occurrence of what we usually report by 'I'm in pain', and if, in so doing, we would be making more accurate reports, then both cases would be perfectly parallel to the case of pink-rat-reports in the relevant respects, because using 'I see a pink-rat-appearance' is more accurate than using 'I see a pink rat'. Rorty thinks this parallel is enough to make his case: just as we do not need 'pink rat', we need neither 'pain', nor 'water' nor any other sensation-terms and observation terms to report and describe what occurs.

FIRST OBJECTION: SENSATION-TERMS NEEDED FOR REPORTING

We can grant that if 'stimulation of C-fibers' and 'pain' refer to the same things, then there is a clear sense in which we would lose no ability to refer to anything and, consequently, a clear sense in which we would lose no ability to report something if we dropped 'pain' and all other psychological terms that refer to what 'pain' refers to. That is, although our ability to refer to things would be diminished in the

[17] *Ibid.*, p. 160.

sense that we would have fewer nonsynonymous terms to use to refer to things, our ability to identify in *some* way each thing there is would not be diminished. And, it is clear that it is the latter ability that is relevant to Rorty's claim about our reporting ability.

The problem is, however, whether 'stimulation of C-fibers', or some other physicalistic term, and 'pain' do refer to the same things. If they do not, then our ability to identify in some way each thing there is would be diminished if we were to drop 'pain' and all other psychological terms that refer to what 'pain' refers to. Rorty, then, can establish his claim about our undiminished reporting ability, only if he has reason to think that some physicalistic terms refer to what sensation-terms refer to. But this identity of reference is just what Rorty is trying to establish. Thus he cannot use his claim about our undiminished reporting ability to help justify his identity of reference claim as he tries to do.

Two replies might be made at this point. First, someone might claim that although J. J. C. Smart was wrong to think that topic neutral language could be used to give the meaning of sensation-sentences,[18] his mistake can be converted into a sound point. Namely, topic neutral expressions, although not synonymous with sensation-expressions, can be used to identify in some way each thing we now use sensation-terms to identify. Thus, contrary to the previous objection to Rorty, we can drop sensation-terms without diminishing our ability to identify each thing in some way.

The problem for this reply is whether there is reason to think topic neutral terms will do the job of replacing the reporting function of sensation-terms. Consider first an attempt derived from Smart's suggested translation of 'I have a pain', a suggestion he later claims is merely an attempt to give "the general purport of sensation-reports." [19] Thus we might try to replace 'pain' by:

> Something that happens to someone like what happens when he is stuck with a pin.

This is neutral because there is no implication about whether this something is mental or physical. But the problem is that this reporting-expression is not specific enough to pick out from several things

[18] For Smart's attempted analysis, see J. J. C. Smart, pp. 41–42. I have discussed problems facing his analysis in *Metaphysics, Reference and Language*, pp. 42–45.
[19] J. J. C. Smart, "Brain Processes and Incorrigibility," *Australasian Journal of Philosophy* (1962), p. 69.

that happen in such situations just what we identify using 'pain'. A more specific phrase might be used, such as:

> Something that happens to someone when and only when his C-fibers are stimulated.

This would identify one kind of thing which might well be what we identify using 'pain', if there is only one kind of thing that happens when and only when C-fibers are stimulated. But the problem is whether there is only one such kind of thing. Thus although this attempt might work, it cannot be decided merely by philosophers, for it cannot be decided without scientific investigation. We cannot, then, rely on this reply to the previous objection.

If the second reply is sound, however, we need not worry about finding suitable topic neutral expressions to take over the reporting functions of sensation-terms. There is reason to think that pains occur when and only when C-fibers are stimulated, and so, according to this reply, we can use 'stimulation of C-fibers' to report what we now use 'pain' to report: Thus "My C-fibers are stimulated!" could be used to report what "I have a pain!" reports. The immediate objection to this is that nothing can be solved this way for there is no more reason to think that 'stimulation of C-fibers' with this new reporting role has univocal reference than to think that it has ambiguous reference, referring to certain brain states and, in addition, pains. But, in the spirit of Rorty's argument, a materialist might well reply that if the *only* thing that *might* be lost is univocal reference, and there is no reason to conclude it would be lost, then we are justified in assuming that the reference is univocal. And, consequently, we can also assume that our ability to identify in some way each thing there is would remain undiminished if sensation-terms were dropped from language. This brings us finally to the central question of whether the only thing that might be lost is an unverifiable ambiguity of reference. To see that there is reason to think more would be lost than that, we can turn to the second objection to Rorty's claim.

SECOND OBJECTION: SENSATION-TERMS NEEDED FOR TRUE DESCRIPTIONS

For the purposes of considering the present objection, let us grant Rorty one more point, that not only can we explain and predict everything that occurs without sensation-terms and observation terms, but also we can report, in the sense of identify, everything there is without such terms. Although Rorty may think we have granted him all he needs to make this point, we shall find that we have not. We have not settled the question of whether or not our ability to describe what there is would be diminished if we dropped these terms from our language. In order to answer this question, we must again be clear about what kind of ability is relevant to Rorty's claim. We can distinguish at least three different kinds of descriptive ability:

(1) The ability to make many different sorts of descriptions of what there is.
(2) The ability to make accurate descriptions of what there is.
(3) The ability to make true descriptions, i.e., use true sentences to describe what there is.

It is clear that the first kind of ability would be diminished if we dropped sensation-terms and observation terms, but it is also clear that having only this ability diminished would not affect Rorty's point. If the second and third kinds of abilities remain undiminished his point is sound. If, however, either of these two kinds of abilities are diminished, then Rorty's argument fails.

Consider first the second kind of ability. If we would lose accuracy in our descriptions by dropping certain terms, then we could not justify the claim that they are needed only for convenience. This may be the kind of ability Rorty considers, and, if so, we might well agree with him that descriptions without sensation-terms and observation terms would be no less accurate and precise, no more vague and unclear, than if we used such terms. Indeed using only mathematically formulated descriptions would seem to result in more accuracy rather than less. Let us assume, then, that Rorty is right concerning the second kind of descriptive ability.

Descriptions of what there is would be no less accurate if we dropped sensation-terms and observation terms. But would they be complete? Would there be any true descriptive sentences we would be unable to formulate? If there would be some, then one kind of descriptive ability relevant to what there is would be lost and Rorty's argument would fail. We cannot justify eliminating terms needed for making true descriptions. It seems clear that concerning this kind of descriptive ability a parallel holds between sensation-terms and observation terms, but this is the wrong parallel for Rorty's argument.

A theoretical statement will provide the same description as an observation sentence only if the two statements are synonymous. Thus the observation description of water, or H_2O, as a clear, wet fluid can be made only by a sentence synonymous with 'Water (H_2O) is a clear, wet fluid'. But there is reason to think that no purely theoretical sentence is synonymous with this sentence. Observation sentences seem to be unanalyzable by theoretical sentences. Thus to eliminate all observation terms would result in our being unable to ascribe to water those observable properties it surely seems to have, and our ability to make true descriptions of water would seem to be considerably diminished.

The same conclusion applies to sensation-terms. Even if we grant that a pain is identical with a stimulation of C-fibers, it would seem we shall still need sensation-terms to make the true description of certain pains, or stimulation of C-fibers, as, for example, intense, sharp and throbbing. No neurophysiological sentence is synonymous with 'This pain (stimulation of C-fibers) is intense, sharp, and throbbing'; and thus no neurophysiological sentence can be used to make the same true description. Thus to eliminate the sensation-terms we apply to what we experience would seem to diminish our ability to describe considerably. Rorty, although he may be correct about explaining and predicting, and even if we grant he is right about reporting, seems wrong about describing. It would be more than convenience that would be lost if we were to eliminate sensation-terms and observation terms. The eliminative materialist cannot justify the elimination of sensations in the way Rorty claims he can.

FIRST REPLY: NON-SYNONYMY OF EXPRESSIONS IS MERELY CONTINGENT

It might be replied to the previous objection that it is based on a contingent fact dependent on the present state of language. There is no reason why in the future theoretical terms could not take on the descriptive roles of both observation terms and sensation-terms. When that time comes, according to this reply, the last obstacle to the acceptance of the 'sensation'-elimination theory will disappear and the theory will be acceptable. And, it might be added, because there is nothing, except perhaps ingrained usage and convenience, to stop theoretical terms from acquiring these roles, it does not matter whether they actually ever do acquire them. If observation terms and sensation-terms are in principle eliminable, then the 'sensation'-elimination theory is justified.

This reply does point to one clear way terms can be eliminated, but, unfortunately, it is not a kind of elimination that will help an eliminative materialist. Let us assume that 'Jones' C-fibers are very stimulated' has acquired the descriptive role of 'Jones' pain is intense', and that it also retains its theoretical role. Let us also grant that if this role change occurs, then 'Jones' pain is intense' is no longer needed to make a true description of Jones because 'Jones' C-fibers are very stimulated' gives us this description of Jones and more. The objection to such a reply is not, as has been suggested, that "conjectured future concepts" are irrelevant to the question of materialism because the question is about our present concepts.[20] The question is about what there is. Questions about concepts whether past, present, or future, are relevant only in so far as they help answer the question of what there is. The objection is, rather, that the reason we would no longer need 'Jones' pain is intense' is that what it states would be entailed by 'Jones' C-fibers are very stimulated'. Consequently, we could no longer even make certain physiological claims about the brain without implying that there are sensations. This is surely a move in the wrong direction for an eliminative materialist.

The faliure of the previous kind of linguistic elimination to help the eliminative materialist points to the kind of elimination of terms he requires. The elimination must accomplish at least two things. First, as we have already seen, it must show the terms eliminated are not needed for any true description. Second, as the present discussion emphasizes, it must also show that all of the descriptive roles played by the eliminated terms in true statements can be played by purely physicalistic terms, that is, terms that can be used to describe physical phenomena without implying the existence of anything mental. It is not important, then, which words we use now or ever. What matters is which descriptive roles they play. Merely to eliminate or change terms, and thus to leave untouched the descriptive roles they play, has no ontological significance. Thus because 'stimulation of C-fibers' taking on the descriptive role of 'pain' accomplishes only the elimina-

[20] Cf. N. Malcolm, "Scientific Materialism and the Identity Theory," *Dialogue* (1964); reprinted in this volume, pp. 72–81. Subsequent page references to Malcolm's article are to the reprint in this volume.

tion of 'pain' and not its role in true descriptions, such an elimination of sensation-terms fails to help the eliminative materialist. Indeed, if this is the only way sensation-terms can be eliminated, we should reject eliminative materialism, because we must either keep sensation-terms to make true descriptions or change physicalistic terms in such a way that using them descriptively implies that there are sensations.

SECOND REPLY: H_2O WITHOUT WATER AND SENSING WITHOUT SENSATIONS

The previous discussion leads to the conclusion that, contrary to Rorty, the case of water and pain are not "perfectly parallel to the case of demons and hallucinations." There is, however, a new move that would make the cases of water and pink rats perfectly parallel. This is a move a scientific realist might make, that is, to claim that, although we commonly suppose the referents of observation-expressions to be physical objects and their sensible qualities, what they actually refer to are sense impressions caused in us by physical objects. What refer to physical objects and then properties are the theoretical terms of science; they provide the most accurate and comprehensive description of physical objects that is available.[21] If we were to adopt this position, then we could agree that although our ability to describe would be diminished in one way by eliminating observation terms, it would not be the relevant way. Nothing would be lost for the purposes of making accurate and complete descriptions. We would still have available all the terms needed to make accurate and true descriptions: theoretical terms to describe physical objects and their properties, and nonobservation terms, such as 'clear-wet-appearance' to describe the sense impressions and their sensible qualities we experience.

This move by a scientific realist makes the cases of water and pink rats parallel because in both cases when we ascribe sensible qualities to what we experience, we are describing sense impressions rather than physical objects. But this move destroys the parallel between the cases of water and sensations. If we make this move, then, although the only thing lost by eliminating observation terms is convenience, it seems clear that our ability to describe truly would be vastly dimin-

[21] See W. Sellars, *Science, Perception and Reality* (London: Routledge & Kegan Paul, 1963), esp. chs. 1 and 3, for a position much like this one.

ished if all sensation-words were eliminated. We would then be unable to make descriptions of what we experience. Indeed, we would be unable to describe sense impressions in the ways we ordinarily and "mistakenly" describe physical objects when we use observation terms.

A 'sensation'-elimination theorist is not finished yet, however. He might claim that, contrary to what is said above, we do not need sensation-terms such as 'pink-rat-appearance' to describe our sensory experiences. He could defend this claim by denying any descriptive need for the appearance terminology, and thus any need for sensation-terms to attribute properties to impressions, or appearances. This defense requires that he replace the appearance terminology with another equally adequate to describe sensory experience. If R. M. Chisholm is right, this can be done. We can use an adverbial sensing terminology instead. Chisholm says,

> When we say "The appearance of the thing is white," our language suggests that we are attributing a certain property to a substance. But we could just as well have said "The thing appears white," using the verb "appear" instead of the substantive "appearance." And in "The thing appears white," as already noted, the word "white," in what we have called its sensible use, tells us something about the way in which the object appears, just as "slowly" tells us something about the way in which an object moves.[22]

And where we do not wish to imply there is an object appearing to someone we can say "He senses whitely" instead of "He senses a white appearance." In saying the former,

> we are not committed to saying that there *is* a thing—an appearance—of which the word "white," in its sensible use, designates a property. We are saying, rather, that there is a certain state or process—that of being appeared to, or sensing, or experiencing—and we are using . . . the adverb "whitely," to describe more specifically the way in which the process occurs.[23]

If Chisholm is right, then no descriptive ability would be lost by eliminating the appearance terminology if we adopted, instead, the adverbial sensing terminology. This move, then, would provide for the elimination of sensation-terms required by the 'sensation-elimina-

[22] R. Chisholm, *Theory of Knowledge* (Englewood Cliffs, N.J.: Prentice-Hall, 1966), pp. 95–96.
[23] *Ibid.*, p. 96.

tion theory. Have we finally reached a point of elimination sufficient to justify some form of eliminative materialism? Clearly we have not. It surely seems we cannot also eliminate the sensing terminology without considerably diminishing our descriptive ability, because we often truly describe someone in saying that he is sensing whitely and no purely physicalistic statement makes the same description.

FINAL REPLY: WHAT EXPLAINS BEST DESCRIBES BEST

The conclusion we have now reached is that although it may be that neither observation terms nor sensation-terms are needed for accurate and true descriptions of what there is—because the function of the former can be taken over by the joint use of theoretical terms and sensation-terms, and the function of the latter taken over by sensing-terms—the elimination seems unable to go further. We seem left with a residue of terms, and it surely seems phenomena, that cannot be eliminated. There is, however, one last move an eliminative materialist might try. He might adopt an extreme version of scientific realism, one which holds that in all cases those pure theoretical terms of science that provide the best available explanations of behavior also provide the best available descriptions of the things whose behavior they explain. That is, not only is each theoretical sentence at least as accurate a means of description as any other sentence available for describing the same thing, but all theoretical sentences that explain a particular phenomenon, when taken together, provide a true description of what they explain that is more accurate and more comprehensive than any other description of the same phenomenon. If also, as this kind of scientific realist believes, the theoretical terms of neurophysiology provide the best available explanation of the behavior that sensing-terms are used to explain, then some set of neurophysiological sentences would provide a true description of someone that is more accurate and comprehensive than any set that includes sentences such as 'He sensed a white appearance' or 'He sensed whitely'. Strictly speaking, there would be no sensations and no sensings, but only a misapprehension by us of what really occurs, perhaps some brain process with only physicalistic properties.

The objection to this extreme move is that at least with regard to his own sensory phenomena, many a man is fully aware of at least some of their features, for example, that a certain sensing is a sensing whitely rather than a sensing redly. It may be at least plausible to claim physical objects are quite different from what most of us believe, because they are best described by the theoretical terms of science, and it may be plausible to claim that our sensory phenomena have some (e.g., neurophysiological) features we do not experience. But it is most implausible to claim that a man's sensory phenomena have nothing like the features he experiences them to have, with the consequence that he has no special epistemological status even regarding those features he believes his sensory phenomena have.

CONCLUSION: A HOBBESIAN MATERIALISM WITHOUT PHANTASMS?

The previous objection cannot be ignored, and I am not sure how it is to be met. If it cannot be met, then I think a materialist must at some point abandon eliminative materialism, and embrace reductive materialism if he is finally to solve the problems bequeathed to him by Hobbes. He must turn to the identity theory, and, consequently, must face the property objection confronting it. It may be, however, he can avoid one problem inherited from Hobbes. If the materialist can adopt the adverbial metaphysical position associated with the sensing terminology, then he need not worry about Hobbes' phantasms, or sensations, and the problem about the properties sensations have but brain phenomena lack, and those brain phenomena have and sensations lack. This would be an important gain, because this problem seems intractable. He is indeed left with the problem of the properties which sensings and Hobbes' "internal motions," or brain events, might not have in common,[24] but this problem may be solvable.

[24] Cf. R. Chisholm, pp. 99–102.

11 *Jaegwon Kim*

On the Psycho-Physical Identity Theory

Jaegwon Kim was born on September 12, 1934, in Taegu, Korea. He was educated at Dartmouth College and Princeton University and is now Associate Professor of Philosophy at the University of Michigan. He works primarily in the philosophy of science and the theory of knowledge and has published articles in several important journals.

This paper aims at an interpretation and evaluation of the so-called Psycho-Physical Identity Theory of mind. In Part I, I examine one group of arguments often offered in support of the theory. These arguments share the characteristic of being based upon considerations of theoretical simplicity in science; roughly, they contend that the Identity Theory leads to a simpler and more fruitful structure of scientific theory than its rival theories. Thus, these arguments can be called "arguments from scientific simplicity." I dispute the cogency and strength of these arguments. In Part II, I raise some questions concerning the interpretation of the Identity Theory—in particular, questions concerning the notion of identity of events and states—and suggest some tentative answers. I then examine another type of argument offered in support of the theory to the effect that it leads to a simpler scheme of entities than its rival theories. An argument of this type can be called "an argument from ontological simplicity."

FROM *American Philosophical Quarterly*, III (1966), pp. 227–35. Reprinted by permission of the author and the editors.

I

1. The Psycho-Physical Identity Theory asserts that the so-called mental states, such as feelings of pain and the having of an after image, are just states of the brain. Pain, for example, is taken to be just some not as yet completely understood state or process in the brain. Let us refer to this brain state allegedly identical with pain as "brain state *B*." The identity in question is explained as the "strict identity" of reference, and this notion is illustrated by examples such as the identity of the Morning Star and the Evening Star. Thus, the two expressions "pain" and "brain state *B*" are said to refer to or denote the same event or state, just as the expressions "the Morning Star" and "the Evening Star" refer to the same planet. Further, the pain-brain state *B* identity is said to be an empirical fact subject to factual confirmation and not something that can be ascertained *a priori.*

If pain is identical with brain state *B*, there must be a concomitance between occurrences of pain and occurrences of brain state *B*—and presumably not between occurrences of pain in me and occurrences of brain state *B* in someone else, but between my pains and my brain states *B*. Thus, a necessary condition of the pain-brain state *B* identity is that the two expressions "being in pain" and "being in brain state *B*" have the same extension; namely, the following equivalence must hold: "For every x, x is in pain at time t if and only if x is in brain state *B* at time t." An equivalence statement of a similar sort will correspond to each particular psycho-physical identity statement. I shall refer to a statement of this kind as "a psycho-physical correlation statement."

It is clear that a psycho-physical correlation statement does not entail the corresponding identity statement—at least, the identity must be understood in such a way that it is not entailed by a mere correlation. For otherwise the Identity Theory would fail to be a significant thesis distinguishable from other theories of mind such as some forms of Interactionism and the Double-Aspect Theory. It is perhaps clearer that the identity entails the corresponding correlation, and at least to this extent, the identity statement has a factual component. Further, the correlation is the *only* factual component of the identity; the factual content of the identity statement is exhausted by the corresponding correlation statement.

It is often emphasized that a particular psycho-physical identity (e.g., pain and brain state *B*) is a factual identity. From this some philosophers seem to infer that the Identity Theory is an empirical theory refutable or confirmable by experience. This is misleading, however. To begin with, a particular psycho-physical identity statement is not confirmable or refutable *qua* identity statement; it is confirmable or refutable insofar as, and only insofar as, the corresponding correlation statement entailed by it is confirmable or refutable by observation and experiment. There is no conceivable observation that would confirm or refute the identity but not the associated correlation. Moreover, not only the psycho-physical identity statement, but also the corresponding "psycho-physical interaction statement," the corresponding "psycho-physical double-aspect statement," and so on, are all confirmable or refutable by fact. And the very same evidence will confirm all of them or none of them; the very same evidence will refute all of them or none of them. Thus, the pain-brain state *B* identity statement is not an empirical hypothesis vis-à-vis the corresponding correlation, interaction, and double-aspect statements.

An essentially similar comment is in order for the claim that the Identity Theory itself is an empirical theory. It is asserted [1] that the Identity Theory would be "empirically false" if there were mental states not associated with the brain, namely "disembodied" mental states. This is true, although how the existence of such states could be ascertained *empirically* is a mystery. However, what is often not noticed is that the existence of disembodied mental states would refute not only the Identity Theory but also the Double-Aspect Theory, Parallelism, Epiphenomenalism, and some forms of Interactionism; for it would contradict the general hypothesis of psycho-physical correlation, a fact assumed, and to be explained, by philosophical theories of mind and body. If there were no correlation at all between mental and physical events, there would be no need for a theory of mind-body relation. So, within the context of philosophical discussion, it is of no significance that the Identity Theory is a factually refutable theory: it is not an empirical hypothesis vis-à-vis its rival theories.

2. The proponents of the Identity Theory, however, will be quick

[1] See Jerome A. Shaffer, "Recent Work on the Mind-Body Problem," *American Philosophical Quarterly*, II (1965), pp. 81–104, esp. pp. 93–94.

to point out that the foregoing considerations issue from an excessively narrow conception of "factual support." They will probably concede that an identity statement has no more direct observational consequences than the corresponding correlation statement. But it may be that the inclusion of such statements within a scientific theory will effect significant simplification of the structure of the theory and lead to new laws and theories, new explanations and predictions. If these conjectures turn out to be true, it would be proper to claim a broad factual support for the Identity Theory. Arguments of this kind have been offered by most adherents of the theory; even some critics of the theory have argued that certain developments and discoveries in science would increase the plausibility of the theory.

In "Minds and Machines," [2] Hilary Putnam offers an argument of this nature. He cites two advantages for identifying the mental and the physical:

> (1) "It would be possible . . . to derive from physical theory the classical laws (or low-level generalizations) of common-sense 'mentalistic' psychology, such as: 'People tend to avoid things with which they have had painful experiences.'
>
> (2) "It would be possible to predict the cases (and they are legion) in which common-sense 'mentalistic' psychology fails." [3]

Briefly, the argument is that we ought to identify—or, at least, we are permitted to identify—the mental with the physical to make possible the reduction of mentalistic psychology to some physical theory of the body, presumably neurophsiology. Such a reduction is claimed to have two benefits: to unify and simplify scientific theory, and to make new predictions possible. The benefits of theoretical reduction in science cannot be questioned; in particular, the reduction of mentalistic psychology to a physical theory of the body, if carried out, would be a major scientific achievement. The question, however, is whether or not such a reduction presupposes the identification of the mental with the physical.

The reduction of one scientific theory to another involves the derivation of the laws of the reduced theory from the laws of the theory to which it is reduced.[4] If the reduction is to be genuinely

[2] In S. Hook, ed., *Dimensions of Mind* (New York: New York University Press, 1960).

[3] *Ibid.*, pp. 170–71.

[4] For an illuminating discussion of the problem of reduction in science, see Ernest Nagel, *The Structure of Science* (New York: Harcourt, Brace & World, 1961), ch. 11.

inter-theoretic, the reduced theory will contain concepts not included in the vocabulary of the reducing theory, and these concepts will occur essentially in the laws of the reduced theory. Hence, if these laws are to be derived from the laws of the reducing theory in which those concepts do not occur, we shall need, as auxiliary premisses of derivation, certain statements in which concepts of both theories occur. We may refer to these statements as "connecting principles." Thus, the reduction of mentalistic psychology to neurophysiology will require connecting principles in which both mentalistic and neurophysiological concepts occur; they will enable us to move from neurophysiological premisses to mentalistic conclusions.

Putnam's claim, then, may plausibly be taken as asserting that psycho-physical identity statements can serve as such connecting principles, just as statements like "Gas is a collection of molecules" and "Temperature is the mean kinetic energy of molecules" serve as connecting principles in the reduction of classical thermodynamics to statistical mechanics. This is plausible enough, but it alone does not support the psycho-physical identification. What needs to be shown is that *unless* the identification is made, the derivation of mentalistic laws from neurophysiological laws is impossible. That is, it has to be shown that nothing less than psycho-physical identity statements will do as psycho-physical connecting principles. But it is dubious that this can be shown; in fact, psycho-physical correlation statements seem sufficiently strong to function as the requisite connecting principles.

Consider a simple example: the usual derivation of the Boyle-Charles law of the gas from certain statistical-mechanical assumptions about gas. Essential to this derivation is the assertion that the temperature of a body of gas is a constant times the mean translational kinetic energy of the molecules of the gas—that is, $(1/2)M\bar{v}^2 = (3/2)RT$. Now, in order to derive the Boyle-Charles law, it is sufficient to interpret this equation as asserting a mere correlation between the temperature and the mean kinetic energy of a gas, namely to the effect that whenever a gas has such-and-such temperature, it has such-and-such mean kinetic energy, and conversely. It is not necessary to interpret the equation to the effect that temperature *is* mean kinetic energy. The equation clearly does not assert this; it only asserts that the *value* of temperature is the same as the *value* of mean kinetic energy.

Similarly, it is plausible to suppose that, without identifying the mental with the physical, mentalistic psychology can be reduced to physical theory in the sense that given a suitable set of psycho-physical correlation statements, laws of mentalistic psychology can be derived from physical theory. If psycho-physical identity statements are sufficient for such derivation, the corresponding psycho-physical correlation statements will do just as well. It is not easy to demonstrate this conclusively for the reason that it is not clear exactly what an identity statement asserts over and above the corresponding correlation statement. In Part II of this paper I shall claim that an identity statement involves the identification of properties; for example, the pain-brain state *B* identity involves the identification of the property of being in pain with the property of being in brain state *B*. On the other hand, I shall claim that the corresponding correlation statement involves only extensional identity of the two properties. If this construal is correct, it is evident that the correlation statement can do everything that the identity statement does on the further reasonable assumption that there are no "intensional" contexts in neurophysiology.

3. Herbert Feigl and J. J. C. Smart have offered a somewhat different reason for identifying the mental with the physical.[5] They have argued that by such identification we are able to eliminate what they call "nomological danglers," irreducible and unexplainable psycho-physical laws. It is argued that the identification of pain with a brain process is justified by some kind of methodological principle of "parsimony" or "simplicity" in science. The reasoning behind this argument seems to be as follows.

A correlation statement cries out for an explanation: Why is it that whenever and wherever there is water, there is H_2O? Why is it that whenever and only whenever a person has pain he is in some specific brain state? Now, according to this line of reasoning, we can answer these questions if, and perhaps only if, we accept the corresponding identity statements. That is, we shall answer: Because water

[5] H. Feigl, "The 'Mental' and the 'Physical,'" in H. Feigl, M. Scriven, and G. Maxwell, eds., *Minnesota Studies in the Philosophy of Science*, II (Minneapolis: University of Minnesota Press, 1958); J. J. C. Smart, "Sensations and Brain Processes," *The Philosophical Review*, LXVIII (1959), pp. 141–56 (reprinted in this volume, pp. 32–47; subsequent page references to Smart's article are to the reprint in this volume; J. J. C. Smart, *Philosophy and Scientific Realism* (London: Routledge & Kegan Paul, 1963).

is H_2O, because pain *is* brain state *B*, and so on. But how can we explain these facts of identity? The answer is that they are not in need of explanation, that they cannot be explained—not because we lack relevant factual or theoretical information, but because they are not the sort of thing that can be explained. It is nonsense to ask for an explanation of why Cicero *is* Tully, or why the Evening Star *is* the Morning Star; it is equally nonsensical to ask for an explanation of why water *is* H_2O, or why pain *is* brain state *B*. Water just is H_2O, and pain just is brain state *B*. Generally, most identity statements do not seem to be capable of functioning as the explananda of scientific explanations; and psycho-physical identity statements are not in need of any explanation at all. On the other hand, psycho-physical laws, not being identity statements, must either be explained by deduction from higher laws or be taken as fundamental, unexplainable laws of nature. And if they are to be deduced from higher laws, then at least some of these higher laws in turn must be psycho-physical statements, and so in any case we are left with fundamental and irreducible psycho-physical laws.

Thus, it turns out that by moving from correlation statements to identity statements we do not explain facts that were previously unexplained; rather, we make them "non-explainable." Now, the question is this: In what sense does this achieve scientific or theoretical simplicity of the sort desired in science? In what respect does it contribute to the unity and fruitfulness of the system of scientific laws and theories?

I think that the simplicity thus achieved is rather trivial and of minimal significance from a scientific point of view. To begin with, the explanation of a correlation by an identity—"Why is pain correlated with brain state *B*?" "Because pain *is* brain state *B*"—is trivial. The factual cash value of the identity is simply the correlation, and in terms of factual information we are simply repeating in the explanans what is supposed to be explained. This is a far cry from the usual kind of scientific explanation in which a fact or a regularity is explained by invoking more general and more comprehensive laws and theoretical principles far richer in factual implication and theoretical power than the explanandum. But further, the introduction of these identity statements does not produce simplicity in a theoretically meaningful sense. The essential import of reduction in science lies in that it achieves a more parsimonious set of primitive concepts and primitive assumptions. When optics is reduced to electromagnetic theory, we thereby reduce the number of independent factual commitments about the world; the reduction of thermodynamics to statistical mechanics yields the same kind of simplification. Previously we had two theories, each with its own postulates; now we have one.

But merely to replace correlation statements by identity statements does not effect this sort of simplicity. First, such replacement does not reduce the number of primitive concepts, for mentalistic concepts remain nonsynonymous with physicalistic concepts. Second, it does not reduce the number of independent primitive assumptions, for factual identity statements simply replace the corresponding factual correlation statements. It yields neither economy of concepts nor economy of assumptions.

4. If the foregoing considerations are correct, why should we, it might be asked, accept such apparently noncontroversial identity statements as "Water is H_2O" and "Temperature is the mean kinetic energy of molecules"? Should we not in these cases, too, stop short of identification and be satisfied with correlation? I would claim that the water-H_2O identity is, indeed, disanalogous with the pain-brain state *B* case, and that the temperature-energy case is rather like the pain-brain state *B* case.

"Water" and "H_2O" (in the sense of "substance whose molecular structure is H_2O") are both substantive expressions referring to physical things and not to properties, events, states, or the like. Any bit of water has a decomposition into H_2O molecules; the two occupy the same spatio-temporal volume. The reduction of macro-chemistry to micro-chemistry, which is in part based on such identities as that of water and H_2O, is an example of micro-reduction:[6] the things in the domain of the reduced theory have a decomposition into proper parts that belong in the domain of the reducing theory. In this sense, water has a decomposition into H_2O molecules; gas a decomposition into molecules and atoms. The net effect of micro-reduction is the explanation of the properties of some entity on the basis of the properties of the parts of the entity. So, water is literally made up of H_2O molecules, and a body of gas, of molecules and atoms.

Temperature, however, is unlike water and gas. Temperature is not

[6] See P. Oppenheim and H. Putnam, "Unity of Science as a Working Hypothesis," in H. Feigl, M. Scriven, and G. Maxwell, *op. cit.*

a thing that is made up of certain parts; we cannot pick out a bit of temperature or an instance of it and say that it is made up of mean kinetic energy. The domain of classical thermodynamics does not contain temperature in the way the domain of macro-chemistry contains water; rather, it contains gas, or bodies of gas, and temperature is a state variable whose values are used to characterize the thermodynamic states of a system—in other words, it is a property of the things in the domain. But it in itself is not a thing: it has no decomposition into mean kinetic energy.

Take pain: again, pain is not a thing. It is supposed to be an event or state; and we may take it as a property of living organisms. A pain has no parts—it has no decomposition into parts of the brain or into neurons. It only has a "participant," the person (or the biological organism) who has the pain. This person has a decomposition into parts of his body, organs, tissues, cells, and so on. So, there is almost an exact analogy between the temperature-energy case and the pain-brain state case. A physical thing, such as a body of gas, has temperature, and temperature itself is not a thing. The physical thing having temperature has a decomposition into molecules, and these molecules collectively have a certain property, namely a certain value of mean kinetic energy. And there is a definite correlation between this property of the molecules and the property temperature of the physical thing. A biological organism, such as a man, has pain, and pain itself is not a thing. The biological organism having the pain has a decomposition into organs, tissues, and so on—and, in particular, into the brain and the nervous system as a whole. The brain and the nervous system have a certain property, say some patterns of electric pulses ("brain state *B*"), and there is a definite correlation between the two properties, the property of being in pain and the property of being in this kind of brain state.

Thus, on this view, micro-reduction is still possible, and the unification of the domains of various scientific disciplines is also possible by repeated micro-reduction of one discipline to another. What should be noticed here is that the micro-reduction of one theory to another does not require—nor does it sanction—the reduction of properties in the sense of identifying macro-properties with correlated micro-properties. I conclude, therefore, that the adherents of the Identity Theory can find no support in the considerations of simplicity or unity in the structure of scientific theory.

II

1. The Identity Theory asserts that pain is identical with brain state *B*. But what does this mean?

To say that pain is identical with brain state *B* is to make a general statement that each particular occurrence of pain is identical with some particular occurrence of brain state *B*, and also, conversely, that each particular occurrence of brain state *B* is identical with some particular occurrence of pain. It is clearly not intended that Plato's pain is identical with Socrates' brain state *B*; but rather that Plato's pain is identical with his own simultaneous brain state *B*. Hence, to claim that pain is identical with brain state *B* is to claim, among other things, that the two statements "Plato is in pain (at time *t*)" and "Plato is in brain state *B* (at time *t*)" *describe* or *refer to* the same event or state.

But what are we to understand by this assertion that two statements describe the same event or state? Under what conditions do two singular statements—restricting ourselves to singular statements—describe or refer to the same event or state of affairs? An answer to this question will have the general form: "Statement A describes event *a* and statement B describes event *b*, and *a* is identical with *b*." So two problems emerge: first, what particular event or state does a given singular statement describe or refer to, and second, under what conditions does the identity of events obtain?

To be told that event *a* and event *b* are the same event if and only if *a* and *b* share all properties in common gives us no real enlightenment; it gives us a definition, no doubt a valid one, but not a practically usable *criterion*, of the identity of events. I would like to see someone apply this definition to Plato's being in pain and Plato's being in brain state *B* and deliver an opinion as to their identity or non-identity. To say that two singular statements refer to or describe the same event if and only if they are logically equivalent is clearly inadequate for the purposes of the Identity Theory.[7] For the identity of the mental and the physical is assumed to be a factual one and not a matter of logic or meaning.

I suggest the following procedure. First, what is an event or state?

[7] K. Popper appears to have this concept of event in *The Logic of Scientific Discovery* (New York: Basic Books, 1959), pp. 88–90. However, a precise interpretation of Popper is uncertain.

An event or state can be explained as a particular (substance) having a certain property, or more generally a certain number of particulars standing in a certain relation to one another. Suppressing reference to time, we may take the expressions of the following kind as designating-expressions for events and states: "*a*'s being *F*," "*b*'s being *G*," "*a* standing in relation *R* to *b*," etc., where '*a*' and '*b*' refer to particulars and 'F', 'G' and 'R' to properties and relations. Thus, Socrates' being in pain, Socrates' being in brain state *B*, and Socrates speaking to Theaetetus are all events or states. Although we normally distinguish between events and states, or between events, states, and processes, I shall not attempt such a distinction here; in discussing the mind-body problem, philosophers speak indifferently in terms of events, states, and processes, and the fate of the Identity Theory does not hinge on whether mental events or states are identified with physical events, states, or processes. It suffices if the Identity Theorist concedes, as I think he would, that among the things that he wants to identify are Socrates' being in pain and Socrates' being in brain state *B*. With this understanding let us hereafter speak in terms of events for the sake of brevity.

Under this conception of event, the following criterion of the identity of events naturally comes to mind: The event *a's being F* and the event *b's being G* are the same event if and only if either the statements "*a* is *F*" and "*b* is *G*" are logically equivalent, or else the particular *a* is identical with the particular *b* and the property of being *F* (*F*-ness) is identical with the property of being G (G-ness). The criterion can be generalized in obvious directions so as to cover "relational events" and "compound events"; but the simple special case is all we need for the purposes at hand. Thus, on this criterion, Cicero's being a bachelor is the same event (state) as Tully's being an unmarried adult male; the Morning Star emitting yellow light is the same event as Venus emitting light of the color of the sunflower.

A singular atomic statement involving a one-place predicate—again we need not consider more general cases—has the form "*a* is *F*," and we may say that the statement, if true, describes or refers to the event *a's being F*. It follows that two singular statements "*a* is *F*" and "*b* is G" describe or refer to the same event if the event *a's being F* and the event *b's being* G are the same. Or we may say: Two singular statements describe the same event if they assert truly of the same particular that the same property holds for it.

In identifying a mental event with a physical event, the identity of the particulars involved in the events presumably is not at issue, unless one would want to say that the Socrates who has pain is different from the Socrates who is in brain state *B*. A radical Cartesian Dualist would claim that mental events necessarily occur to mental substance and physical events necessarily occur to material substance. Let us disregard this problem for the moment, however, and assume that both pain and brain state *B* can be attributed to the biological organism, Socrates. Then the problem of the identity of Socrates' being in pain and Socrates' being in brain state *B* reduces to the problem whether or not the property of being in pain and the property of being in brain state *B* are the same property.[8]

2. The problem of the identity of properties is a difficult one. Most writers[9] take logical equivalence or cointensivity as the criterion of property identity. Under such a criterion, all property-identity statements would be either logically or necessarily true, if true, and logically or necessarily false, if false. This shows that logical equivalence or cointensivity is obviously too strong as a criterion of property identity for the Identity Theory.

On the other hand, if cointensivity is too strong, mere coexten-

[8] The foregoing, wh ch is a fragment of what is hoped to be a full systematic analysis, not here presented, of the concept of event, admittedly does not precisely coincide with the ordinary presystematic notion. (But then it is not clear that there is *one*, ordinary notion of event.) Some of the points at which my analysis deviates from it may be noted here. For example, Brutus' killing Caesar and Brutus' stabbing Caesar turn out, on the proposed criterion of event identity, to be different events, and similarly, "Brutus killed Caesar" and "Brutus stabbed Caesar" describe different events. Notice, however, that it is not at all absurd to say that Brutus' killing Caesar is *not the same as* Brutus' stabbing Caesar. Further, to explain Brutus' killing Caesar (why Brutus killed Caesar) is not the same as to explain Brutus' stabbing Caesar (why Brutus stabbed Caesar); also, to postdict one is not to postdict the other.

Such common notions as one description of event being more detailed than another description of the *same* event, one description being more informative than another, and so on, have no immediate meaning under the proposed analysis. If these notions are to be clarified, a more comprehensive notion of event (say, "happening"), namely one in terms of which "Brutus killed Caesar" and "Brutus stabbed Caesar" can be said to be *about the same happening*, would have to be constructed, hopefully on the basis of the more atomistic concept of event used in this paper. Anyhow, the critical portions of the present paper do not depend on a full acceptance of the proposed analysis (see the end of the following section).

[9] For example, Rudolf Carnap in *Meaning and Necessity* (Chicago: University of Chicago Press, 1947), pp. 16 ff.

sivity is too weak. In asserting that pain is identical with brain state *B*, the Identity Theorist intends to assert more than that there is a concomitance between occurrences of pain and occurrences of brain state *B*. These considerations put the Identity Theorist in a quandary: In order to state his theory in an intelligible and nontrivial way, he must produce a criterion of property identity that is weaker than cointensivity but stronger than coextensivity. Can such a criterion be found?

The task seems difficult but perhaps not impossible. The Identity Theorist may take heart in the fact that there are prima facie cases of nonanalytic and contingent property identity. The following are some of the representative examples:[10]

(1) Blue is the color of the sky.
(2) Black is the color of ravens.
(3) The property designated by the English word "redness" is the same as the property designated by the German word "Rot."
(4) Goodness is Plato's favorite property (i.e., the property Plato liked best).

I have tried to enumerate as many different kinds of factual property identity as I can think of. If we inspect these cases, one common characteristic is seen to emerge: in each case, at least one of the terms of the identity refers to a property via some particular(s) that stands in a certain definite relation to it. In the first two examples, properties are referred to on the basis of the particulars that *exemplify* them, as in "the color of the sky" and "the color of ravens." In the third, a property is referred to on the basis of a word that *designates* it. In the last example, reference is made to a property by way of an "intentional relation" in which a particular, Plato, stands to that property. Hence, a reasonable conjecture is that all contingent statements of property identity contain, essentially, some expression that refers to a particular or individual. This seems true, but I have no general argument to prove it. The converse of the conjecture seems more intuitively plausible: if a statement of property identity includes an essential reference to a particular, then it is nonanalytic and contingent.

These considerations are admittedly inconclusive; but perhaps it is not unwarranted to suppose that the identity of pain and brain

[10] Some of the examples are adapted from N. L. Wilson, "The Trouble with Meanings," *Dialogue*, III (1964), pp. 52–64.

state *B*, if there is such identity, is unlikely to turn out to be a contingent and nonanalytic identity of properties. Here, there is no mention of particulars in referring to the properties; nor any mention or use, implicit or explicit, of such relations as exemplification and designation, or of any intentional relation. At any rate, it seems evident that if the pain-brain state *B* identity is a case of factual property identity, it is unlike the usual examples of such identity and would require an explanation and justification of a special nature. And if the Identity Theorist objects to our entire procedure leading to this problem of the factual identity of properties, he is invited to propose a more reasonable alternative analysis of the concepts of event and of event identity.

The analysis of event proposed above explains why some Identity Theorists[11] are anxious to eliminate mental properties or "features" as well as mental events and states. For to allow irreducible mental properties that are exemplified is to allow irreducible mental events and states. Indeed, the problem of the identity of properties seems to be one of the central problems that confront the adherents of the Identity Theory. Whether or not my analysis of event is generally acceptable, we can argue as follows: Suppose that the property of being in pain is not the same as the property of being in brain state *B*. Then, surely, Socrates' being in pain and Socrates' being in brain state *B* would have to count as distinct events. Presumably, the former is a mental event and the latter its correlated physical event, and the two are distinct. This contradicts the Identity Theory.[12]

3. The so-called location problem for mental events and states has perhaps been the strongest obstacle to the Identity Theory; the alleged difficulties raised by it seem to have persuaded more philosophers against the theory than any other single difficulty.[13] As formulated by the critics of the theory, the objection runs as follows. If a mental state is to be identical with a physical state, the two must share all properties in common. But there is one property, spatial

[11] For example, see Smart, "Sensations and Brain Processes," *op. cit.*, pp. 39–42.
[12] J. A. Shaffer writes: ". . . we cannot avoid admitting at the least the existence of *nonphysical properties* or *features*, even if we give up nonphysical events as a different class from physical events" (Shaffer's italics); "Mental Events and the Brain," *The Journal of Philosophy*, LX (1963), p. 162. My claim is that we cannot admit nonphysical properties without admitting nonphysical events.
[13] See Norman Malcolm, "Scientific Materialism and the Identity Theory," *Dialogue*, III (1964), pp. 115–25 (reprinted in this volume, pp. 72–81); J. A. Shaffer, "Recent Work on the Mind-Body Problem," *op. cit.*, pp. 96–98.

localizability, that is not so shared; that is, physical states and events are located in space, whereas mental events and states are not. Hence, mental events and states are different from physical ones. When it is retorted that some mental events like itches and some cases of pain have fairly determinate spatial locations, it is answered that a pain or an itch may be locatable but not *having a pain* or *being itchy.* An obvious rejoinder to this move is to point out that having a hand, weighing 145 pounds, having a temperature of 97 degrees, and other so-called physical states and events have no clear spatial locations either. A hand can be located in space, but having a hand cannot; a brain can be located in space, but not a brain state; my body can be located in space, but not my body's weighing 145 pounds.

Thus, the inconclusiveness and weakness of this objection to the Identity Theory stems not so much from the possible locatability of mental states and events as from the vagueness of the general concept of spatial location for events and states. Of course, it must be admitted that we do locate explosions, fires, and deaths; but it takes only a moment's reflection to notice that we do not locate events as such. Rather, we locate events by locating the particulars or things that "undergo" them. Something explodes in an explosion, and the explosion is located where the thing that explodes is located; when there is a fire, something burns, and the fire is where the burning thing is; and, similarly, a death takes place where the dying man is located. Particulars are located first; events and states are located relatively to particulars. Or, we may say, particulars are the primary localizable entities; events and states are localizable only derivatively.[14]

In terms of our analysis of the concept of event and state, we may say that an event *a's being F* can be located derivatively at the place where the particular *a* is located. Then, what the critic of the Identity Theory who takes the location problem seriously must show is that a mental event *a's being B*, where *M* is some mental property, is non-spatial in that the particular *a* to which *M* is attributed is not a spatially localizable entity. Namely, in order to show that Socrates' being in pain is not spatially localizable, it must be shown, on this construal of the location of an event, that Socrates to whom the property of being in pain is attributed is not a spatially localizable

[14] This point is anticipated by P. F. Strawson. See his *Individuals* (London: Methuen, 1959), p. 57.

entity. But in order to show this one must show or assume that the subjects of mental properties—or the subjects of mental events and states—are immaterial souls or mental substances in the full-fledged Cartesian sense.

The situation, therefore, seems to be this. Insofar as the notion of the location of an event is unclear and vague, it is not clear that all physical events and states have locations; and insofar as it is made clear—in terms of the location of particulars—the assertion that mental events and states lack spatial locations implies the Cartesian thesis of the immaterial soul and unextended mental substance. Hence, the objection based on the location problem is unclear and therefore inconclusive, or it begs the question at issue.

4. Can the Identity Theory claim to involve a simpler, more parsimonious ontology than the Dualist Theories? Under that theory, there would be only one system of events, namely physical ones some of which are also mental events, rather than two distinct interacting, correlating, or paralleling systems of events. And there would be fewer events, too, pain and the corresponding brain state being counted as one. It must be granted, I think, that the scheme of entities countenanced by the Identity Theory is clearly simpler than, and at least as simple as, that to be assumed by any alternative theory. But exactly what sort of ontological economy is effected by the Identity Theory? Or, equivalently, what does "fewer events" mean? The analysis of event given earlier suggests an answer to this question.

We assume an ontological scheme that includes particulars (substances) and properties as basic entities or one that includes events in addition to particulars and properties. In either case, an event can be understood in the manner explained in earlier sections on the basis of particulars and properties; and the identity of events can be explained on the basis of the identity of particulars and of properties. Let *M* be some mental property and *P* some physical property, and let *a* and *b* be particular substances. Then, factual identification of the mental event *a's being M* and the physical event *b's being P* involves (1) the identification of the properties *M* and *P*, and (2) the identification of the particulars *a* and *b*. Accordingly, the identification of the two events results in the reduction of both particulars and properties.

However, the net amount of economy thus achieved will vary depending on the alternative theory of mind that is taken as the point of comparison. An opponent of the Identity Theory may be one of the following two kinds: (a) one who rejects both (1) and (2) above, and (b) one who rejects (1) but is willing to accept (2). Philosophers of the first kind can be called "Cartesians"; they deny not only that mental properties and physical properties are identical but also that the "subjects" of physical properties or events can be the "subjects" of mental properties or events. On this view, nothing that has some mental property can have a physical one, nor vice versa; unextended mental substances are the subjects of mental happenings and the extended, unthinking matter is the substratum of physical properties. Thus, the Cartesians represent the opposite extreme of the Identity Theory: their theory involves a bifurcated system of particulars and a bifurcated system of properties, and either bifurcation is sufficient to generate a bifurcated system of events.

But a radical Dualism of this form is not the only alternative to the Identity Theory. A sort of Dualistic Materialism results if one accepts the identity of the particulars involved in the two events but not the identity of the properties. A theory of this form is materialistic in that it allows only spatio-temporally localizable particulars; and it is dualistic in that mental events are countenanced as a distinct system of events from the system of physical events. Over such a theory, the net simplicity of entities effected by the Identity Theory lies merely in the reduction of properties. Whether such an economy of entities is of much philosophical significance is a difficult question that cannot be settled here; perhaps, it cannot be settled at all. But we will do well to remind ourselves that the economy in question would have to be attained in the face of the extreme implausibility besetting the factual identification of mental properties with physical ones, and also, as I tried to show in Part I, that the economy has no scientific import and hence cannot be supported by scientific considerations. The slogan of ontological economy does not by itself sanction the identification of any two factually correlated properties. We clearly do not think that ontological economy of this kind would justify the identification of, say, thermal conductivity and electrical conductivity as one property on the basis of the Wiedemann-Franz law.

12 Richard Brandt and Jaegwon Kim

The Logic of the Identity Theory

Richard Brandt was born on October 17, 1910, in Wilmington, Ohio. He attended Denison, Cambridge, and Tübingen universities and received his Ph.D. from Yale in 1936. He is now Professor of Philosophy at the University of Michigan. His major work is in ethics and epistemology. He is the author of *Ethical Theory*, the editor of *Value and Obligation*, and the co-editor of *Meaning and Knowledge.*

We take it that the Identity Theory (IT, hereafter) is the thesis that phenomenal or conscious events (e.g., sensations like itches) are physical occurrences in the body of the person to whom the phenomenal events belong.

This theory may or may not be true; whether it is, is obviously of interest. We are unhappy, however, with current statements of the theory. For one thing, we are unhappy with formulations in which such events as something looking red to me or my being in pain, in the ordinary sense of these terms, disappear from the actual world, as they appear to do in the proposals of Smart [1] and Feyerabend.[2] Moreover, we have difficulty in understanding what is meant by a

FROM *The Journal of Philosophy*, LXIV (September, 1967), pp. 515–37. Reprinted by permission of the authors and the editors.

[1] J. J. C. Smart, "Sensations and Brain Processes," *The Philosophical Review*, LXVIII, 2 (April, 1959), pp. 141–56; reprinted in this volume, pp. 32–47. Subsequent page references to Smart's article are to the reprint in this volume.
[2] P. Feyerabend, "Materialism and the Mind-Body Problem," *The Review of Metaphysics*, XVII, 1 (September, 1963), pp. 49–66; reprinted in this volume, pp. 82–98. Subsequent page references to Feyerabend's article are to the reprint in this volume.

"theoretical identity" of phenomenal and physical events, which does not require identity of all nonintensional and nonmodal properties (see T. Nagel[3]); nor is it clear to us that such "theoretical identity" is a strong enough relation to resolve puzzles about the relation of the phenomenal to the physical which have bothered philosophers historically.

In what follows we attempt to provide a formulation of the theory which we think everyone can at least understand, which affirms that phenomenal events like being-looked-red-to and itching are retained as ultimate items in the furniture of the world, and which construes "identity" in a way sufficiently strong to remove the traditional philosophical puzzles. At the same time we attempt to make clear the relation of this theory to the correlations between phenomenal and physical events which brain physiologists have in fact discovered or which in principle they might possibly discover, and whether the existence of such correlations either is a commitment of IT or constitutes a confirmation of IT. Finally, we consider what other considerations might justify accepting IT, if it is concluded—as we shall conclude—that correlations alone cannot conclusively disconfirm alternative theories.

THE PHENOMENAL AND THE PHYSICAL

We shall concern ourselves with IT construed as a thesis about only one subclass of mental occurrences, viz., phenomenal occurrences. Intuitively, phenomenal occurrences are events like itches, tickles, daydreams, thoughts,[4] and afterimages, as distinct from quasi-dispositional states like desiring or believing, which are mental occurrences in a broad sense, but not phenomenal ones. We do not, of course,

[3] Thomas Nagel, "Physicalism," *The Philosophical Review*, LXXIV, 3 (July, 1965), pp. 339–56; reprinted in this volume, pp. 99–116. Subsequent page references to Nagel's article are to the reprint in this volume.

[4] We assume that a thought can be characterized as a purely physical event, as a kind of occurrence which is introspectible, and that such characterization is distinct from a semantic description of it—an account of what it is about, what role the symbols that occur in the thought have in the speaker's language system, the connection of these with expectations, and so on. We are concerned here only with thoughts as purely physical events. How IT may be defended consistently with a satisfactory account of the semantic dimension is another story which we do not attempt to tell. We do not believe, however, that anyone has demonstrated that IT is not consistent with a satisfactory account of the semantic dimension.

deny that sudden impulses or longings, or judgments ("it occurred to me that . . .") are phenomenal events.

We do not expect the concept of a "phenomenal event" to be clear to everyone, and therefore we shall begin with an explanation of this term and of 'physical event'. We feel that clarity about these concepts is essential for an intelligible formulation of IT. Our concern, however, is not restricted to the meanings of 'phenomenal' and 'physical'; we are equally concerned to make clear what we shall mean by 'event' and 'is the same event as'. These concepts, also, are crucial for a formulation of IT.

We begin with the concept of "event." To say that there is an event of a certain kind is to say that some logically contingent property (set of properties) is instantiated at a specific time and "location." Thus we consider that an event can always be described by a triplet of the form $(U_i t_i L_i)$ where U_i is a property, and t_i and L_i are a time and a location, respectively. We use the term 'location' very broadly as a technical term which may be, but need not be, construed to refer to physical position. We are supposing that a philosopher will have his conception of what are the fundamental individuals of the world, by reference to which any event may be uniquely identified. "Location" is to be construed as the set of these identifying relations to the fundamental individuals. For instance, if we take the human being Socrates as one of the fundamental individuals of the world, we could construe the "location" of an instance of Wisdom as just being "of Socrates." A person might hold that every event could be located simply by specifying the substance that the property characterized, along with the time. One might, however, take events such as momentary sensibilia or sense data as the fundamental individuals, in which case one would presumably identify an instance of a property through quasi-spatiotemporal relations to a given phenomenal field. It is our purpose in this paper to avoid choice among various ontologies. In particular, we have no objection if one wishes to "locate" an afterimage by taking, say, "having a red afterimage in the center of one's visual field" as a property in a broad sense, and assigning this property to the human being Socrates at a particular time. Equally, however, we have no objection to taking "is red" as the property, and identifying the instance by its centrality in a visual field identifiable in various ways, e.g., by a description of its content or its causal relation to the body of Socrates, etc.; in this case the instance is not identified as being a property of some substance. The IT can be stated more simply if one regards human persons as among the basic individuals and construes phenomenal events as temporary properties of these individuals,[5] but we state the theory in a more complex way so as, we think, to make it intelligible to a wider group of philosophers. It will be noticed that in our usage of 'event' no line is being drawn between events, states, processes, and the like; we believe that no such distinction is needed for our purposes, since the adherents of IT will want to affirm that not only phenomenal *events* in the more usual but narrower sense of 'event' but also phenomenal *states* and *processes* are physical ones. Also, in our usage we do not mean to imply that an event is necessarily a momentary occurrence; we permit 'at a time' to refer to a segment of time, of whatever duration is convenient.

Given this conception of "event", there follows an important consequence for the identity of events: that two events are not rendered identical merely by having the same "location." And surely this consequence is one that we want. For obviously, the fact that some substance exemplifies two distinct properties F and G at the same time (i.e., F and G are instantiated at the same "location") is compatible with F-being-instantiated not being the same event as G-being-instantiated. For F to be instantiated at a certain time and location is not the same thing as for G to be instantiated at the same time and location unless F and G happen to be the same property. Evidently, one event (U_i,t_i,L_i) is the same as another event (U_j,t_j,L_j) if and only if $U_i = U_j$, $t_i = t_j$, and $L_i = L_j$.

This requirement for event identity may seem strong, but it is hard to see how any weaker conception can be framed that avoids

[5] Some sympathizers with IT (e.g., Smart, T. Nagel) have used this formulation with a view to avoiding commitments to what may be called "phenomenal particulars," e.g., sense data, as entities in the world. Thus it is felt that this maneuver resolves puzzles about spatial location of phenomenal events, as well as others (see Nagel, pp. 101–04). Whatever the merits of this formulation may be, one should be wary of the philosophical commitments it itself carries; for instance, it would seem to rule out an analysis of the concept of a person along Humean lines.

The precise form of the definition of 'phenomenal property', which we used below to define 'phenomenal event', depends in part on how this problem of "location" for phenomenal events is resolved. Since we wish to make our proposals independent of these issues, we shall try to be neutral on this point in defining 'phenomenal property', although in particular passages we may seem to favor some specific formulation of "location" over others.

trivializing IT, in the sense of formulating IT in a way that leaves unresolved most of the puzzles about the relation of the mind and the body that have agitated philosophers historically. For instance, we obviously want to explain "event identity" in such a way that IT asserts something stronger and more interesting than the thesis that any individual which exemplifies some phenomenal property (say, being in pain) *also* exemplifies some physical property (say, being in some neural state) at the same time—viz., the thesis merely that the "subjects" (or "locations") of phenomenal events are the "subjects" (or "locations") of certain types of physical events. Moreover, our conception of event identity makes clear in what sense IT makes a stronger claim than merely that there is a pervasive phenomenal-physical correlation, a thesis which can be accepted by various different theories of the mind-body relation: if one event (U_i,t_i,L_i) is to be identical with another (U_j,t_j,L_j), the two universals or properties U_i and U_j must in fact be the same universal—mere coextensivity of the two is not enough.

We have said that IT is the thesis that phenomenal events are identical with physical events. Obviously it is of the first importance that we explain carefully the conceptions of "phenomenal" and "physical"; these terms could be defined in such a way as to render IT self-contradictory. Obviously, we want to explain these terms in such a way as to capture the essential notions of the phenomenal and the physical, as they have figured in historical philosophical puzzlement.

First the term 'phenomenal'. We shall call an event "phenomenal" if and only if two conditions are satisfied. First, the property instantiated must be a *phenomenal property*, which is a property designated by a *phenomenal predicate*, where a "phenomenal predicate" is one which the person in whose experience the phenomenal event occurs might define for himself ostensively, to refer to the features of events of which he is directly aware. (We take for granted the epistemological notion of "direct awareness," which we think, despite all the usual protests to the contrary, philosophers understand quite well.[6]) Second, the instance of the property must be one of which ex-

[6] If one repudiated this concept one would be repudiating at least one important philosophical conception of mental events, and the question would then arise whether there is any definite mind-body problem to worry about. Instead of 'direct awareness' some philosophers would prefer 'knowing without observation', 'having privileged access to', and the like.

actly one person is directly aware.[7] Thus, if something is a phenomenal event, there is one and only one person *S* and some phenomenal property *F*, such that there is an instance of *F* at a time and "location" and *S* is directly aware of this instance of *F*.

We would propose—although we shall not be using the concept in this paper—to explain 'mental property' and 'mental event' by reference to the above conception of the phenomenal, in such a way that every phenomenal event (property) is a mental event (property), but not conversely. A *mental property* is a property designated by a mental predicate; a *mental predicate* is one that can be fully explained only by a clause which makes some reference to phenomenal events of the person to whom the predicate is to be ascribed. For instance, "wanting that *p*" counts as a mental predicate because a full explanation of it involves pointing out that under certain conditions the person to whom the predicate is ascribed would experience feelings of disappointment.

Now as to the meaning of 'physical event'. We have suggested that an event is the instancing of a property at a time and location. So a physical event may be thought of as the instancing of a physical property at a time and location. But what is a physical property? Some philosophers have tried to explain this in terms of *spatiality*; others have tried to use the notion of *public observability;* and still others have used the notion of *nonintensionality*. But in view of the well-known difficulties, we shall not attempt to work these ideas into a generally adequate definition of 'physical', but operate with something less ambitious than a precise general definition. We propose to specify a concept that is no wider than that of a physical property. For this we turn to the contemporary physical and biological sciences of human and animal organisms and propose that we so use the term 'physical property' that the nonlogical terms of these sciences stand for physical properties. It will be conceded that under any adequate definition of 'physical' these properties will turn out to be physical properties.[8]

[7] A person at least *may* be directly aware of an instance of some property *F* at a certain time and "location," without being directly aware of what are the time and the location. That is, we see no inconsistency in this, although we are making no affirmation one way or the other.

If certain alleged facts of telepathy or co-personality turned out to be substantiated, this explanation might have to be modified. We propose not to face that problem until we come to it.

[8] If a general definition of 'physical' is desired, one could perhaps use the notion

It is important to notice that, given this notion of "physical," it is not self-contradictory that one and the same event might be both physical and phenomenal. This possibility is crucial for IT. But is it possible that the same property might be both phenomenal and physical, as we understand 'phenomenal' and 'physical'—and hence that the same event, which is an instancing of it, be both phenomenal and physical? For instance, might not itchiness be a property designated by some physical predicate? There may seem faint hope that the answer to these questions is affirmative; but at any rate these questions seem to us the important ones, and how to answer them is the problem we wish to explore.

Before turning to the main issues, one comment on a secondary point. We know of no adequate general definition of 'physical event' relevant to the mind-body problem under which every physical event must have size, shape, or color, or even location in a simple sense (although it must have "location" in the sense of standing in some uniquely identifying relation to the fundamental individuals of the world).[9] Moreover, one might argue that it does not make sense to speak of the color, size, or shape of an event, either physical or mental, any more than it does to speak of the color, etc., of a fact. It is often glibly assumed that physical events necessarily have such properties and that phenomenal events, which are thought not to have such properties, cannot be physical events. At the very least this assumption needs to be defended. Therefore we do not feel we must take on the burden of explaining how a ruler might mark the spatial boundaries of a dream, since it is by no means obvious that IT commits one to saying that this could be done.

---

of "inorganic," although this approach would yield a concept of "physical" that is narrower than that we have explained. H. Feigl, for example, writes: "By 'physical$_2$' I mean the type of concepts and laws which suffice in principle for the explanation and prediction of inorganic processes." In "The 'Mental' and the 'Physical'," in H. Feigl *et al.*, eds., *Minnesota Studies in the Philosophy of Science*, II (Minneapolis: University of Minnesota Press, 1958), p. 377. See also P. E. Meehl and W. Sellars, "The Concept of Emergence," in *Minnesota Studies*, I (1956), p. 252.

[9] It is not obvious that the sun's gravitational attraction on the earth at a given time has a location in any simple sense. For more detailed discussion, see J. Kim, "On the Psycho-Physical Identity Theory," part II, sec. 3, *American Philosophical Quarterly*, III, 3 (July, 1966), 227–35; reprinted in this volume, pp. 195–211.

THE PRINCIPLE OF SIMULTANEOUS ISOMORPHISM

Many philosophers have thought that IT has empirical commitments, and would be falsified by certain factual observations. We wish to assess this view. For this purpose we shall, in the present section, formulate as precisely as we can a principle of psychophysical correspondence which is generally thought to be entailed by IT, under the title, "the Principle of Simultaneous Isomorphism."

As a start, consider the following:

> For every kind of phenomenal event *M*, there is a kind of physical event *P* such that an *M*-event occurs to a person *x* at a time *t* if and only if a *P*-event occurs in the body of *x* at *t*.

We believe that this approximates fairly closely to what most philosophers have taken to be the principle of psychophysical correspondence.[10] There is, however, a difficulty with this formulation: that, as stated, it is capable of being trivially satisfied, provided there are no "disembodied" phenomenal events—namely, for each particular phenomenal event there is a simultaneous physical event occurring to the organism to which the phenomenal event occurs. For take any kind *M* of phenomenal events, say pain sensations. Then, for each occurrence *m* of *M*, there will be some physical event *p* simultaneous with it. Now, the set *P* of these physical events, *p*'s, can be taken as the physical correlate of *M* as required. Evidently, what we need is some kind of restriction on the choice of *M* and *P*; we think the following will do:

> PSI: For every *phenomenal property* *M*, there is a physical property *P* such that it is *lawlike* and true that for every *x* and every *t* an *M*-event (i.e., an event involving the instancing of *M*) occurs to *x* at *t* if and only if a *P*-event occurs in the body of *x* at *t*; further, distinct phenomenal properties have distinct physical correlates.

[10] For instance, J. A. Shaffer writes: ". . . for each particular mental event there is some particular physical event which always occurs and is such that whenever that physical event occurs then the mental event occurs" (93). "Recent Work on the Mind-Body Problem," *American Philosophical Quarterly*, II, 2 (April, 1965), pp. 81–104. Presumably, he means each particular *kind* of event by 'each particular event'. We also have 'if and only if' where he has just 'if'.

The requirement of lawlikeness entails that the correlation between each *M* and *P* be nonanalytic (that is, that *M* and *P* be specified logically independently of each other); that the descriptions of *M* and *P* be given in "purely qualitative predicates" without essential reference to any particular individual object, and so on.[11]

There are some features in the epistemological status of PSI which merit attention. The first is that the principle makes what one might call "transcendent" use of phenomenal predicates. That is, it contains a variable '*M*' whose place is to be taken by specific phenomenal predicates, which have been defined above as predicates a person might ostensively define for himself by noticing the contents of his direct awareness. There are well-known puzzles about whether such terms can be explained to other persons. Yet PSI presumes that it is meaningful to talk of a correlation between the property designated by such a predicate and some physical property, for all persons. So, if there is an epistemological problem about the explanation, to other persons, of the meaning of "private" phenomenal predicates, there is a corresponding epistemological problem about the confirmation of PSI.

A second feature of PSI is that it has a logical status rather more like that of a Principle of Universal Causation than that of any particular causal law in science. PSI is synthetic (for one thing, it implies the clearly synthetic principle that there are no "disembodied" phenomenal events), but its empirical basis is much more complex and indirect than that of specific laws. In effect, it asserts that there are specific laws of a certain kind. As such, it cannot be refuted by observations that upset particular laws; although this is not to say that the facts could not force its abandonment—say, in the light of persistent failures to discover even approximate correlations of the required kind.

There is a third question of some interest about PSI: whether the particular psychophysical laws under PSI are "causal laws." On the answer to this question depend, in part, its logical relations to such "causal theories" as Epiphenomenalism and Interactionism.

(a) One might say that two events correlated by laws of the kind

[11] On lawlikeness, purely qualitative predicates, and projectability, see N. Goodman, *Fact, Fiction, and Forecast* (Cambridge, Mass.: Harvard University Press, 1955); C. G. Hempel, *Aspects of Scientific Explanation* (New York: Free Press, 1965), pp. 264–70, 338–47; E. Nagel, *The Structure of Science* (New York: Harcourt, Brace & World, 1961), ch. 4.

PSI envisages *are* (or, at least, *can be*) causally related—presumably because one thinks that, in general, two simultaneous events can be causally related, and that a law of the form "$(x)(t)[Fx$, at $t \equiv Gx$, at $t]$" is (or, at least, can be) a causal law. Among the paradigm cases of laws of this sort are the gas laws which relate the pressure, volume, and temperature of a gas. The trouble with this view, however, is that our use of the concept of cause does not permit us to say that each of two events is the cause of the other; and on the other hand, it is puzzling to pick out arbitrarily a change in one of these parameters as the cause or effect of changes in the other—one feels rather like saying that the parameters causally interact without saying which is the cause of which. The kind of "causation" permitted on such assumptions is different from the classical forms, which require an asymmetry, temporal and otherwise, between cause and effect. Moreover, if the existence of a law of the form "$(x)(t)[Mx$, at $t \equiv Px$, at $t]$" is taken as a sufficient reason for saying that there is a causal relation between *M*-events and *P*-events, then the causal theories of mind would be indistinguishable from such noncausal theories as IT, Parallelism, and the Double-Aspect Theory.

(b) Alternatively, one might say that the laws envisaged by PSI are not causal laws. The question then arises whether PSI is consistent with the claims of either Epiphenomenalism or Interactionism, to the effect that at least for many (for the Epiphenomenalist, all) specific mental events, of any kind *M*, there is some causal law that relates them to an *earlier* brain state of kind *P*. Thus, we may conceive of a principle, analogous to PSI, which asserts the existence of "temporally staggered" psychophysical laws (these laws need not be biconditional in form); we may call it a "Principle of Temporally Staggered Isomorphism" (PTI). There is no incompatibility between PSI and PTI; in fact, if PSI holds and, further, if there is a prior physical causal condition in the brain for each brain event correlated by PSI with some phenomenal event, then PTI, too, would hold. If PTI holds, that should cause the Identity theorist no great concern; he would simply take the staggered psychophysical laws as cases of physical-physical causation.

There is a view closely related to traditional Epiphenomenalism—we might call it "Methodological Epiphenomenalism"—which is supported by PSI, whether or not we take PSI as a causal thesis. This is the thesis that phenomenal events need not figure at all in the explanation of events of human behavior. The support arises from the fact that, if PSI is true, whenever a phenomenal event plays a role in an explanation or prediction, one could in principle replace it by the corresponding physical-brain event without destroying the logical structure of the explanation or prediction. Hence, phenomenal events could drop out of the explanatory-causal chain of human behavior. There is an obvious analogy between loss of explanatory efficacy and loss of causal efficacy.

For the same reason, PSI seems to undermine Interactionism—or what we might call "Methodological Interactionism." For the Interactionist thinks that there is some necessity in framing causal laws in such a way that some phenomenal event, say of the kind M, at t appears as at least part of the cause of some physical event P, at $t + k$. But since, by PSI, there is a physical event at t of some kind P' correlated with M, it is not obvious why the phenomenal event, rather than this correlated physical event, should be taken as the cause of the physical event at $t + k$. So, while PSI is not inconsistent with the assertion of such causal relations, it is inconsistent with the assertion that such causal relations must be countenanced.

A quite different way of interpreting the relation of PSI to Epiphenomenalism would be to assert that there could be no empirical reason for distinguishing the two—if we construe Epiphenomenalism as involving a form of PTI that is like PSI with the modification that a very small time lag is assigned to the occurrence of the phenomenal event as compared with the associated physical event.

How would one decide, in one's own case, whether PSI or PTI (of the kind just mentioned) were true—assuming that one were provided with an adequate supply of electrodes in one's brain, and that a screen in front of one depicted the state of one's brain as indicated by the electrodes (like H. Feigl's "autocerebroscope")? Under PSI the picture as seen will appear a bit later than the correlated phenomenal event m, and this time lag T may be broken up as follows: (1) the time T_1 needed for the associated physical event p to interact with the apparatus and be projected on the screen, and (2) T_2 needed for the image on the screen to interact with one's nervous system and cause a physical event p' which is simultaneously correlated with the phenomenal event m' (seeing the image on the screen). Thus, $T = T_1 + T_2$. On the other hand, the time lag T' under PTI would be as follows: (1) T_1 needed for p to cause the image on the screen (the same as under PSI), (2) T_2 for the image on the screen to cause the physical event p' in the brain, and (3) T_3 (> 0) for p' to cause the phenomenal event m'. However, T' is not equal to $T_1 + T_2 + T_3$; for there is another time interval to be taken into account, namely, (4) T_4 needed for p to cause m, and this must be subtracted from the total. Thus, we have: $T' = T_1 + T_2 + T_3 - T_4$. Now, there seems to be no good reason to suppose that there can be any difference (or, at least, any perceptible difference) between T_3 and T_4, the "critical time lag" in physical-psychological causation. Thus, if T_3 is taken to be the same as T_4, we have that $T = T'$. Hence, between Epiphenomenalism so construed and PSI, it appears there could be no empirical reason for making a choice.

THE IDENTITY THEORY

In our introductory remarks we stated that we construe IT as affirming that phenomenal events are physical events. In the light of our explanations of 'event', 'phenomenal', and 'physical', what does this come to? A phenomenal event, we saw, is an instantiation, of which exactly one person is directly aware, of a property designatable by a predicate which is ostensibly definable by reference to the content of direct awareness. A physical event, we said, is an instantiation of a property designated by some descriptive predicate of the physical and biological sciences. It turns out, then, that what is necessary and sufficient for a phenomenal event to be physical is for the property instantiated to be both designatable by an ostensively definable predicate and also designatable by some descriptive predicate of the physical and biological sciences. IT requires that phenomenal properties be physical properties, which thus means that the properties designated by ostensively definable predicates like 'being itchy', 'being painful', and 'being a red afterimage' must be designatable by physical predicates.

If IT entails that every phenomenal property is identical with some physical property, then, since the identity of properties entails their extensional equivalence, it further entails that:

(A) For every phenomenal property M there is a physical property P such that for all persons x, an M-event occurs to x at t if and only if a P-event occurs to x at t.

If it is assumed that each phenomenal-physical equivalence statement falling under (A) is nonanalytic and lawlike (for this we need only assume that *M* and *P* can be given by purely qualitative predicates and that no phenomenal predicate is synonymous with, or analytically related to, any physical predicate), then (A) logically entails PSI. This assumption is needed for the entailment. Moreover, the first part of the assumption—that the specific phenomenal-physical equivalence be nonanalytic—is what prevents IT from being interpreted as logically true; it thus permits the thesis often expressed by the adherents of IT that psychophysical identity is a "de facto" or "factual" identity as contrasted with a logical or analytic identity.

What, then, is the essential difference between PSI and IT? It is that, whereas PSI affirms the simultaneous nomic equivalence of each kind of phenomenal event with some kind of physical event, IT affirms the identity of the two. IT does not, of course, tell us specifically what kind of physical event a given kind of phenomenal event is. It only affirms the existence of the requisite kinds of physical events. Presumably the identification of the specific types of physical events with which types of phenomenal events are to be identified will be based on the correlation laws whose existence is affirmed by PSI.

The crucial task for IT, therefore, is to explain precisely what this modification introduced by it amounts to and how it can be justified. What is asserted by PSI seems clear enough; what must be explained is exactly what IT is adding, and why. Under our conceptions of "event" and "event identity," which require identity of properties for event identity, the crucial thing to be explained is IT's move from extensional equivalence of each phenomenal predicate with some physical predicate, via a law, to the assertion that each phenomenal predicate designates a property which is also designated by some physical predicate. How can predicates, apparently so different in meaning as phenomenal and physical predicates, designate one and the same property? And is it true that they do? We take these to be the fundamental problems for IT. We understand, of course, what it is for different predicates, say 'is a bachelor' and 'is an unmarried adult male', to designate the same property, when they are synonymous. And the same for predicates like 'red' and 'rot', drawn from different languages. But how can phenomenal and physical predicates designate one and the same property?

It is a beginning of the answer to note that two nonsynonymous predicates can ascribe the same property to something. Take 'is garnet' and 'has the color of transparent almandite'. Or consider 'red' and 'the color generally believed to excite bulls to fury'. Obviously, nonsynonymous expressions can ascribe one and the same property to something, or name (designate, refer to, express) the same property. Designation of one property does not require synonymy of predicates; we should no more expect to be able to tell, by mere meaning analysis, whether two given predicates designate the same property than expect to be able to tell, by the same method, whether two definite descriptions refer to the same object.

But this general point does not by itself explain how phenomenal predicates and some physical predicates can designate the same properties. We believe that an understanding of how this is possible may be had by attending to the language of neurology, or indeed simply to physical-object language generally, as compared with phenomenal language, i.e., language whose basic descriptive predicates are phenomenal predicates. The point has often been made that IT is essentially a "two-languages" or "two-vantage points" theory. We believe that this is a suggestive point and is the key to an understanding of the possible truth of IT.

So let us now consider how certain physical predicates ascribed to the brain of a person can be construed to designate certain phenomenal properties for that person.

In order to be realistic, we assume that these physical predicates are in terms of "theoretical constructs" or neurology and the associated sciences. For instance, a correlation law of the kind falling under PSI might connect a pain in a certain phenomenal location with a flow of current of certain intensity in a specified neuronal circuit in the hypothalamus. Schematically, let us suppose that the terms used by the neurologist to describe events in the brain are '*E*', '*F*', and '*G*', and that these are parameters or variables that can take on different values from certain specified ranges of values, numerical or otherwise. We may then assume that a neurological description of a particular state of the brain, or a brain event (more precisely, the associated physical property) would take the form of assigning particular values to these parameters. Now these terms (they could be 'amplitudes of brain waves', 'second time-derivative of a proportion of instantaneously activated synaptic knobs on cells of type *X* in cell assemblies of structure *S'*, etc.)[12] are used with a certain meaning, and what this meaning is, is fixed in part by the embedding of these terms in a theoretical system, accepted by the neurologist, which ideally contains "correspondence rules" or an "interpretative system"[13] relating them to the observation terms of the physical language. Namely, the properties designated by the theoretical terms of the system are "unobservable," and can be determined only by their interconnections with other theoretical terms of the system, and ultimately by their interconnections with the observable properties designated by the observation terms of the theory; and the correspondence rules of the system specify what these theoretical-observational interconnections are.

It is important to be clear about just what it means to say that the theoretical predicates are "interpreted" by being embedded in a system of laws and correspondence rules. What the laws and correspondence rules in which a theoretical predicate appears do by way of providing an "interpretation" for it is merely to *set restrictions* on what property the term may be taken to designate. In effect, they tell us that the property designated is one of which such-and-such must hold—as spelled out in the laws and correspondence rules. One is free to choose any property one likes as the designatum of the predicate so long as these things are true of it; in fact, the only thing one knows about its designatum is that these things are true of it. What specific property one chooses makes no difference to the theory in question, for the use which the theory makes of it goes no further than the laws or rules of correspondence in which the term appears. So we may say that what the laws and correspondence rules do is to define a "relational property" to be satisfied by any potential designatum of the predicate; so long as the designatum satisfies this relational property it may be freely chosen or, alternatively, left blank, since it makes no difference what is selected.

The neurological theory up to this point contains only physical predicates, both theoretical and observational. But suppose that the neurologist discovers some psychophysical laws of the kind the ex-

[12] This example is taken from Paul Meehl, "The Compleat Autocerebroscopist," in P. K. Feyerabend and G. Maxwell, eds., *Mind, Matter, and Method: Essays in Philosophy and Science in Honor of Herbert Feigl* (Minneapolis: University of Minnesota Press, 1966), p. 109.

[13] On correspondence rules, see E. Nagel, *op. cit.*, ch. 5. On interpretative systems, see C. G. Hempel, "The Theoretician's Dilemma," in *op. cit.*

istence of which is asserted by PSI, and that he adds these to his theory. That is, his total theory would now contain laws of the form "If and only if *E*, *F*, and *G*, have the values . . . , then there would be a phenomenal event involving the phenomenal property *M* for the organism of whose brain this is true." Thus, the expanded theory contains, for selected configurations P_1, P_2, . . . of physical predicates, the psychophysical laws, '$(x)(P_1x \equiv M_1s)$', '$(x)(P_2x \equiv M_2x)$', . . . , where 'x' ranges over organisms and 'M_1', 'M_2', . . . are phenomenal predicates (these are all assumed to be simultaneity laws; we suppress reference to time, for brevity). The addition of these laws, therefore, achieves in effect a *phenomenal reinterpretation* of these complexes of theoretical predicates, the laws serving as rules of *theoretical-phenomenal correspondence*; namely, it achieves a partial interpretation, in the phenomenal language, of the theoretical terms of the neurological theory—only partial, for what the added psychophysical laws affirm is that the various theoretical variables *jointly* taking *certain specified* values is correlated with a specified phenomenal event. The expanded theory need not provide, and, as a rule, will not provide, a phenomenal interpretation for each value of the theoretical variables; moreover, these variables individually may not receive any such interpretation. We can think of no reason to believe that a reinterpretation of this kind is incompatible with the usual physicalistic interpretation of these predicates; the predicates can consistently receive the two types of interpretation.

When psychophysical laws of the sort under discussion are viewed as a special variety of theoretical-observational correspondence rules, namely, theoretical-phenomenal correspondence rules, the particular complexes of physical predicates for which phenomenal correlates are provided by them are seen to receive a *full* observational interpretation in the sense that each of them is provided with an observationally necessary and sufficient condition in the phenomenal observation language; and in consequence the physical properties they designate are more narrowly circumscribed. That is, we now have for each of these properties a nomically coextensive phenomenal property, a property which, as a matter of lawlike connection, is exemplified if and only if (and when and only when) the physical property is exemplified. Still, this does not by itself pinpoint the physical property in question: what exactly is this property so correlated with the phenomenal property? To say that it just is that property which is nomically coextensive with the phenomenal property is like specifying the property of electric conductivity by saying that it just is that property of substance which correlates in such-and-such fashion (as specified by the Wiedemann-Franz law) with thermal conductivity.

The positive proposal of IT may be construed as a strengthening, or replacement, of these correlation laws by corresponding identities. What IT asserts is "For *E*, *F*, *G* to have values . . . in the brain of the organism *S*, is the occurrence in *S* of an instance of the phenomenal property *M*." This is not to add another restriction on the interpretation of '*E*', '*F*', and '*G*'. It is to assert that there is in fact one and only one property, namely the phenomenal property *M*, which meets all the interpretative constraints imposed by the laws and correspondence rules of the neurological theory. It says boldly that what it is for these variables to have certain values at a certain time and location is just for a phenomenal event, instancing a certain specified phenomenal property, to occur in connection with the brain of the organism in question. It treats the phenomenal property as an irreducible kind of property in nature and says that this kind of property is what is instanced when certain physical variables take on certain values at a time and location. The physical property we have been looking for is one and the same thing as this phenomenal property. This is the heart of the Identity Theory.

There is an important difference between predicates like 'is garnet' and 'has the color of transparent almandite', on the one hand, and the predicate pairs of special interest to us, on the other. That there is one and only one color which is the color of transparent almandite, and that it is garnet, is something that is known by observation. But that there is one and only one property which is the property satisfying some neurological description and that this property is in fact a certain phenomenal property, cannot be known by simple observation. It is true that knowing this latter fact is partly an empirical matter—that of knowing the relevant correlation law. But it involves more than this: it involves knowing, also, that when a correlation law of the appropriate type is true, the phenomenal property is identical with the physical property. And to know this is just to know that IT is true. What grounds we have for thinking IT is true is a separate question which we shall consider in the next section; all we are considering now is what IT means, or asserts.

Can IT, so conceived, lead to inconsistency? We should note, first, that the replacement of correlation laws by identities does not in any way diminish the factual content of the neurological theory (including the correlation laws). The only question is whether the possible excess content introduced by the phenomenal-physical identification might lead to an internal inconsistency or inconsistency with physical data. But we do not believe that either could happen. In the first place, since the identity statements have no more empirically verifiable content than their associated correlations, the theory with identities will fare as well as the theory with correlation laws, in confrontation with observational fact. In the second place, it seems clear that the theory with the identities will not be internally inconsistent, unless the theory with correlation laws actually implies that phenomenal events are not identical with physical events. But we see no reason to think there are such implications.

Historically, IT has been referred to as a "two-languages" theory or "two-vantage points" theory. A person observes his phenomenal events directly; he has "private" and "privileged" access to them. But he can also observe these same events in another way, in the way in which anyone else can observe them—by looking at his brain, by placing electrodes in it and observing the readings of instruments. In this case he observes his phenomenal events by means of his eyes, and instruments, just as other persons observe them. He uses "phenomenal language" to report his phenomenal events observed in the first way; and he uses physical language to report his observations made in the second way. The two languages are different in that the epistemic conditions of ascriptions of their descriptive predicates are different, but IT affirms that the designata of the phenomenal predicates are the designata of certain complex physical predicates. If there were not these two modes of observation, there would be no mind-body problem.

So far, however, we have not considered the question what reason there might be for regarding IT as true. It is all very well to say that it is consistent to say that the property designated by a certain configuration of physical predicates is in fact a phenomenal property. But why should we believe that this is true?

REASONS FOR ACCEPTING THE IDENTITY THEORY

The present is not the place for mentioning the various possible forms of mind-body theory and examining whether each has difficulties, as a way of leading up to IT as the sole survivor. We propose simply to ask whether, if one already supposes that PSI has reasonable evidential backing, there is any good reason to go on and assert that the correlation laws subsumed under it should be construed as identity assertions. We have already conceded that no observation could require taking this step.

If the step is not taken, one could be a Parallelist—presumably one who does not say that every physical event has a mental correlate, but rather only that certain brain events do. One would then simply assert PSI as a fundamental fact about nature. People find temporally staggered psychophysical correlation laws intelligible enough. Why not this principle?

The only reason we see for taking the step is that of parsimony. To refrain from taking it is to countenance a larger number of events and properties. In other words, IT is a step in the direction of ontological simplicity. The Parallelist has to admit neurophysical properties, the values of the parameters *E*, *F*, and G of his theory; on the other hand he tells us that there are distinct phenomenal events involving the phenomenal property *M*, which are correlated with these physical parameters taking certain specific values. The Identity Theory effects a simplification, at least by identifying the property *M* and these parameters taking on certain values. (He does not, presumably, succeed in giving a phenomenal interpretation to these parameters for more than certain of their values.) It is true that, when we think of an empirical scientific theory of the mind and the body, in a sense there is no simplification: the total number of basic postulates and of distinct concepts remains the same. Nor is there a gain in the "hard" factual explanatory and predictive power of the theory, for its total factual content remains unchanged. Nevertheless, one has reduced the total number of one's commitments to entities.

The factual basis of the identification of the mental property *M* with the physical property *P* is the nomic correlation between *M* and

P. One might raise here an objection to the effect that such an argument based on simplicity considerations would justify the identification of any two nomologically correlated properties, and that this would lead to such unappealing conclusions as (1) that thermal conductivity is the same property as electrical conductivity, and (2) that for a simple pendulum to have such-and-such a period of oscillation is the same as its having such-and-such length. But we think that there are two important features in the case of phenomenal-physical identification which are lacking in these alleged counterexamples. First, we note, with regard to the case involving thermal and electrical conductivity, that the correlation law (namely, the Wiedemann-Franz law) is explainable by appeal to more fundamental structures of material substance; that is, the fact that there is a correlation of this kind between the two properties can be explained by reference to the micro-structures of matter which are neither thermal nor macro-electrical. On the other hand, in the case of phenomenal-physical correlation laws, there is no deeper structure which is neither physical nor phenomenal, and to which we can appeal to explain them.

With regard to case (2) above concerning the period and length of a simple pendulum, we would point out that this correlation seems to be a more or less isolated case; there is no *general* correlation between the length of an object and the period of its oscillation. But PSI assures us that in the phenomenal-physical case there exists a comprehensive and pervasive system of phenomenal-physical correlations. If there were a correlation law for throbbing pains and the occurrence of some brain state, but none for dull pains, we would feel little temptation to say that throbbing pains are brain states. Similarly, if there should turn out to be certain phenomenal events for which no nomically correlated physical events existed, we would hardly say that those phenomenal events which do have physical correlates, at any rate, are physical events.

But why should the existence of a systematic and pervasive correlation of the kind affirmed by PSI be a reason for identifying the properties involved? The answer seems to be that simplification of an ontological scheme counts most when there is a *systematic* reduction of entities applying to a whole comprehensive class of entities; piecemeal and isolated reductions have little philosophical or conceptual interest. Most well-known cases of reduction seem to be of this kind: e.g., the Frege-Russell reduction of arithmetic, the reduction of macro-chemical and thermodynamic properties to microphysical ones.

As far as we can see, parsimony of this sort is the only reason for taking the step from PSI to IT. As a result, one has to admit that the ground for accepting IT is less than overpowering. But in fact, the decision is not very important, since the theories are not very different.[14] Why would one want some overwhelmingly powerful ground for a choice of one rather than another?

J. J. C. Smart, in the final paragraphs of his "Sensations and Brain Processes" (46–47), seems to agree that the choice between IT and Epiphenomenalism must be made on grounds of "parsimony and simplicity." But he says that the issue is rather like that between the evolutionary theory of fossils, etc., and the thesis "that the universe just *began* in 4004 B.C. . . . with sediment in the rivers, eroded cliffs, fossils in the rocks, and so on." Now, if this were correct, there would be no question whether a rational person must accept IT. But we fail to see the analogy. Smart seems to suggest that the difference between IT and Epiphenomenalism is that the latter "involves a large number of irreducible psychophysical laws . . . of a queer sort, that just have to be taken on trust." His thought seems to be that IT avoids these, just as the theory of evolution enables us to avoid having to accept just as a brute fact the sediments, eroded cliffs, and fossils. Unfortunately, there is no diminution of laws on IT; each particular psychophysical identity, in our view, logically entails a correlation law,[15] and in this sense the identity is at least as queer as the correlation law. After all, one would not guess, by inspecting a mental event of kind M, that a brain event of kind P is identical with it. If a correlation law has to be taken "on trust," so must the corresponding identity.

[14] Most of the popular mind-body theories such as Parallelism, Epiphenomenalism, the Double-Aspect Theory, and some forms of Interactionism, have the same implications as IT for such problems as the survival of bodily death and free will. The crucial question for these philosophical problems is whether or not one accepts PSI (or some principle like PTI); for example, if PSI holds, disembodied mental events are ruled out.

[15] Smart holds that the identity *excludes* the corresponding correlation law for the reason that "you cannot correlate something with itself" (*op. cit.*, p. 34). We should not, however, be dazzled by this verbal maneuver; whether or not we call it a "correlation law," an identity such as "Pain is brain state P" logically entails the law "A pain occurs at t if and only if a brain state P occurs at t."

Smart and others seem to think that IT explains PSI. We doubt, however, that anything is here explained in the sense in which there are explanations in science. Take a particular correlation law: "An *M*-event occurs at *t* if and only if a *P*-event occurs at *t*." In what way is this explained by invoking the identity "An *M*-event is identical with a *P*-event"? Recall that the only possible evidential ground for thinking the identity to be true is the reason we have for thinking the correlation to be true. This "explanation" does not look like any ordinary scientific explanation. Nor do we think that IT explains PSI, both taken as general propositions. Of course, IT logically entails PSI, just as a particular identity implies the corresponding correlation; but we do not see how this fact alone can be construed as showing that there is an explanatory connection. You can call this an explanation if you like; but if you do, you should not think that IT has the status of atomic theory, or the theory of evolution (as Smart suggests); this sort of talk is pernicious in that it lends, or at least tends to lend, a false air of scientific respectability to what is essentially a philosophical and speculative interpretation of PSI.

There is also the argument to the effect that, given the psychophysical identities, the laws of neurology and of the sciences presupposed by it might enable us to explain the familiar laws of psychology (e.g., "People have anxiety feelings when in a situation that resembles one in which there were caused severe pains in the past") and to predict new laws. Would this not be reason for holding that IT is a genuinely explanatory and predictive theory? The trouble with this argument[16] is that the deduction of the psychological laws from neurological theory would proceed just as well if the correlation laws were regarded just as correlation laws, and not as identities. Anyone who uses this argument for IT must show that the deduction succeeds *only if* identity statements are used in the deduction, and not correlation laws. This has certainly not been done.

Our view, then, is that the reason for adopting IT as contrasted with affirming one of its rival theories, given that PSI is true, is solely one of parsimony of a rather metaphysical sort. Perhaps, this is not a very strong reason. But we feel intuitively that the reason for accepting IT is *not* compelling, as compared with the molecular

[16] See the more detailed discussion in J. Kim, *op. cit.*

theory of temperature or the theory of evolution. Surely this is correct.[17]

SOME MISTAKES TO BE AVOIDED

There are certain mistakes about the Identity Theory which seem to have considerable currency at present. We wish to point out that they are mistakes.

1. Various objections to IT may be labeled "epistemological objections"; they all assume some fundamental epistemological difference between the phenomenal and the physical; and from this it is concluded that the phenomenal cannot be identical with the physical. The following argument would be typical: "If IT were true, anyone who is directly aware of a phenomenal event, say a pain, would also be directly aware of some cerebral event—which presumably no one is. Hence, IT must be false." Obviously, the crucial assumption in this argument is the principle that 'directly aware' is *extensional,* namely that, if x is identical with y and a person is directly aware of x, then he is directly aware of y. But is this true?

We think that there is a sense of 'directly aware' in which this principle does hold; the notion of a person being *acquainted with* a sense datum or a sense datum being *presented to* a person, as used in some sense-datum theories, seems similar to this sense of 'directly aware'. In any case, *if* we interpret 'directly aware' in a manner that renders the principle true—that is, *if* the position 'x' in "S is directly aware of x" is treated as a purely referential position open to substitution by identity and accessible to quantification—then the price we must pay is that the concept of direct awareness becomes *noncognitive*: from the fact that a person is directly aware of x, we cannot infer that he has any knowledge of x; in fact, we cannot infer that he has any belief or makes any judgment about x. A person can be directly aware of x in this sense and yet there may be no sentence '. . . x . . .' involving the name 'x' such that he knows or believes that . . . x . . . For the following kind of situation is possible: Jones is directly aware of the blue patch in front of him; the blue

[17] Some of the above points have been made in Kim, *op. cit.*, and some in Brandt, "Doubts about the Identity Theory" in S. Hook, ed., *Dimensions of Mind* (New York: New York University Press, 1960).

patch = the square patch in front of Jones reflecting light of such-and-such wavelengths; so, by the extensionality of 'directly aware', Jones is directly aware of the square patch in front of him reflecting light of such-and-such wavelengths; but Jones has never even heard of wavelengths.[18]

Thus, in this noncognitive sense, a person who is directly aware of a phenomenal event would, according to IT, be directly aware of a cerebral event. But we do not believe this is absurd. For this does not imply that the person has any knowledge or belief, or makes any judgment, about the cerebral event. Under the extensional and non-cognitive interpretation of 'directly aware', it is perfectly consistent to say of a person that he is directly aware of a cerebral event and yet has no conception of a cerebral event, or even of a brain.

Isn't it prima facie paradoxical to say that a person can be directly aware of something and not know or believe anything about it? We agree that this is paradoxical. But the reason for this is, surely, that 'directly aware' is ordinarily used in the *cognitive* or *epistemic* sense in which to say of a person that he is directly aware of x does entail the existence of some sentence '. . . x . . .' such that he knows that . . . x . . . Under this interpretation of 'directly aware', however, the position 'x' in 'S is directly aware of x' is no longer open to substitution by identity; as the example of Jones above shows, it is no longer true that if $x = y$ and a person is directly aware of x, he is directly aware of y. Thus, if one wants to make "directly aware" a cognitive concept, one must give up its extensionality; and, conversely, if one wants to interpret it extensionally, one must accept that direct awareness does not entail knowledge or belief.

To say, in the cognitive sense, that a person is directly aware of a phenomenal event is, according to our analysis of 'event' presented in section I, to say that, for some phenomenal property M, time t, and "location" L, a person is directly aware that M is instanced at t in L. But given that a person is directly aware that M is instanced at t in L and that phenomenal property M = physical property P, one cannot infer that the person is directly aware that P is instanced at t in L. This has nothing to do with the fact that M is a phenomenal property and P is a physical one; rather, it is due to the fact that the

[18] On an analogous noncognitive sense of 'sensing a sense content', see W. Sellars' illuminating discussion in "Empiricism and the Philosophy of Mind," in his *Science, Perception and Reality* (London: Routledge & Kegan Paul, 1963), pp. 127–34.

law of substitutivity of identity fails to be operative in the context governed by the epistemological prefix '*S* is directly aware that'. It is well known that epistemological and psychological verbs of propositional attitude are "intensional" and govern "referentially opaque" contexts; e.g., '*S* knows that', 'It is evident to *S* that', and '*S* is pleased that'.

In summary, our answer to the epistemological objection is this: either "directly aware" is extensional or it is intensional. If it is extensional, it is true that IT implies that anyone who is directly aware of a phenomenal event is directly aware of a cerebral event. But this conclusion is not absurd, for it does not imply that the person has any knowledge or belief about the cerebral event. On the other hand, if "directly aware" is intensional, then IT does not imply that a person who is directly aware of a phenomenal event is directly aware of a cerebral event. Thus, the objection is either harmless or fallacious,

2. A related epistemological objection argues that IT would abolish the unique epistemological authority a person has with respect to his own phenomenal states; it is thought that the evidence of encephalograms, etc., could, according to IT, override his own beliefs about his phenomenal states, and that this consequence must be avoided. But the answer to this objection obviously is that it is indeed true, that if we knew the relevant laws for certain and also knew what a person's brain state was, for certain, we would not need to bother with his testimony about his phenomenal states. But in fact a person's testimony is evidence we have to use to establish these laws, and if one's testimony or introspection conflicted with the conclusions about his phenomenal states drawn from the data about his brain and the correlation laws accepted at the time, this would be good reason either for reviewing the data about the brain state or for revising our tentative set of laws. Moreover, what is often overlooked is the fact that IT is no worse off in this respect than Interactionism, Epiphenomenalism, or Parallelism, theories which imply the existence of general psychophysical laws. The objection merely points to the difficulty of establishing the correlation laws, and is not a special problem of IT.

3. Smart wishes to hold that a "full description" of human life can be given without mentioning any mental events, or at any rate any "irreducible" ones; Farrell and Feyerabend affirm that the concept of

mental events can be abandoned altogether as a piece of outworn mythology.[19] These views, however plausible they may be, are not commitments of IT as we have stated it. The fact that what is referred to by a certain expression in physical language is a pain does not make the concept of a pain generally dispensable. We do not find the notion of a "full description" of something clear, but, whatever that might be, it is not obvious why we should not say that, if IT is true, a "full description" of human life can be given without mentioning certain physical events, namely those which are identical with phenomenal events. Identity is a symmetric relation; it does not favor one of its terms at the expense of the other.

IT is sometimes classified as a form of "materialism." But the logical connection between IT and materialism (whatever this may be taken to affirm) is by no means obvious. What is clear is that one cannot both assert that mental events are physical events and pretend at the same time that somehow we are rid of mental events, unless one is prepared to get rid of some physical events as well. If materialism is the thesis that all events are physical, IT undoubtedly supports it; but it is important to remember that IT also entails that some physical events are mental (assuming, of course, that there are mental events). It is true that, if IT is correct, mentalistic laws and concepts are not *needed* to explain events and phenomena involving sentient creatures (so much is implied by PSI alone); but if this is correct, it is equally true that, if IT is correct, certain physical laws and concepts are dispensable in exactly the same sense in favor of mentalistic ones.

[19] Smart, *op. cit.*, p. 34; Feyerabend, *op. cit.*; B. A. Farrell, "Experience," *Mind*, LIX, 234 (April 1950), pp. 179–98, also reprinted in Chappell, *op. cit.*

13 Hilary Putnam

Robots: Machines or Artificially Created Life?

Hilary Putnam was born in Chicago, Illinois on July 31, 1926. He was educated at the University of Pennsylvania and the University of California at Los Angeles and is now Professor of Philosophy at Harvard University. He is primarily interested in the philosophy of science and mathematical logic and is the co-editor of *Philosophy of Mathematics: Selected Readings*. He has contributed many articles to philosophical journals and anthologies.

Those of us who passed many (well- or ill-spent?) childhood hours reading tales of rockets and robots, androids and telepaths, galactic civilizations and time machines, know all too well that robots—hypothetical machines that simulate human behavior, often with an at least roughly human appearance—can be friendly or fearsome, man's best friend or worst enemy. When friendly, robots can be inspiring or pathetic—they can overawe us with their superhuman powers (and with their greater than human virtue as well, at least in the writings of some authors), or they can amuse us with their stupidities and naiveté. Robots have been "known" to fall in love, go mad (power- or otherwise), annoy with oversolicitousness. At least in the literature of science fiction, then, it is possible for a robot to be "conscious"; that means (since 'consciousness,' like 'material object' and 'universal,' is a philosopher's stand-in for more substantial words) to have feel-

FROM *The Journal of Philosophy*, LXI (November, 1964), pp. 668–91. Reprinted by permission of the author and the editors. This paper was presented in a symposium on "Minds and Machines" at the sixty-first annual meeting of the American Philosophical Association, Eastern Division, December 28, 1964.

ings, thoughts, attitudes, and character traits. But is it really possible? If it is possible, what are the necessary and sufficient conditions? And why should we philosophers worry about this anyway? Aren't the mind-body problem, the problem of other minds, the problem of logical behaviorism, the problem: What did Wittgenstein really mean in the private-language argument? (and why should one care?), more than enough to keep the most industrious philosopher of mind busy without dragging in or inventing the Problem of the Minds of Machines?—These are my concerns in this paper.

The mind-body problem has been much discussed in the past thirty-odd years, but the discussion seems to me to have been fruitless. No one has really been persuaded by *The Concept of Mind* that the relation of university to buildings, professors, and students is a helpful model for the relation of mind to body, or even for the relation of, say, *being intelligent* to individual speech-acts. And Herbert Feigl informs me that he has now himself abandoned his well-known "identity theory" of the mind-body relation. The problem of other minds has been much more fruitful—the well-known and extremely important paper by Austin is ample testimony to that—but even that problem has begun to seem somewhat stale of late. What I hope to persuade you is that the problem of the Minds of Machines will prove, at least for a while, to afford an exciting new way to approach quite traditional issues in the philosophy of mind. Whether, and under what conditions, a robot could be conscious is a question that cannot be discussed without at once impinging on the topics that have been treated under the headings Mind-Body Problem and Problem of Other Minds. For my own part, I believe that certain crucial issues come to the fore almost of their own accord in this connection—issues which *should* have been discussed by writers who have dealt with the two headings just mentioned, but which have not been—and, therefore, that the problem of the robot becomes almost obligatory for a philosopher of mind to discuss.

Before starting I wish to emphasize, lest any should misunderstand, that my concern is with how we should speak about humans and not with how we should speak about machines. My interest in the latter question derives from my just-mentioned conviction: that clarity with respect to the "borderline-case" of robots, if it can only be achieved, will carry with it clarity with respect to the "central area" of talk about feelings, thoughts, consciousness, life, etc.

MINDS AND MACHINES

In an earlier paper,[1] I attempted to show that a problem *very* analogous to the mind-body problem would automatically arise for robots. The same point could easily have been made in connection with the problem of other minds. To briefly review the argument: conceive of a community of robots. Let these robots "know" nothing concerning their own physical make-up or how they came into existence (perhaps they would arrive at a robot Creation Story and a polytheistic religion, with robot gods on a robot Olympus). Let them "speak" a language (say, English), in conformity with the grammatical rules and the publicly observable semantic and discourse-analytical regularities of that language. What might the role of psychological predicates be in such a community?

In the paper referred to, I employed a simple "evincing" model for such predicates. Since this model is obviously *over*-simple, let us tell a more complicated story. When a robot sees something red (something that evokes the appropriate internal state in the robot) he calls it "red." Our robots are supposed to be capable of inductive reasoning and theory construction. So a robot may discover that something he called red was not really red. Then he will say "well, it looked red." Or, if he is in the appropriate internal state for red, but knows on the basis of cross-inductions from certain other cases that what he "sees" is not really red, he will say "it *looks* red, but it isn't really red." Thus he will have a distinction between the physical reality and the visual appearance, just as we do. But the robot will never say "that looks as if it looked red, but it doesn't really look red." That is, there is no notion in the robot-English of an *appearance of an appearance of red*, any more than there is in English. Moreover, the reason is the same: that any state which cannot be discriminated from "looks-red" *counts* as "looks-red" (under normal conditions of linguistic proficiency, absence of confusion, etc). What this illustrates, of course, is that the "incorrigibility" of statements of the form "that looks red" is to be explained by an elucidation of the logical features of such discourse, and not by the metaphor of "direct" access.

If we assume that these robots are unsophisticated scientifically,

[1] "Minds and Machines," in Sidney Hook, ed., *Dimensions of Mind* (New York: New York University Press, 1960), pp. 148–79.

there is no reason for them to know more of their own internal constitution than an ancient Greek knew about the functioning of the central nervous system. We may imagine them developing a sophisticated science in the course of centuries, and thus eventually arriving at tentative identifications of the form: "when a thing 'looks red' to one of us, it means he is in internal state 'flip-flop 72 is on'." If these robots also publish papers on philosophy (and why should a robot not be able to do considerably better than many of our students?), a lively discussion may ensue concerning the philosophical implications of such discoveries. Some robots may argue, "*obviously*, what we have discovered is that 'seeing red' *is* being in internal state 'flip-flop 72 on' "; others may argue, "*obviously*, what you made was an *empirical* discovery; the *meaning* of 'it looks red' isn't the same as the *meaning* of 'flip-flop 72 is on'; hence the *attributes* (or states, or conditions, or properties) 'being in the state of seeming to see something red' and 'having flip-flop 72 on' are *two* attributes (or states, or conditions, or properties) and not *one*"; others may argue "when I have the illusion that something red is present, nothing red is physically there. Yet, in a sense, I *see* something red. What I see, I *call* a sense datum. The sense datum is red. The flip-flop isn't red. So, *obviously*, the sense datum can't be identical with the flip-flop, on or off." And so on. In short, robots can be just as bad at philosophy as people. Or (more politely), the *logical* aspects of the Mind-Body Problem are aspects of a problem that *must* arise for any computing system satisfying the conditions that (1) it uses language and constructs theories; (2) it does not initially "know" its own physical make-up, except superficially; (3) it is equipped with sense organs, and able to perform experiments; (4) it comes to know its own make-up through empirical investigation and theory construction.

SOME OBJECTIONS CONSIDERED

The argument just reviewed seems extremely simple. Yet some astonishing misunderstandings have arisen. The one that most surprised me was expressed thus: "As far as I can see, all you show is that a robot could simulate human *behavior*." This objection, needless (hopefully) -to-say, misses the point of the foregoing *completely*. The point is this: that a robot or a computing machine can, *in a sense*, follow rules (Whether it is the same sense as the sense in which a man follows rules, or only analogous, depends on whether the particular robot can be said to be "conscious," etc., and thus on the central question of this paper.); that the meaning of an utterance is a function of the rules that govern its construction and use; that the rules governing the *robot* utterances 'I see something that looks red' and 'flip-flop 72 is on' are quite different. The former utterance may be correctly uttered by any robot which has "learned" to discriminate red things from non-red things correctly, judged by the consensus of the other robots, and which finds itself in the state that signals the presence of a red object. Thus, in the case of a normally constructed robot, 'I see something that looks red' may be uttered whenever flip-flop 72 is on, *whether the robot "knows" that flip-flop 72 is on or not.* 'Flip-flop 72 is on' may be correctly (reasonably) uttered only when the robot "knows" that flip-flop 72 is on—i.e., only when it can *conclude* that flip-flop 72 is on from empirically established theory together with such observation statements as its conditioning may prompt it to utter, or as it may hear other robots utter. 'It looks red' is an utterance for which it does not and cannot give reasons. 'Flip-flop 72 is on' is an utterance for which it can give reasons. And so on. Since these semantic differences are the same for the robot as for a human, any argument from the semantic nonequivalence of internal (physical) -state statements and "looks" statements to the character of mind or consciousness must be valid for the robot if it is valid for a human. (Likewise the argument from the alleged fact that there is "a sense of *see*" in which one can correctly say "I see something red" in certain cases in which nothing red is physically present.)

Besides the misunderstandings and nonunderstandings just alluded to, some interesting objections have been advanced. These objections attempt to break the logical analogy just drawn by me. I shall here briefly discuss two such objections, advanced by Prof. Kurt Baier.

Baier's first argument[2] runs as follows: The connection between my visual sensation of red and my utterance 'it looks as if there is something red in front of me' (or whatever) is *not* merely a causal one. The sensation does not *merely* evoke the utterance; I utter the utterance because I *know* that I am having the sensation. But the robot utters the utterance because he is *caused* to utter it by his internal

[2] These arguments come from an unpublished paper by Baier, which was read at a colloquium at the Albert Einstein College of Medicine in 1962.

state (flip-flop 72 being on). Thus there is a fundamental disanalogy between the two cases.

Baier's second argument is as follows: Certain *qualia* are *intrinsically* painful and others are *intrinsically* pleasurable. I cannot conceive of an intrinsically unpleasant quale *Q* being exactly the same for someone else "only he finds it pleasurable." However, if a robot is programmed so that it *acts as if* it were having a pleasant experience when, say, a certain part of its anatomy jangles, it could easily be reprogrammed so that it would act as if it were having a painful, and not a pleasant, experience upon those occasions. Thus the counterparts of "qualia" in the robot case—certain physical states—lack an essential property of qualia: they cannot be *intrinsically* pleasurable or painful.

Can a robot have a sensation? Well, it can have a "sensation." That is, it can be a "model" for any psychological theory that is true of human beings. If it is a "model" for such a theory, then when it is in the internal state that corresponds to or "realizes" the psychological predicate "has the visual sensation of red," it will act as a human would act (depending also on what other "psychological" predicates apply). That is, "flip-flop 72 being on" does not have to *directly* (uncontrollably) "evoke" the utterance 'It looks as if there is something red in front of me.' I agree with Baier that so simple an "evincing" model will certainly not do justice to the character of such reports—but not in the case of robots either!

What is it for a person to "know" that he has a sensation? Since only philosophers talk in this way, no uniform answer is to be expected. Some philosophers identify having a sensation and knowing that one has it. Then "I know I have the visual sensation of red" just means "I have the visual sensation of red," and the question "Can the robot *know* that he has the 'sensation' of red?" means "Can the robot have the 'sensation' of red?"—a question which we have answered in the affirmative. (I have not argued that "sensations" are *sensations*, but only that a thorough-going logical analogy holds between sensation-talk in the case of humans and "sensation"-talk in the case of robots.) Other philosophers (most recently Ayer, in *The Concept of a Person*) have argued that to *know* one has a sensation one must be able to describe it. But in this sense, too, a robot can know that he has a "sensation." If knowing the *p* is having a "multi-tracked disposition" to appropriate sayings and question-answerings and behavings, as urged by Ryle in *The Concept of Mind*, then a robot can know anything a person can. A robot, just as well as a human, could participate in the following dialogue:

A. Describe the visual sensation you just mentioned.
B. It is the sensation of a large red expanse.
A. Is the red uniform—the same shade all over?
B. I think so.
A. Attend carefully!
B. I am!

Unfortunately for this last argument, Ryle's account of knowing is incorrect; no specifiable disposition to sayings and behavings, "multi-tracked" or otherwise, can *constitute* a knowing-that in the way in which certain specifiable arrangements and interrelationships of buildings, administrators, professors, and students will constitute a university. "Knowing that," like being in pain and like preferring, is only mediately related to behavior: knowing that *p* involves being disposed to answer certain questions correctly *if I want to, if I am not confused*, etc. And wanting to answer a question correctly is being disposed to answer it correctly *if I know the answer, if there is nothing I want more*, etc.—Psychological states are characterizable only in terms of their relations to each other (as well as to behavior, etc.), and not as dispositions which can be "unpacked" without coming back to the very psychological predicates that are in question. But this is not fatal to our case. A robot, too, can have internal states that are related to each other (and only indirectly to behavior and sensory stimulation) as required by a psychological theory. Then, when the robot is in the internal state that realizes the predicate "knows that *p*" we may say that the robot "knows" that *p*. Its "knowing" may not be *knowing*—because it may not "really be conscious"—that is what we have to decide; but it will play the role in the robot's behavior that *knowing* plays in human behavior. In sum, for any sense in which a human can "know that he has a sensation" there will be a logically and semantically analogous sense in which a robot can "know" that he has a "sensation." And this is all that my argument requires.

After this digression on the logical character of "knowing," we are finally ready to deal with Baier's first argument. The argument may easily be seen to be a mere variant of the "water-on-the-brain" argument (you can have water on the brain but not water on the mind; hence the mind is not the brain). One can know that one has a sensation without knowing that one is in brain-state S; hence the sensation cannot be identical with brain-state S. This is all the argument comes to. But, since "knowing that" is an intensional context, a robot can correctly say "I don't know that flip-flop 72 is on (or even what a 'flip-flop' is, for that matter)," even in situations in which it can correctly assert, "I have the 'sensation' of red." It can even assert: "I 'know' that I have the 'sensation' of red." If it follows in the human case that the sensation of red is not identical with the brain-state S, then by the same argument from the same semantical premises, the robot philosopher can conclude that the "sensation" of red is not identical with "flip-flop 72 being on." The robot philosopher too can argue: "I am not merely *caused* to utter the utterance 'It looks as if there is something red in front of me' by the occurrence of the 'sensation'; part of the causation is also that I '*understand*' the words that I utter; I 'know' that I am having the 'sensation'; I 'wish' to report my 'sensation' to other robots; etc." And, indeed, I think that Baier and the robot philosopher are both right. Psychological attributes, whether in human language or in robot language, are simply *not* the same as physical attributes. To say that a robot is angry (or "angry") is a quite different predication from the predication "such and such a fluid has reached a high concentration," even if the latter predicate "physically realizes" the former. Psychological theories say that an organism has certain states which are *not* specified in "physical" terms, but which are taken as primitive. Relations are specified between these states, and between the totality of the states and sensory inputs ("stimuli") and behavior ("responses"). Thus, as Jerry Fodor has remarked,[3] it is part of the "logic" of psychological theories that (physically) *different* structures may obey (or be "models" of) the *same* psychological theory. A robot and a human being may exhibit "repression" or "inhibitory potential" in exactly the same sense. I do not contend that 'angry' is a primitive term in a psychological theory; indeed, this account, which has been taken by some as a reaction to Ryle-ism, seems to me to create puzzles where none should exist (if 'angry' is a theoretical term, and "I am angry" must be a *hypothesis!*); but I do contend that the patterns of correct usage, in

[3] "Psychological Explanation," to appear in a . . . collection edited by Max Black [*Philosophy in America* (Ithaca, N.Y.: Cornell University Press, 1965)].

the case of an ordinary-language psychological term, no more presuppose or imply that there is an *independently* specifiable state which "realizes" the predicate, or, if there is one, that it is a *physical* state in the narrow sense (definable in terms of the vocabulary of present-day physics), or, if there is one, that it is the *same* for all members of the speech community, than the postulates of a psychological theory do. Indeed, there could be a community of robots that did *not* all have the same physical constitution, but did all have the same *psychology*; and such robots could *univocally* say "I have the sensation of red," "you have the sensation of red," "he has the sensation of red," even if the three robots referred to did not "physically realize" the "sensation of red" in the same way. Thus, the *attributes:* having the "sensation" of red and "flip-flop 72 being on" are simply *not* identical in the case of the robots. If Materialism is taken to be the denial of the existence of "nonphysical" attributes, then Materialism is false even for robots!

Still, Baier might reply: if I say that a robot has the "sensation" of red, I mean that he is in *some* physical state (a "visual" one) that signals to him the presence of red objects; if I say that a human has the sensation of red, I do not mean that he is necessarily in some special *physical* state. *Of course,* there is a *state* I am in when and only when I have the sensation of red—namely, the state of having a sensation of red. But this is a remark about the logic of 'state,' and says *nothing* about the meaning of 'sensation of red.'

I think that this is right. When *we* say: "that robot has the 'sensation' of red," there are (or would be) implications that are not present when we talk about each other. But that is because we think of the robots *as* robots. Let us suppose that the robots do *not* "think" of themselves as robots; according to their theory, they have (or possibly have) "souls." Then, when a robot says of another robot "he has the 'sensation' of red" (or something in more ordinary language to this effect), the implication will *not* be present that the other robot must be in any special *physical* state. Why should it not be an open possibility for the robot scientists and philosophers that they will *fail* to find "correlates" at the physical level for the various sensations they report, just as if it is an open possibility for us that we will fail to find such correlates? To carry the analogy one final step further: if the robots go on to manufacture ROBOTS (i.e., robots that the robots themselves regard as *mere* robots), a robot philosopher will sooner or later argue: "when I say that a ROBOT 'thinks that something is red,' or that something 'looks red' to a ROBOT, all that I mean is that the ROBOT is in a certain kind of *physical* state (admittedly, one specified by its *psychological* significance, and not by a direct physical-chemical description). The ROBOT must be able to discriminate red from non-red things, and the state in question must figure in a certain rather-hard-to-describe way in the discrimination process. But when I say that a fellow *person* (robot) 'thinks that something is red,' etc., I do not mean that he is necessarily in any special kind of physical state. Thus, in the only philosophically interesting sense of 'sensation,' persons (robots) have 'sensations' and ROBOTS do not." I conclude that Baier's first argument does not break my analogy.

The second argument seems to me to rest on two dubious premises. Granted, if the physical correlate of a given painful quale Q is something peripheral, then my brain could be "reprogrammed" so that the event would become the physical correlate of some pleasurable psychological state; if the correlate is a highly structured state of the whole brain, then such reprogramming may well be impossible. Thus the premise: Let S be the state of the robot's brain that "realizes" some "pleasure quale"; then, in principle, the robot's brain could always be reprogrammed so that S would "realize" a "painful quale" instead—seems to be simply false. (The other dubious premise is the existence of *intrinsically* pleasant and painful qualia. This is supposed to be introspectively evident, but I do not find it so.)

SHOULD ROBOTS HAVE CIVIL RIGHTS?

Throughout this paper I have stressed the possibility that a robot and a human may have the same "psychology"—that is, they may obey the same psychological laws. To say that two organisms (or systems) obey the same psychological laws is not at all the same thing as to say that their behavior is similar. Indeed, two people may obey the same psychological laws and exhibit *different* behavior, even given similar environments in childhood, partly because psychological laws are only statistical and partly because crucial parameters may have different values. To know the psychological laws obeyed by a species, one must know how *any* members of that species *could* behave, given the widest variation in all the parameters that are capable of variation at all. In general, such laws, like all scientific laws, will involve abstractions—terms more or less remote from direct behavioral observation. Examples of such terms have already been given: repression, inhibitory potential, preference, sensation, belief. Thus, to say that a man and a robot have the same "psychology" (are *psychologically isomorphic,* as I will also say) is to say that the behavior of the two *species* is most simply and revealingly analyzed, at the psychological level (in abstraction from the details of the internal physical structure), in terms of the *same* "psychological states" and the same hypothetical parameters. For example, if a human being is a "probabilistic automaton," then any robot with the same "machine table" will be psychologically isomorphic to a human being. If the human brain is simply a neural net with a certain program, as in the theory of Pitts and McCulloch, then a robot whose "brain" was a similar net, only constructed of flip-flops rather than of neurons, would have exactly the same psychology as a human. To avoid question-begging, I will consider psychology as a science that describes the behavior of any species of systems whose behavior is amenable to behavioral analysis, and intrepretation in terms of molar behavioral "constructs" of the familiar kind (stimulus, response, drive, saturation, etc.). Thus, saying that a robot (or an octopus) has a *psychology* (obeys psychological laws) does not imply that it is necessarily conscious. For example, the mechanical "mice" constructed by Shannon have a psychology (indeed, they were constructed precisely to serve as a model for a certain psychological theory of conditioning), but no one would contend that they are alive or conscious. In the case of Turing Machines, finite automata, etc., what I here call "psychological isomorphism" is what I referred to in previous papers as "sameness of functional organization."

In the rest of this paper, I will imagine that we are confronted with a community of robots which (who?) are psychologically isomorphic to human beings in the sense just explained. I will also assume that "psychophysical parallelism" holds good for human beings and that, if an action can be explained psychologically, the corresponding "trajectory" of the living human body that executes that action can be explained (in principle) in physical-chemical terms. The possibility of constructing a robot psychologically isomorphic to a human being does not depend on this assumption; a robot could be psychologically isomorphic to a disembodied spirit or to a "ghost in a machine" just as well, if such there were; but the conceptual situation will be a little less confusing if we neglect *those* issues in the present paper.

Let Oscar be one of these robots, and let us imagine that Oscar is having the "sensation" of red. Is Oscar having the sensation of red? In more ordinary language: is Oscar *seeing* anything? Is he thinking, feeling anything? Is Oscar Alive? Is Oscar Conscious?

I have referred to this problem as the problem of the "civil rights of robots" because that is what it may become, and much faster than any of us now expect. Given the ever-accelerating rate of both technological and social change, it is entirely possible that robots will one day exist, and argue "we *are* alive; we *are* conscious!" In that event, what are today only philosophical prejudices of a traditional anthropocentric and mentalistic kind would all too likely develop into conservative political attitudes. But fortunately, we today have the advantage of being able to discuss this problem disinterestedly, and a little more chance, therefore, of arriving at the correct answer.

I think that the most interesting case is the case in which (1) "psychophysical parallelism" holds (so that it can at least be contended that *we* are just as much "physical-chemical systems" as robots are), and (2) the robots in question are psychologically isomorphic to us. This is surely the most favorable case for the philosopher who wishes to argue that robots of "a sufficient degree of complexity" would (not just *could*, but necessarily *would*) be conscious. Such a philosopher would presumably contend that Oscar had sensations, thoughts, feelings, etc., in just the sense in which we do and that the use of "raised-eyebrows" quotes throughout this paper whenever a psychological predicate was being applied to a robot was unnecessary. It is this contention that I wish to explore, not with the usual polemical desire to show either that materialism is correct and, hence (?), that such robots as Oscar would be conscious or to show that all such questions have been resolved once and for all by *Philosophical Investigations,* God but give us the eyes to see it, but rather with my own perverse interest in the logical structure of the quaint and curious bits of discourse that philosophers propound as "arguments"—and with a perhaps ultimately more serious interest in the relevant semantical aspects of our language.

ANTI-CIVIL-LIBERTARIAN ARGUMENTS

Some of the arguments designed to show that Oscar *could not* be conscious may be easily exposed as bad arguments. Thus, the *phonograph-record argument:* a robot only "plays" behavior in the sense in which a phonograph record plays music. When we laugh at the joke of a robot, we are really appreciating the wit of the human programmer, and not the wit of the robot. The *reprogramming argument:* a robot has no real character of its own. It could at any time be reprogrammed to behave in the reverse of the way it has previously behaved. But a human being who was "reprogrammed" (say, by a brain operation performed by a race with a tremendously advanced science), so as to have a new and completely predetermined set of responses, would no longer be a human being (in the full sense), but a monster. The *question-begging argument:* the so-called "psychological" states of a robot are in reality just physical states. But *our* psychological states are *not* physical states. So it could only be in the most Pickwickian of senses that a robot was "conscious."

The first argument ignores the possibility of robots that *learn.* A robot whose "brain" was merely a library of predetermined behavior routines, each imagined in full detail by the programmer, would indeed be uninteresting. But such a robot would be incapable of learning anything that the programmer did not know, and would thus fail to be psychologically isomorphic to the programmer, or to any human. On the other hand, if the programmer constructs a robot so that it will be a model of certain psychological laws, he will *not,* in general, know how it will behave in real-life situations, just as a psychologist might know all of the *laws* of human psychology, but still be no better (or little better) than anyone else at predicting how humans will behave in real-life situations. Imagine that the robot at "birth" is as helpless as a new-born babe, and that it acquires our culture by being brought up with humans. When it reaches the stage of inventing a joke, and we laugh, it is simply not true that we are "appreciating the wit of the programmer." What the programmer invented was not a joke, but a system which could one day produce new jokes. The second argument, like the first, assumes that "programmed" behavior must be wholly predictable and lack all spontaneity. If I "reprogram" a criminal (via a brain operation) to become a good citizen, but without destroying his capacity to learn, to develop, to change (perhaps even to change back into a criminal some day), then I have certainly not created a "monster." If Oscar is psychologically isomorphic to a human, then Oscar can be "reprogrammed" to the extent, and only to the extent, that a human can. The third argument assumes outright that psychological predicates never apply to Oscar and to a human in the same sense, which is just the point at issue.

All these arguments suffer from one unnoticed and absolutely crippling defect. They rely on just two facts about robots: that they are artifacts and that they are deterministic systems of a physical kind, whose behavior (including the "intelligent" aspects) has been preselected and designed by the artificer. But it is purely contingent that these two properties are *not* properties of human beings. Thus, if we should one day discover that *we* are artifacts and that our every utterance was anticipated by our superintelligent creators (with a small "c"), it would follow, if these arguments were sound, that *we* are not conscious! At the same time, as just noted, these two properties are *not* properties of *all* imaginable robots. Thus these arguments fail in two directions: they might "show" that *people* are *not* conscious—because people might be the wrong sort of robots—while simultaneously failing to show that some robots are not conscious.

PRO-CIVIL-LIBERTARIAN ARGUMENTS

If the usual "anti-civil-libertarian" arguments (arguments against conceding that Oscar is conscious) are bad arguments, *pro*-civil-libertarian arguments seem to be just about nonexistent! Since the nineteenth century, materialists have contended that "consciousness is just a property of matter at a certain stage of organization." But as a semantic analysis this contention is hopeless (psychophysical parallelism is certainly not *analytic*), and as an identity theory it is irrelevant. Suppose that Feigl had been correct, and that sensation words *referred* to events (or "states" or "processes") definable in the language of physics. (As I remarked before, Feigl no longer holds this view.) In particular, suppose 'the sensation of red' *denotes* a brain process. (It is, of course, utterly unclear what this supposition comes to. We are taught the use of "denotes" in philosophy by being told that 'cat' denotes the class of all cats, and so on; and then some philosophers say " 'the sensation of red' denotes a class of brain processes," as if *this* were now supposed to be clear! In fact, all we have been told is that " 'the sensation of red' denotes a brain process" is true just in case " 'the sensation of red' *is* a brain process" is true. Since this latter puzzling assertion was in turn explained by the identity theorists in terms of the distinction between *denotation* and *connotation*, nothing has been explained.) Still, this does not show that Oscar is conscious. Indeed, Oscar may be psychologically isomorphic to a human without being at all similar in physical-chemical construction. So we may suppose that Oscar does not have "brain processes" at all and, hence, (on this theory) that Oscar is *not* conscious. Moreover, if the physical "correlate" of the sensation of red (in the case of a human) is P_1, and the physical correlate of the "sensation" of red (in the case of Oscar) is P_2, and if P_1 and P_2 are *different* physical states, it can nonetheless be maintained that, when Oscar and I both "see something that looks red" (or "have the sensation of red," to use the philosophical jargon that I have allowed myself in this paper), we are in the *same* physical state, namely the *disjunction* of P_1 and P_2. How do we decide whether "the sensation of red" (in the case of a human) is "identical" with P_1 or "identical" with $P_1 \vee P_2$? Identity theorists do not tell me anything that helps me to decide.

Another popular theory is that ordinary-language psychological terms, such as 'is angry' (and, presumably, such quasi-technical expressions as 'has the sensation of red') are *implicitly defined by a psychological theory*. On this view, it would follow from the fact that Oscar and I are "models" of the same psychological (molar behavioral) theory that psychological terms have *exactly the same sense* when applied to me and when applied to Oscar.

It may, perhaps, be granted that there is something that could be called an "implicit psychological theory" underlying the ordinary use of psychological terms. (That an angry man will behave aggressively, unless he has strong reasons to repress his anger and some skill at controlling his feelings; that insults tend to provoke anger; that most people are not very good at controlling strong feelings of anger—are examples of what might be considered "postulates" of such a theory. Although each of these "postulates" is quasi-tautological, it might be contended that the conjunction of a sufficient number of them has empirical consequences, and can be used to provide empirical explanations of observed behavior.) But the view that the whole meaning of such a term as 'anger' is fixed by its place in such a theory seems highly dubious. There is not space in the present paper to examine this view at the length that it deserves. But one or two criticisms may indicate where difficulties lie.

To assert that something contains phlogiston is (implicitly) to assert that certain laws, upon which the concept of phlogiston depends, are correct. To assert that something is electrically charged is in part to assert that the experimental laws upon which the concept of electricity is based and which electrical theory is supposed to explain, are not radically and wholly false. If the "theory" upon which the term anger "depends" really has empirical consequences, then even to say "I am angry" is in part to assert that these empirical consequences are not radically and wholly false. Thus it would not be absurd, if 'anger' really *were* a theoretical term, to say "I think that I am very angry, but I'm not sure" or "I think that I have a severe pain, but I'm not sure" or "I think that I am conscious but I'm not sure," since one might well not be sure that the experimental laws implied by the "psychological theory" implicit in ordinary language are in fact correct. It would also not be absurd to say: "perhaps there is not really any such thing as anger" or "perhaps there is not really any such thing as pain" or "perhaps there is not really any such thing as being conscious." Indeed, no matter how certain I might be that I have the sensation of red, it might be proved *by examining other people* that I did *not* have that sensation and that in fact there was no such thing as having the sensation of red. Indeed, "that *looks like* the sensation of red" would have a perfectly good use—namely, to mean that my experience is as it would be if the "psychological theory implicit in ordinary language" were true, but the theory is not in fact true. These consequences should certainly cast doubt on the idea that "psychological terms in ordinary language" really are "theoretical constructs."

It is obvious that "psychological terms in ordinary language" have a *reporting use*. In the jargon of philosophers of science, they figure in *observation statements*. "I am in pain" would be such a statement. But clearly, a term that figures in observational reports has an observational use, and that use must enter into its meaning. Its meaning cannot be fixed merely by its relation to other terms, in abstraction from the actual speech habits of speakers (including the habits upon which the reporting use depends).

The first difficulty suggests that the "psychological theory" that "implicitly defines" such words as 'anger' has in fact *no* nontautological consequences—or, at least, no empirical consequences that could not be abandoned without changing the meaning of these words. The second difficulty then further suggests that the job of fixing the meaning of these words is only partially done by the logical relationships (the "theory"), and is completed by the reporting use.

A third difficulty arises when we ask just what it is that the "psychological theory implicit in ordinary language" is supposed to be *postulating.* The usual answer is that the theory postulates the existence of certain *states* which are supposed to be related to one another and to behavior as specified in the theory. But what does 'state' mean? If 'state' is taken to mean physical state, in the narrow sense alluded to before, then psychophysical parallelism would be implied by an arbitrary "psychological" assertion, which is obviously incorrect. On the other hand, if 'state' is taken in a sufficiently wide sense so as to avoid this sort of objection, then (as Wittgenstein points out) the remark that "being angry is being in a certain psychological state" *says nothing whatsoever.*

In the case of an ordinary scientific theory (say, a physical theory), to postulate the existence of "states" S_1, S_2, . . . , S_n satisfying certain postulates is to assert that one of two things is the case: either (1) physical states (definable in terms of the existing primitives of physical theory) can be found satisfying the postulates; or (2) it is necessary to take the new predicates S_1, . . . , S_n (or predicates in terms of which they can be defined) as additional primitives in physical science, and widen our concept of "physical state" accordingly. In the same way, identity theorists have sometimes suggested that "molar psychological theory" *leaves it open* whether or not the states it postulates are physical states or not. But if physical states *can* be found satisfying the postulates, then they are the ones referred to by the postulates. 'State' is then a methodological term, so to speak, whose status is explained by a perspicuous representation of the procedures of empirical theory construction and confirmation. This solution to our third difficulty reduces to the identity theory under the supposition that psychophysical parallelism holds, and that physical states *can* be found "satisfying" the postulates of "molar behavioral psychology."

Even if this solution to the third difficulty is accepted, however, the first two difficulties remain. To be an empirically confirmable scientific theory, the "molar behavioral theory" implicit in the ordinary use of psychological terms must have testable empirical consequences. If the ordinary-language psychological terms really designate states postulated by this theory, then, if the theory is radically false, we must say there are no such "states" as being angry, being in pain, having a sensation, etc. And this must always remain a possibility (on this account), no matter what we observe, since no finite number of observations can deductively establish a scientific theory properly so-called. Also, the reporting role of "psychological" terms in ordinary language is not discussed by this account. If saying "I am in pain" is simply ascribing a *theoretical* term to myself, then this report is in part a *hypothesis,* and one which may always be false. This account—that the ordinary use of "psychological" terms presupposes an empirical theory, and one which may be radically false—has recently been urged by Paul Feyerabend. Feyerabend would accept the consequence that I have rejected as counterintuitive: that there may not really be any pains, sensations, etc., in the customary sense. But where is this empirical theory that is presupposed by the ordinary use of "psychological" terms? Can anyone state *one* behavioral law which is clearly empirical and which is presupposed by the concepts of sensation, anger, etc.? The empirical connection that exists, say, between being in pain and saying "ouch," or some such thing, has sometimes been taken (by logical behaviorists, rather than by identity theorists) to be such a law. I have tried to show elsewhere,[4] however, that no such law is really required to be true for the application of the concept of pain in its customary sense. What entitles us to say that a man is in pain in our world may not entitle one to say that he is in pain in a different world; yet the *same* concept of pain may be applicable. What I contend is that to understand any "psychological" term, one must be implicitly familiar with

[4] In "Brains and Behavior." The character of psychological concepts is also discussed by me in "The Mental Life of Some Machines," in Hector-Neri Castañeda, ed., *Intentionality, Minds, and Perception* (Detroit: Wayne State University Press, 1966), pp. 177–200; reprinted in this volume, pp. 263–81.

a network of *logical* relationships, and one must be adequately trained in the reporting use of that word. It is also necessary, I believe, that one be prepared to accept first-person statements by other members of one's linguistic community involving these predicates, at least when there is no *special* reason to distrust them; but this is a general convention associated with discourse, and not part of the meaning of any particular word, psychological or otherwise. Other general conventions associated with discourse, in my opinion, are the acceptance of not-too-bizarre rules of inductive inference and theory confirmation and of certain fundamental rules of deductive inference. But these things, again, have to do with one's discourse *as a whole* not being linguistically deviant, rather than with one's understanding any particular word. If I am not aware that someone's crying out (in a certain kind of context) is a sign that he is in pain, I can be *told.* If I refuse (without good reason), to believe what I am told, it can be pointed out to me that, when I am in that context (say, my finger is burnt), *I* feel pain, and no condition known by me to be relevant to the feeling or nonfeeling of pain is different in the case of the Other. If I *still* feel no inclination to ascribe pain to the Other, then my whole concept of discourse is abnormal—but it would be both a gross understatement and a misdiagnosis to say that I "don't know the meaning of 'pain.'"

I conclude that "psychological" terms in ordinary language are *not* theoretical terms. Moreover, the idea that, if psychophysical parallelism is correct, then it is analytic that pain *is* the correlated brain-state is not supported by a shred of linguistic evidence. (Yet this is a consequence of the combined "identity theory-theoretical term" account as we developed it to meet our third difficulty.) I conclude that any attempt to show that Oscar is conscious (analytically, relative to our premises) along these lines is hopeless.

ZIFF'S ARGUMENT

So far all the arguments we have considered, on both sides of the question: Is Oscar conscious? have been without merit. No sound consideration has been advanced to show that it is false, given the meaning of the words in English and the empirical facts as we are assuming them, that Oscar is conscious; but also no sound consideration has been advanced to show that it is true. If it is a violation of the rules of English to say (without "raised-eyebrow quotes") that Oscar is in pain or seeing a rose or thinking about Vienna, we have not been told *what* rules it violates; and if it is a violation of the rules of English to *deny* that Oscar is conscious, given his psychological isomorphism to a human being, we have likewise not been told what rules it violates. In this situation, it is of interest to turn to an ingenious ("anti-civil-libertarian") argument by Paul Ziff.[5]

Ziff wishes to show that it is false that Oscar is conscious. He begins with the undoubted fact that if Oscar is not alive he cannot be conscious. Thus, given the semantical connection between 'alive' and 'conscious' in English, it is enough to show that Oscar is not *alive*. Now, Ziff argues, when we wish to tell whether or not something is alive, we do *not* go by its *behavior*. Even if a thing looks like a flower, grows in my garden like a flower, etc., if I find upon taking it apart that it consists of gears and wheels and miniaturized furnaces and vacuum tubes and so on, I say "what a clever mechanism," not "what an unusual plant." It is *structure*, not *behavior* that determines whether or not something is alive; and it is a violation of the semantical rules of our language to say of anything that is clearly a mechanism that it is "alive."

Ziff's argument is unexpected, because of the great concentration in the debate up to now upon *behavior*, but it certainly calls attention to relevant logical and semantical relationships. Yet I cannot agree that these relationships are as clear-cut as Ziff's argument requires. Suppose that we construct a robot—or, let me rather say, an *android*, to employ a word that smacks less of mechanism—out of "soft" (protoplasm-like) stuff. Then, on Ziff's account, it may be perfectly correct, if the android is sufficiently "life-like" in structure, to say that we have "synthesized life." So, given two artifacts, both "models" of the same psychological theory, both completely deterministic physical-chemical systems, both designed to the same end and "programmed" by the designer to the same extent, it may be that we must say that one of them is a "machine" and not conscious, and the other is a "living thing," (albeit "artificially created") and conscious, simply because the one consists of "soft stuff" and the other consists of "hardware." A great many speakers of English, I am sure (and I am one of them), would find the claim that this dogmatic decision is required by the meaning of the word 'alive'

[5] I take the liberty of reporting an argument used by Ziff in a conversation. I do not wish to imply that Ziff necessarily subscribes to the argument in the form in which I report it, but I include it because of its ingenuity and interest.

quite contrary to their linguistic intuitions. I think that the difficulty is fundamentally this: a plant does not exhibit much "behavior." Thus it is natural that criteria having to do with *structure* should dominate criteria having to do with "behavior" when the question is whether or not something that looks and "behaves" like a plant is really a living thing or not. But in the case of something that looks and behaves like an *animal* (and especially like a *human being*), it is natural that criteria having to do with behavior—and not just with actual behavior, but with the *organization* of behavior, as specified by a psychological theory of the thing—should play a much larger role in the decision. Thus it is not unnatural that we should be prepared to argue, in the case of the "pseudo-plant," that "it isn't a living thing because it is a mechanism," while some are prepared to argue, in the case of the robot, that "it isn't a *mere* mechanism, because it is *alive*," and "it is alive, because it is conscious," and "it is conscious because it has the same behavioral organization as a living human being." Yet Ziff's account may well explain why it is that many speakers are not convinced by these latter arguments. The tension between conflicting criteria results in the "obviousness," to some minds, of the robot's "machine" status, and the equal "obviousness," to other minds, of its "artificial-life" status.

There is a sense of 'mechanism' in which it is clearly analytic that a mechanism cannot be alive. Ziff's argument can be reduced to the contention that, on the normal interpretation of the terms, it is analytic in English that something whose *parts* are all mechanisms, in this sense, likewise cannot be alive. If this is so, then no English speaker should suppose that he could even *imagine* a robot *thinking*, being *power-mad, hating humans*, or *being in love*, any more than he should suppose that he could imagine a married bachelor. It seems evident to me (and indeed to most speakers) that, absurdly or not, we *can* imagine these things. I conclude, therefore, that Ziff is wrong: it may be *false*, but it is not a *contradiction*, to assert that Oscar is alive.

THE "KNOW-NOTHING" VIEW

We have still to consider the most traditional view on our question. According to this view, which is still quite widely held, *it is possible that Oscar is conscious, and it is possible that he is not conscious.*

In its theological form, the argument runs as follows: I am a creature with a body and a soul. My body happens to consist of flesh and blood, but it might just as well have been a machine, had God chosen. Each voluntary movement of my body is correlated with an activity of my soul (how and why is a "mystery"). So, it is quite possible that Oscar has a soul, and that each "voluntary" movement of his mechanical body is correlated in the same mysterious way with an activity of his soul. It is also possible—since the laws of physics suffice to explain the motions of Oscar's body, without use of the assumption that he has a soul—that Oscar is but a lifeless machine. There is absolutely no way in which we can know. This argument can also be given a nontheological (or at least apparently nontheological) form by deleting the reference to God, and putting 'mind' for 'soul' throughout. To complete the argument, it is contended that I know what it *means* to say that Oscar has a "soul" (or has a pain, or the sensation of red, etc.) *from my own case.*

One well-known difficulty with this traditional view is that it implies that it is also possible that other humans are not really conscious, even if they are physically and psychologically isomorphic to me. It is contended that I can know with *probability* that other humans are conscious by the "argument from analogy." But in the inductive sciences, an argument from analogy is generally regarded as quite weak unless the conclusion is capable of further and independent inductive verification. So it is hard to believe that our reasons for believing that other persons are conscious are very strong ones if they amount simply to an analogical argument with a conclusion that admits of *no* independent check, observational, inductive, or whatever. Most philosophers have recently found it impossible to believe *either* that our reasons for believing that other persons are conscious are that weak *or* that the possibility exists that other persons, while being admittedly physically and psychologically isomorphic (in the sense of the present paper) to myself, are not conscious. Arguments on this point may be found in the writings of all the major analytical philosophers of the present century. Unfortunately, many of these arguments depend upon quite dubious theories of meaning.

The critical claim is the claim that it follows from the fact that I have had the sensation of red, I can imagine this sensation, "I know what it is like," that I can understand the assertion that Oscar has the sensation of red (or any other sensation or psychological state). In a sense, this is right. I *can,* in one sense, understand the *words.* I can parse them; I don't think "sensation of red" means *baby carriage,* etc. More than that: I know what I would experience if I were conscious and psychologically as I am, but with Oscar's mechanical "body" in place of my own. How does this come to be so? It comes to be so, at least in part, because we have to learn from experience what our own bodies are like. If a child were brought up in a suitable kind of armor, the child might be deceived into thinking that it was a robot. It would be harder to fool him into thinking that he had the internal structure of a robot, but this too could be done (fake X-rays, etc.). And when I "imagine myself in the shoes of a (conscious) robot," what I do, of course, is to imagine the sensations that I might have if I were a robot, or rather *if I were a human who mistakenly thought that he was a robot.* (I look down at my feet and see bright metal, etc.)

Well, let us grant that in this sense we *understand* the sentence "Oscar is having the sensation of red." It does not follow that the sentence possesses a truth value. We understand the sentence "the present King of France is bald," but, on its normal interpretation in English, the sentence has no truth value under present conditions. We can give it one by adopting a suitable convention—for example, Russell's theory of descriptions—and more than one such suitable convention exists. The question really at issue is *not* whether we can "understand" the sentences "Oscar is conscious" (or "has the sensation of red" or "is angry") and "Oscar is not conscious," in the sense of being able to use them in such contexts as "I can perfectly well picture to myself that Oscar is conscious," but whether there really is an intelligible sense in which one of these sentences is true, on a normal interpretation, and the other false (and, in that case, whether it is also true that we can't tell which).

Let us revert, for a moment, to our earlier fantasy of ROBOTS—i.e., second-order robots, robots created by robots and regarded by robots as *mere* ROBOTS. As already remarked, a robot philosopher might very well be led to consider the question: Are ROBOTS conscious? The robot philosopher "knows," of course, just what "experiences" he would have if he were a "conscious" ROBOT (or a robot in a ROBOT suit). He can "perfectly well picture to himself that a ROBOT could have "sensation." So he may perfectly well arrive at the position that it is logically possible that ROBOTS have sensations (or, rather, "sensations") and perfectly possible that they do not, and moreover he can never know. What do we think of this conclusion?

It is clear what we should think: we should think that there is not the slightest reason to suppose (and every reason not to suppose) that there is a special property, "having the 'sensation' of red," which the ROBOT may or may not have, but which is inaccessible to the robot. The robot, knowing the physical and psychological description of the ROBOT, is in a perfectly good position to answer all questions about the ROBOT that may reasonably be asked. The idea that there is a further question (class of questions) about the ROBOT which the robot cannot answer, is suggested to the robot by the fact that these alleged "questions" are grammatically well formed, can be "understood" in the sense discussed above, and that the possible "answers" can be "imagined."

I suggest that our position with respect to robots is *exactly* that of robots with respect to ROBOTS. There is not the slightest reason for us, either, to believe that "consciousness" is a well-defined property, which each robot either *has* or *lacks*, but such that it is not possible, on the basis of the physical description of the robot, or even on the basis of the psychological description (in the sense of "psychological" explained above), to *decide* which (if any) of the robots possesses this property and which (if any) fail to possess it. The rules of "robot language" may well be such that it is perfectly possible for a robot to "conjecture" that ROBOTS have "sensations" and also perfectly possible for a robot to conjecture that ROBOTS do not have "sensations." It does not follow that the physical and psychological description of the ROBOTS is "incomplete," but only that the concept of "sensation" (in "raised-eyebrow quotes") is a well-defined concept only when applied to robots. The question raised by the robot philosopher: Are ROBOTS "conscious"? calls for a decision and not for a discovery. The decision, at bottom, is this: Do I treat ROBOTS as fellow members of my linguistic community, or as machines? If the ROBOTS are accepted as full members of the robot community, then a robot can find out whether a ROBOT is "conscious" or "unconscious," "alive" or "dead" in just the way he finds out these things about a fellow robot. If they are rejected, then nothing *counts* as a ROBOT being "conscious" or "alive." Until the decision is made, the statement that ROBOTS are "conscious" has no truth value. In the same way, I suggest, the question: Are robots conscious? calls for a decision, on our part, to treat robots as fellow members of our linguistic community, or not to so treat them. As long as we leave this decision unmade, the statement that robots (of the kind described) are conscious has no truth value.

If we reject the idea that the physical and psychological description of the robots is incomplete (because it "fails to specify whether or not they are conscious"), we are not thereby forced to hold either that "consciousness" is a "physical" attribute or that it is an attribute "implicitly defined by a psychological theory." Russell's question in the philosophy of mathematics: If the number 2 is not the set of all pairs, then what on earth is it? was a silly question. Two is simply the second number, and nothing else. Likewise, the materialist question: If the attribute of "consciousness" is not a physical attribute (or an attribute implicitly defined by a psychological theory) then what on earth is it? is a silly question. Our psychological concepts in ordinary language are as we have fashioned them. The "framework" of ordinary-language psychological predicates is what it is and not another framework. *Of course* materialism is false; but it is so *trivially* false that no materialist should be bothered!

CONCLUSION

In this paper, I have reviewed a succession of failures: failures to show that we *must* say that robots are conscious, failures to show that we *must* say they are not, failures to show that we *must* say that we can't tell. I have concluded from these failures that there is no correct answer to the question: Is Oscar conscious? Robots may indeed have (or lack) properties unknown to physics and undetectable by us; but not the slightest reason has been offered to show that they do, as the ROBOT analogy demonstrates. It is reasonable, then, to conclude that the question that titles this paper calls for a decision and not for a discovery. If we are to make a decision, it seems preferable to me to extend our concept so that robots *are* conscious —for "discrimination" based on the "softness" or "hardness" of the body parts of a synthetic "organism" seems as silly as discriminatory treatment of humans on the basis of skin color. But my purpose in this paper has not been to improve our concepts, but to find out what they are.

14 Hilary Putnam

The Mental Life of Some Machines

In this paper I want to discuss the nature of various "mentalistic" notions in terms of a machine analog. In an earlier paper,[1] I tried to show that the conceptual issues surrounding the traditional mind-body problem have nothing to do with the supposedly special character of human subjective experience, but arise for any computing system of a certain kind of richness and complexity, in particular for any computing system able to construct theories concerning its own nature. In that paper I was primarily interested in the issues having to do with mind-body identity. In the present paper the focus will be rather in trying to shed light on the character of such notions as preferring, believing, feeling. I hope to show by considering the use of these words in connection with a machine analog that the traditional alternatives—materialism, dualism, logical behaviorism—are incorrect, even in the case of these machines. My objectives are not merely destructive ones; I hope by indicating what the character of these words is in the case of the machine analog to suggest to some extent what their character is in application to human beings.

One question which I shall not discuss, except for these remarks at the outset, is the question to what extent the application of such

REPRINTED from *Intentionality, Minds, and Perception*, ed. Hector-Neri Castañeda, by permission of the author and the Wayne State University Press.

[1] Hilary Putnam, "Minds and Machines," in New York University Institute of Philosophy; Sidney Hook, ed., *Dimensions of Mind* (New York: New York University Press, 1960), pp. 148–79.

terms as "preference" to Turing Machines represents a change or extension of meaning. I shall not discuss this question because, as will become clear, it is not too relevant to my undertaking. Even if the sense in which the Turing Machines I shall describe may be said to "prefer" one thing to another is *very* different in *many* ways from the sense in which a human being is said to prefer one thing to another, this does not run contrary to anything that I claim. What I claim is that seeing why it is that the analogs of materialism, dualism, and logical behaviorism are false in the case of these Turing Machines will enable us to see why the theories are incorrect in the case of human beings, and seeing what these terms might mean in the case of Turing Machines will at least suggest to us important logical features of these terms which have previously been overlooked by philosophers.

In this paper, then, I am going to consider a hypothetical "community" made up of "agents," each of whom is in fact a Turing Machine, or, more precisely, a finite automaton. (Of the many equivalent definitions of "finite automaton," the most useful for present purposes is the one that results if the definition of a Turing Machine is modified by specifying that the tape should be *finite.*) The Turing Machines I want to consider will differ from the abstract Turing Machines considered in logical theory in that we will consider them to be equipped with sense organs by means of which they can scan their environment, and with suitable motor organs which they are capable of controlling. We may think of the sense organs as causing certain "reports" to be printed on the tape of the machine at certain times, and we may think of the machine as being constructed so that when certain "operant" symbols are printed by the machine on its tape, its motor organs execute appropriate actions. This is the natural generalization of a Turing Machine to allow for interaction with an environment.

The fundamental concept we want to discuss will be the concept of *preference.* In order to give this concept formal content with respect to the behavior of these "agents," we will suppose that each of these agents is described by a rational preference function, in the sense of economic theory.[2] We will suppose that our Turing Ma-

[2] John Von Neumann and Oskar Morgenstern, *A Theory of Games and Economic Behavior,* 3rd ed. (Princeton, N.J.: Princeton University Press, 1953), pp. 26 f., 83 *et al.* Von Neumann and Morgenstern think of such a function as

chines are sufficiently complex so as to be able to make reasonably good estimates of the probability of various states of affairs. Given the inductive estimates made by a machine, the behavior of the machine will then be completely determined by the fact that the machine is to obey the rule: act so as to maximize the estimated utility.

The reader should note that the term "utility" is completely eliminable here. What we are saying is that there is associated with each machine a certain mathematical function, called a utility function, such that that function together with another function, the machine's "degree of confirmation" function, completely determines the machine's behavior in accordance with a certain rule and certain theorems of the probability calculus.[3] In short, our machines are *rational agents* in the sense in which that term is used in inductive logic and economic theory. If the rational preference functions of these machines resemble the rational preference functions of idealized human beings, and the computing skills of the machines are approximately equal to the computing skills of human beings, then the behavior of these machines will closely resemble the behavior of (idealized) human beings. We can complicate this model by introducing into the behavior of these machines certain irrationalities which resemble the irrationalities in the behavior of actual human beings (e.g., failure of the transitivity of preference), but this will not be attempted here.

What then does "prefer" mean as applied to one of these machines? As a start it simply means that the function which controls the behavior of the machine (more precisely, the function which together with the machine's inductive logic controls the behavior of the machine) assigns a higher weight to the first alternative than to the second. Even at the outset we can see that the relation of preferring to behavior is going to be quite complicated for these machines. For example, if one of these machines prefers A to B, it does not necessarily follow that in any concrete situation it will choose A rather than B. In deciding whether to choose A rather than B,

---

an assignment of coordinates (in an *n*-dimensional space) to objects, the sum of the coordinates being the "value" of the object. Here it will be convenient to think of it as a function assigning a "utility" to "possible worlds" (or "state descriptions" in the sense of Carnap).

[3] Cf. Rudolf Carnap, *Logical Foundations of Probability* (Chicago: University of Chicago Press, 1950), esp. pp. 253–79.

the machine will have to consider what the consequences of its choice are likely to be in the concrete situation, and this may well bring in "values" of the machine other than the preference that the machine assigns to A over B. We might say that if the machine prefers A to B then that means that *ceteris paribus* the machine will choose A over B, and we might despair of ever spelling out in any precise way the *ceteris paribus* clause. In an analogous way, Miss Anscombe[4] has suggested that if someone intends not to have an accident then that means that, *ceteris paribus,* he will choose methods of driving from one place to another that are likely to minimize the chance of having an accident. She has suggested that in this kind of case the *ceteris paribus* clause could not *in principle* be spelled out in detail. On this basis she has gone on to suggest a fundamental difference between what she calls practical reason and scientific reason. This conclusion should be viewed with some suspicion, however. The fact is that she has shown that certain proposed methods of spelling out the *ceteris paribus* clause in question would not work; but these methods would not work in the case of our machines either. It hardly follows that our machines exhibit in their ordinary "behavior" a form of reasoning fundamentally different from scientific reasoning. On the contrary, given a rational preference function, always acting so as to maximize the estimated utility is exhibiting scientific reasoning of a very high order.

Miss Anscombe might reply that actual human beings do not have rational preference functions. However, Von Neumann and Morgenstern have shown, and this is the fundamental result in the area, that any agent whose preferences are consistent always does behave in a way which can be interpreted in terms of at least one rational preference function. Miss Anscombe might reply that actual human beings do not have consistent preferences; but this would be to say that the difference between practical reason and scientific reason is that practical reason is often in fact more or less irrational—that everyone's practical reasoning is irrational in some areas. This is like saying that deductive logic is different in principle from the logic contained in any textbook because everyone's deductive reasoning is bad in some areas. The fact is that Miss Anscombe's remarks on

[4] G. E. M. Anscombe, *Intention* (Ithaca, N.Y.: Cornell University Press, 1957), esp. pp. 59–61. I wish to emphasize that the view I am critizing occurs in only three pages of what I regard as an excellent book.

intentions are supposed to apply not only to the intentional behavior of more or less irrational human beings but just as much to the intentional behavior of an ideally rational human being with a rich and complex system of values. I think this is quite clear from reading her whole book. But for such an agent one of her major conclusions is just false: the practical reasoning of such an agent would be, as we have seen, not at all unlike scientific reasoning.[5]

The point in a nutshell is that practical reasoning *is* fundamentally different from scientific reasoning if we think of scientific reasoning as consisting of syllogisms, the premises of which can in principle be spelled out exactly, and we think of practical reasoning as consisting of so-called "practical syllogisms" whose premises must in all interesting cases contain ineliminable *ceteris paribus* clauses. However, actual scientific reasoning involves modes of connecting premises and conclusions much more complex than the syllogism, and decision making, either actual or idealized, involves modes of reasoning which are depicted much too inexactly by being forced into the traditional mold of the "practical syllogism." The complex weighing of multitudinous conflicting alternatives and values does admit of deductive schematization; but not the type of deductive schematization considered by Miss Anscombe (and Aristotle).

[5] Some of the differences between practical and theoretical reasoning pointed out by Miss Anscombe do hold. For instance, that the main premise must mention something wanted, and that the conclusion must be an action (although "there is no objection to inventing a form of words by which he *accompanies* this action, which we may call the conclusion in a verbalized form." *Ibid.*, p. 60). What I challenge is the claim that the conclusion (in "verbalized form") does not follow *deductively* from the premises (at least in many cases—cf. her n. 1 on p. 58) and cannot be made to follow, unless the major premise is an "insane" one which no one would accept. This leads Miss Anscombe to the view that Aristotle was really engaged in "describing an order which is there whenever actions are done with intentions" (p. 79). This comes perilously close to suggesting that engaging in practical reasoning is merely performing actions with intentions. Mary Mothersill, in "Anscombe's Account of the Practical Syllogism," *Philosophical Review*, LXXI (1962), pp. 448–61, criticizes Miss Anscombe on this same point but seems to miss the force of her argument. To say, as Mothersill does, that "do everything conducive to not having a car crash" has a "*non*-insane" interpretation is surely true but no help, since *on the noninsane interpretation*, "Do *this*" does not follow deductively from the major premise together with "*this* is conducive to not having a car crash"—*this* may not be an *appropriate* action, and "do everything" means (on the "noninsane" interpretation) "do everything appropriate" (*Ibid.*, p. 455). Mothersill seems to assume that "assuming appropriate conditions" could be spelled out, but this is just what Anscombe is denying.

Before going on, I should like to make one comment which may perhaps prevent some misunderstandings. A Turing Machine is simply a system having a discrete set of states which are related in certain ways. Usually we think of a Turing Machine as having a memory in the form of a paper tape upon which it prints symbols; however, this can be regarded as mere metaphor. Instead, in the case of a finite automaton, i.e., a Turing Machine whose tape is finite instead of potentially infinite, the tape may be thought of as physically realized in the form of any finite system of memory storage. What we mean by a "symbol" is simply any sort of *trace* which can be placed in this memory storage and later "scanned" by some mechanism or other. We can generalize further by allowing the "machine" to "print" more than one symbol at a time and to scan more than one symbol at a time. Turing has shown that these generalizations leave the class of Turing Machines essentially unchanged. Note then that a Turing Machine need not even be a *machine*. A Turing Machine might very well be a biological organism. The question whether an actual human being is a Turing Machine (or rather, a finite automaton), or whether the brain of a human being is a Turing Machine, is an empirical question. Today we know nothing strictly incompatible with the hypothesis that you and I are one and all Turing Machines, although we know some things that make this unlikely. Strictly speaking, a Turing Machine need not even be a physical system: anything capable of going through a succession of states in time can be a Turing Machine. Thus, to the Cartesian dualist, who likes to think of the human mind as a self-contained system in some sort of causal interaction with the body, one can say that from the point of view of pure logic it is entirely possible that the human mind is a Turing Machine (assuming that the human mind is capable of some large but finite set of states, which seems certainly true). To the person who believes that human beings have souls and that personality and memory reside in the soul and survive bodily death, one may say again that from the standpoint of pure logic it is entirely possible that the human soul is a Turing Machine, or rather a finite automaton.

Although it is likely that human brain states form a discrete set no matter what meaning may be given to the somewhat ambiguous notion of a mental state, it is somewhat unlikely that either the mind or the brain is a Turing Machine. Reasoning *a priori* one would think it more likely that the interconnections among the various brain states and mental states of a human being are probabilistic rather than deterministic and that time-delays play an important role. However, empirical evidence is scarce. The reason is that an automaton whose states are connected by probabilistic laws and whose behavior involves time-delays can be arbitrarily well-simulated by the behavior of a Turing Machine. Thus, in the nature of the case, mere empirical data cannot decide between the hypothesis that the human brain (respectively, *mind*) is a Turing Machine and the hypothesis that it is a more complex kind of automaton with probabilistic relations and time-delays.

There is another respect in which our model is certainly oversimplified, however, even if the human brain and mind *are* Turing Machines. As has already been remarked, the necessary and sufficient condition that someone's behavior at a given time should be consistent with the assignment of some rational preference function is that his choices be consistent—e.g., if he prefers A to B and he prefers B to C, then he prefers A to C. But even this very weak axiom of transitivity is violated by the preferences of very many, perhaps all, actual people. Thus, it is doubtful that any actual human being's pattern of choices is consistent with the assignment of a rational preference function. Moreover, even if someone's pattern of preferences is consistent with the assignment of a rational preference function, it is doubtful that people consistently obey the rule: maximize the estimated utility.

And, finally, our model is not dynamical. That is to say, it does not allow for the change of the rational preference function with time—although this last feature can be modified. Thus our model is an overly simple and overly rationalistic one in a number of respects. However, it would be easy, in principle, although perhaps impossible in practice, to complicate our model in all these respects —to make the model dynamical, to allow for irrationalities in preference, to allow for irrationalities in the inductive logic of the machine, to allow for deviations from the rule: maximize the estimated utility. But I do not believe that any of these complications would affect the philosophical conclusions reached in this paper. In other words, I do not believe that the philosophical conclusions of this paper would be changed if we replaced the notion of a Turing Machine by the notion of a K-machine, where the notion of a K-machine were made sufficiently rich and complex so that human brains and minds were, literally, K-machines.

Besides saying that they are Turing Machines and that they have rational preference functions, I shall say nothing about my hypothetical "agents." They could be artifacts, they could be biological organisms, they could even be human beings. In particular then, I shall nowhere specify in this paper that the "agents" in my "community" are alive or not alive, conscious or not conscious. There is, however, a sense in which we may say of these agents, regardless of their physical realization, that they are *conscious of* certain things and *not conscious of* others. Moreover, if they have periods of what answers to sleep, then there is one use of "conscious" and "unconscious" in which we may say that they are "conscious" at certain times and "unconscious" at others.

MATERIALISM

It does not, I think, have to be shown that Cartesian dualism is untenable as a description of the "inner life" of these machines and of the relation of that inner life to their behavior. The "agents" are simply certain systems of states in certain causal interrelations; *all* of their states are causally interrelated. There are not two separate "worlds," a "world" of "inner" states and a "world" of "outer" states in some peculiar kind of correlation or connection. They are not ghosts in Turing Machines, they *are* Turing Machines.

But what of materialism? If materialism as a philosophical doctrine is correct as an account of the mental life of *any* organism, then it should *certainly* be correct as an account of what corresponds to the "mental life" of *these* agents—at least if we imagine the agents to be realized as automata built out of flip-flops, relays, vacuum tubes, and so forth. But even in this last case I shall argue that traditional materialism is incorrect.

Traditional materialism (which is pretty much of a philosopher's straw man by now) holds that mental conduct words are definable in terms of concepts referring to physical-chemical composition. If this is right, then the predicate "T prefers A to B" should be definable in terms of the physical-chemical composition of our Turing Machines. But in fact there is no logically valid inference from the premise that one of our Turing Machines has a certain physical-chemical composition to the conclusion that it prefers A to B, in the sense explained above, nor from the premise that it prefers A to B to the conclusion that it has a certain physical-chemical composition. These are logically independent statements about our Turing Machines even if they are *just* machines.

Let us quickly verify this. Suppose we are given as a premise that T_1 prefers A to B. We can then infer that T_1 must have been programmed in a certain way. In particular, its program must involve a rational preference function which assigns a higher value to A than to B. Suppose that we are given not just this information, but are given the specific machine table of the machine T_1. We can still draw no inference whatsoever to the physical-chemical composition of T_1, for the reason that the *same* Turing Machine (from the standpoint of the machine table) may be physically realized in a potential infinity of ways. Even if in fact a machine belonging to our community prefers A to B when and only when flip-flop 57 is on, this is a purely contingent fact. Our machine might have been exactly the same in all "psychological" respects without consisting of flip-flops at all.

What of inferences in the reverse direction? Suppose that we are given the information that machine T_1 has a certain physical-chemical composition, can we infer that it has a certain rational preference function? This reduces to the question: can we infer the machine table of the machine from its physical-chemical composition? As an empirical matter, there is no doubt that we *can,* at least in simple cases. But we are concerned here with the question of logically valid inferences, not empirically successful ones. In order to know that a machine has a certain machine table, we must know how many significantly different states the machine is capable of and how these are causally related. This cannot be inferred from the physical-chemical composition of the machine unless, in addition to knowing the physical-chemical composition, we also know the *laws of nature.* We don't have to know all the laws of nature, we only have to know some relevant finite set; but there is no way of specifying in advance just what finite set of the laws of nature will have to be given in addition to the physical-chemical composition of the machine before we are able to show that the machine in question has a certain machine table. From the single fact that a machine has a certain physical-chemical composition it does not follow either that it has or that it does not have any particular rational preference function and hence that it does or does not prefer A to B.

Given a description of the physical-chemical composition of a machine *and* a statement of all the laws of nature (for simplicity we will assume these to be finite), can we infer that the machine prefers A to B? Suppose, for the sake of definiteness, the laws of nature are of the classical atomistic kind; that is, they describe how individual elementary particles behave, and there is a composition function which enables us to tell how any isolated complex of elementary particles will behave. Finally, the physical-chemical composition of the machine is described by describing a certain complex of elementary particles. Even in this case, we cannot as a matter of *pure logic* deduce from the statements given that the machine has a particular machine table, or a particular rational preference function, unless in addition to being given the physical-chemical composition of the machine and the laws of nature, we are given the additional premise (which from the formal point of view is a logically independent statement) that we have been given a description of *all* of the machine. Suppose, for the sake of an example, that there exist in addition to elementary particles, entities unknown to physical theory —"bundles of ectoplasm"—and that the whole machine consists of elementary particles and some "bundles of ectoplasm" in some complex kind of causal interrelationship. Then when we give the physical-chemical composition of the machine, in the usual sense, we are only describing a *substructure* of the total machine. From this description of the substructure plus the laws of nature in the ordinary sense (the laws governing the behavior of *isolated systems* of elementary particles) we can deduce how this substructure will behave *as long as there are no interactions with the remainder of the structure* (the "bundles of ectoplasm"). Since it is not a fact of pure logic that the physical-chemical description of the machine is a description of all of the machine, one cannot by pure logic deduce that the machine has any particular machine table or any particular rational preference function from a description of the physical-chemical composition of the machine and the laws of nature.

Logically, the situation just discussed is analogous to the situation which arises when certain philosophers attempt to treat universal generalizations as (possibly infinite) conjunctions, i.e., the proposal has been made to analyze "all crows are black" as "(a_1 is a crow

$\supset a_1$ is black) & (a_2 is a crow $\supset a_2$ is black) & (a_3 is a crow $\supset a_3$ is black) . . ." where a_1, a_2, . . . is a possibly infinite list of individual constants designating all crows. The mistake here is that although this conjunction does indeed follow from the statement that all crows are black, the statement that all crows are black does not follow from the conjunction without the additional universal premise: "a_1, a_2, . . . are all the crows there are." It might be contended that the possibility that there exist causal agents unknown to modern physics and not consisting of elementary particles is so remote that it should be neglected. But this is to leave the context of logical analysis altogether. Moreover we have only to reflect for a moment to remember that today we know of a host of causal agencies which would have been left out in any inventory of the "furniture of the world" taken by a nineteenth-century physicist. Atoms and their solar system-like components, electrons and nucleons, might possibly have been guessed at by the nineteenth-century physicist; but what of mesons, and what of the quanta of the gravitational field, if these turn out to exist? No, the hypothesis that any inventory includes a list of all ultimate "building blocks" of causal processes that there are is a synthetic one and cannot be regarded as true by pure logic.

Materialism, as I admitted before, is today a philosopher's straw man. Modern materialists (or "identity theorists," as they prefer to be called) do not maintain that the *intensions* of such terms as "preference" can be given in physical-chemical terms but only that there is a physical referent. Their formulation would be, roughly, that preferring A to B is *synthetically identical with* possessing certain more or less stable features of the physical-chemical composition (e.g., "preferring A to B is a fairly lasting state of the human cerebral cortex"). This runs into the difficulty that *preference* is a universal, not a particular—preferring A to B is a *relation* between an organism and two alternatives—and the "is" appropriate to *universals* appears to be the *"is" of meaning analysis*. We say, e.g., "*solubility* is the property that something possesses if and only if it is the case that if it were in water it would dissolve." We *don't* say, "solubility is a certain physical-chemical structure," but rather that the solubility of those substances that are soluble is *explained* by their possession of a certain physical-chemical structure. Similarly, in the case of our machines what we would say is that preferring A to B is possessing a rational preference function which assigns a higher value to A than to B. If we say, in addition, that preferring A to B is "synthetically identical with" possessing a certain physical-chemical structure—say, a certain pattern of flip-flops—then we let ourselves in for what seem to me to be remarkable and insufficiently motivated extensions of usage. For instance, if the same Turing Machine is physically realized in two quite different ways, then even though not only the national preference function but the whole machine table is the same in the two cases, we shall have to say "preferring A to B is *something different* in the case of machine 1 and machine 2." Similarly, we shall have to say that "belief" is something different in the two cases, etc. It would be much clearer to say that the realization of the machine table is different in the two cases. There are a number of subtleties here of which it is well to be aware, however.

First of all, what has been said so far suggests the incorrect view that two properties can only be *analytically* identical, not *synthetically* identical. This is false. Let "a_1" be an individual constant designating a particular piece of paper, and suppose I write the word "red" on the piece of paper. Then the statement, "The property *red* is identical with the property designated by the only word written on a_1," is a synthetic statement.[6] However, this is the *only* way in which properties can be "synthetically identical" and the statements "Solubility is a certain molecular structure," "Pain is stimulation of C-fibers" are not of this kind, as one can easily convince oneself.

So far I have suggested that, apart from the kind of synthetic identity statement just cited, the criterion for the *identity* of two properties is *synonymy*, or equivalence in some analytical sense, or the corresponding designators. In my earlier paper I pointed out that for certain other kinds of abstract entities—e.g., situations, events—this does not seem to be correct, and that there might be reasons for giving this up even in the case of properties. I cited in that paper the "*is*" *of theoretical identification* (i.e., the "is" exemplified by such statements as "water is H_2O," "light *is* electromagnetic radiation") and I suggested that some properties might be connectible by this kind of "is." But this would not be of help to the identity theorist. (This represents a change of view from my earlier paper.) Even if

[6] More simply, "blue is the color of the sky" is a synthetic identity statement concerning properties. This example is due to Neil Wilson of Duke University, to whom I am indebted for enlightenment on the subject of identity of properties.

we are willing to say "being P *is* being Q" in some cases in which the designators 'P' and 'Q' are not synonymous, we should require that the designators be equivalent and that the equivalence be *necessary*, at least in the sense of *physically necessary*. Thus, if *one* particular physical-chemical composition should turn out to explain *all* cases of solubility, it would not be a wholly unmotivated extension of ordinary usage to say that solubility *is* the possession of this particular physical-chemical composition. There is an argument in my earlier paper for the view that this would not necessarily be a "change of meaning." This sort of thing cannot happen in the present case. We *cannot* discover laws by virtue of which it is physically necessary that an organism prefers A to B if and only if it is in a certain physical-chemical state. For we already know that any such laws would be false. They would be false because even in the light of our present knowledge we can see that any Turing Machine that can be physically realized at all can be realized in a host of totally different ways. Thus there cannot be a physical-chemical structure the possession of which is a necessary and sufficient condition for preferring A to B, even if we take "necessary" in the sense of *physically* necessary and not in the sense of logically necessary. And to start speaking of properties as "identical in some cases" because they happen to be coextensive in *those cases* would be not only a change of meaning but a rather arbitrary change of meaning at that.

So far we have ascribed to our machines only "multitracked" dispositions such as preference and belief but not such more or less transient states as states of feeling. Of course, we have equipped our machines with sense organs, and if we suppose that these sense organs are not perfectly reliable, then, as I argued in my earlier paper, it is easy to see that the distinction between appearance and reality will automatically arise in the "life" of the machine. We can classify certain configurations of these machines as "visual impressions," "tactile impressions," etc. What of such feelings as pain?

By suitably adapting Stuart Hampshire's discussion in his *Feeling and Expression*,[7] we can introduce into our model a counterpart of pain. Hampshire's idea is that the feelings are states characterized by the fact that they give rise to certain inclinations. For instance, pain is normally, although not invariably, occasioned by damage to part

[7] Stuart Hampshire, *Feeling and Expression* (London: H. K. Lewis and Co., Ltd., 1961).

of the body and gives rise to inclinations to withdraw the part of the body that seems to be damaged and to avoid whatever causes the painful damage in question. These inclinations are in a certain sense *spontaneous* ones—a point that has to be emphasized if this account is not to be open to damaging objections. That is, when X hurts my hand, the inclination to withdraw my hand from X arises at once and without ratiocination on my part. I can answer the question, "Why do you draw your hand away from X?" by saying, "X is hurting my hand." One does not then go on to ask, "But why is that a reason for drawing your hand away from X?" The fact that X's hurting my hand is *ipso facto* a reason for drawing my hand away from X is grounded on and presupposes the spontaneity of the inclination to draw my hand away from X when I am in the state in question.

Let us then equip our machines with "pain signals," i.e., signals which will normally be occasioned by damage to some part of the machine's "body," with "pain fibers," and with "pain states." These "pain states" will normally be caused by damage to some part of the machine's body and will give rise to spontaneous inclinations to avoid whatever causes the pain in question. I think we can see how to introduce the notion of an inclination into our model: inclinations are naturally treated as more or less short-lasting modifications of the rational preference function of the machine. Temporarily, the machine assigns a very high value, as it were, to "getting its arm out of there." This *temporary* change in the machine's rational preference function should not, of course, be confused with the long term change in the machine's behavior occasioned by learning that something it did not previously know to be painful is painful. This last can be built into the machine's rational preference function to begin with, and need not be accounted for by supposing that the pain experience changed the long term rational preference function of the machine (although, in a dynamical model, it may have). In a sense this is a complication of Hampshire's model:[8] pain states are characterized both by the momentary and spontaneous inclinations to which they give rise and by the negative weight assigned by the machine's basic rational preference function to things which the machine has learned from experience put the machine into these states.

[8] Other aspects of Hampshire's model are, however, omitted here: the role of *unconditioned* responses; the "suppression" of inclinations; and the role of imitation.

The above remarks against identifying preference with a particular physical-chemical composition apply equally strongly now against identifying pain with a particular physical-chemical composition. Suppose that the pain fibers of the machines are made of copper and these are the only copper fibers in the machines. It would still be absurd to say, "Pain is stimulation of the copper fibers." If we said that, then we would have to say that pain is something different in the case of machine 1 and the case of machine 2, if machine 1 had copper pain fibers and machine 2 had platinum pain fibers. Again, it seems clearer to say what we said before: that "pain" *is* a state of the machine normally occasioned by damage to the machine's body and characterized by giving rise to "inclinations" to . . . etc., and to eschew the formulation, "Pain is synthetically identical with stimulation of the copper fibers" in favor of the clearer formulation, "The machine is physically realized in such a way that the 'pain' pulses travel along copper fibers."

LOGICAL BEHAVIORISM

We have seen that statements about the preferences of our machines are not logically equivalent to statements concerning the physical-chemical composition of these machines. Are they perhaps logically equivalent to statements concerning the actual and potential behavior of these machines? In answering this question, it is convenient to widen the discussion and to consider not only statements about the preferences of our machines but also statements about their "knowledge," "belief," and "sensory awareness." When we widen the discussion this way, it is easy to see the answer to our question is in the negative. Consider two machines T_1 and T_2 which differ in the following way: T_1 has "pain fibers" which have been cut, so T_1 is incapable of "feeling pain." T_2 has uncut "pain fibers" but has an unusual rational preference function. This rational preference function is such that if T_2 believes a certain event to have taken place, or a certain proposition to be true, then T_2 will assign a *relatively infinite weight* to concealing the fact that its pain fibers are uncut. In other words, T_2 will maintain its pain fibers have been cut when asked, will contend that it is incapable of "feeling pain," and suppress its inclination to give behavioral evidence of feeling pain. If T_2 does not believe that the critical event has taken place or that the critical proposition is true, then T_2 will have, as it were, no reason to conceal the fact that it is capable of "feeling pain" and will then behave quite differently from T_1. In this case, we can tell that a machine is a physical realization of T_2 and not of T_1 by observing its behavior.

However, once T_1 and T_2 have both been informed that the critical event has taken place or that the critical proposition is true, there is then no distinguishing them on behavioral grounds. That is to say, the hypothesis that a machine is an instance of T_1 believes that the critical event has taken place leads to exactly the same predictions with respect to all actual and potential behavior as the hypothesis that a machine is an instance of type T_2 which believes that the critical event has taken place or that the critical proposition is true. In short, certain combinations of beliefs and rational preference functions which are quite different will lead to exactly the same actual and potential behavior.

I have argued in another paper[9] that exactly the same thing is true in the case of human beings. That is to say, two human beings may be inclined to behave in the same way under all possible circumstances, one for the normal reason and the other for a quite abnormal combination of reasons. Once we allow the computing skills or the intelligence of the machine to vary, the point becomes even more clear. Consider the problem of distinguishing between a machine with a normal rational preference function but rather low intelligence and a machine equipped with very high intelligence but with an abnormal rational preference function, which assigns relatively infinite weight to concealing its high intelligence. It is clear the difference is not a wholly untestable one. If we are allowed to take the machines apart and to see what goes on inside them, we can tell whether a given machine is an instance of the first type or an instance of the second type, but it is easily seen that there is no way to tell them apart without examining the internal composition of the machines in question. That is, quite different combinations of computing skills, beliefs, and rational preference functions can lead to exactly the same behavior, not only in the sense of the same actual behavior but in the sense of the same potential behavior under all possible circumstances.

Let T_1 be the machine of low intelligence and let T_2 be the machine of higher intelligence which is simulating the behavior of T_1.

[9] Hilary Putnam, "Brains and Behavior," in *Analytical Philosophy*, R. J. Butler, ed. (Oxford: Basil Blackwell & Mott, Ltd., 1965), pp. 211–35.

It might be asked in what precisely the greater intelligence of T_2 consists. Well, it could consist in two things. First of all, T_2 may be printing many things on its tape which do not contain operant signals and which, therefore, constitute mere interior monolog. T_2 may be solving mathematical problems, analyzing the psychology of the human beings with which it comes in contact, writing caustic comments on human mores and institutions, and so forth. T_2 need not even contain any subsystem of states which at all resembles the states or computations of T_1. T_2 may be sufficiently intelligent to determine what T_1 would do in any particular situation without actually reconstructing the thought processes by which T_1 arrives at the decision to do it. This would be analogous to the case of a human being whose behavior was in no way out of the ordinary but who, unknown to everyone else, enjoyed a rich and unusual inner life.

It will be observed that the machines we have been considering all have, in a sense, *pathological* rational preference functions, i.e., rational preference functions which assign a relatively infinite weight to something. Assigning a relatively infinite weight to something simply means preferring that thing over all alternatives, come what may. Suppose we call a rational preference function *nonpathological* if it does *not* assign a relatively infinite weight to anything except possibly the survival of the machine itself. Let T be the theory that all actually existing intelligent systems possess nonpathological rational preference functions. Then it can be shown that the statement that a machine with fixed computing skills has a particular rational preference function is equivalent under T to saying that it has a certain kind of actual and potential behavior. In fact, to say that a machine has a particular rational preference function is equivalent under T to saying that it behaves under all circumstances exactly as a machine with that particular rational preference function would behave. This does not, however, vindicate logical behaviorism, although it constitutes a kind of "near miss." Logical behaviorism in the case of our machines would be the thesis that the statement that a machine has a particular rational preference function is logically equivalent to some statement about the machine's actual and potential behavior. This is not correct. What is correct is that there is a theory T, which is very likely true (or whose analog in the case of organisms is very likely true), such that in the theory T every statement of the form "T prefers A to B" is equivalent to a statement about T's actual and potential behavior.

But there is all the difference in the world between equivalence as a matter of logic alone and equivalence within a synthetic theory.

In a sense the situation with respect to logical behaviorism is very similar to the situation with respect to materialism. In connection with materialism, we saw that although the statement that a machine has a certain machine table is not logically equivalent to the statement that it has a certain physical-chemical composition, it follows from the latter statement within a synthetic theory, namely the theory consisting of the laws of nature together with the completeness statement, i.e., the statement that there do not exist any causal agencies other than the elementary particles and combinations of elementary particles, and that these possess only the degrees of freedom ascribed to them in physical theory. Indeed, it is easily seen that there is a class C of physical compositions such that the statement that a machine has a particular machine table is equivalent, within the synthetic theory mentioned, to the statement that its physical-chemical composition belongs to the class C. Since the statement that the machine prefers A to B, or that it has a certain belief, or that it "feels pain," etc. is true only if a suitable conjunction of two statements is true, the first of which says that the machine has a certain machine table, while the second describes the total configuration of the machine at the present instant, and since some such conjunction can be true, assuming the synthetic theory alluded to, only if the physical composition of the machine belongs to a very large class C* of physical compositions, we can see that the statement, whatever it may be, will be equivalent within the synthetic theory alluded to, to the statement that the physical composition of the machine is in such a class C*.

Similarly, assuming the synthetic theory alluded to in connection with logical behaviorism—the theory that no machine has a pathological rational preference function—any statement about the "mental life" of one of our machines will be equivalent to some statement about its actual and potential behavior.

Given an "agent" in our hypothetical "community," this is our situation: with enough information about the actual and potential behavior of the agent, we may infer with relative certainty that the agent prefers A to B, or again, with enough information about the physical-chemical composition of the agent (and enough knowledge of the laws of nature), we may infer with relative certainty that the agent prefers A to B. But the two inferences do not support the claims of logical behaviorism and materialism, respectively. Both inferences are synthetic inferences carried out within synthetic theories.

But, it may be asked, how can we even know that either the assumption of the nonexistence of pathological rational preference functions or the completeness assumption with respect to physical theory is correct? I believe that the answer is much the same in both cases. Each assumption is justified as long as there is no good reason to suppose that it might be false. If this is right, then inferences to the mental life of any empirically-given actual system may be perfectly justified; but they are never analytic inferences if the premises only give information about the actual and potential behavior of the system and about its physical-chemical composition. Such inferences are always "defeasible": there are always far-fetched circumstances under which the premises might be retained and the conclusion might be overturned.

On looking over what I have written, I must confess to a certain sense of disappointment. It seems to me that what I have said here is too obvious and trivial to be worth saying, even if there are indeed certain philosophers who would disagree. But at the same time, it seems to me that these remarks, even if they do seem obvious, might suggest something about the nature of our mentalistic concept which it is not at all usual to point out. What is suggested is this: It seems that to know for certain that a human being has a particular belief, or preference, or whatever, involves knowing something about the functional organization of the human being. As applied to Turing Machines, the functional organization is given by the machine table. A description of the functional organization of a human being might well be something quite different and more complicated. But the important thing is that descriptions of the functional organization of a system are logically different in kind either from descriptions of its physical-chemical composition or from descriptions of its actual and potential behavior. If discussions in the philosophy of mind are often curiously unsatisfying, I think it is because just this notion, the notion of functional organization, has been overlooked or confused with notions of entirely different kinds.

Bibliography

Abbreviations

A—*Analysis*
AJP—*Australasian Journal of Philosophy*
APQ—*American Philosophical Quarterly*
ASP—*Aristotelian Society Proceedings*
ASSV—*Aristotelian Society Supplementary Volume*
BJP—*British Journal of Psychology*
BJPS—*British Journal for the Philosophy of Science*
D—*Dialogue*
IPQ—*International Philosophical Quarterly*
JP—*Journal of Philosophy*
M—*Mind*
P—*Philosophy*
PPR—*Philosophy and Phenomenological Research*
PQ—*Philosophical Quarterly*
PR—*Philosophical Review*
PS—*Philosophical Studies*
POS—*Philosophy of Science*
R—*Ratio*
RM—*Review of Metaphysics*
T—*Theories*

Articles

Aaron, R. I., "Dispensing with Mind," *ASP*, LII (May, 1951–52), 225–42.

Albritton, Rogers, "Mere Robots and Others," abstract in symposium "Minds and Machines," *JP*, LXI (November, 1964), 691–94.

Aune, Bruce, "Feigl on the Mind-Body Problem," in *Mind, Matter, and Method: Essays in Philosophy and Science in Honor of Herbert Feigl*, ed. by Paul K. Feyerabend and Grover Maxwell. Minneapolis: University of Minnesota Press, 1966, pp. 17–40.

Baier, Kurt, "Smart on Sensations," *AJP*, XL (May, 1962), 57–68.

Beloff, J., "The Identity Hypothesis: A Critique," in *Brain and Mind: Modern Concepts of the Nature of Mind*, ed. by J. R. Smythies. New York: Humanities Press, 1965, pp. 35–54.

Bernstein, Richard J., "The Challenge of Scientific Materialism," *IPQ*, VIII (June, 1968), 252–75.

Brain, Lord, "Some Aspects of the Brain-Mind Relationship," in *Brain and Mind: Modern Concepts of the Nature of Mind*, ed.

by J. R. Smythies. New York: Humanities Press, 1965, pp. 63–79.

Brandt, Richard B., "Doubts about the Identity Theory," in *Dimensions of Mind*, ed. by Sidney Hook. New York: New York University Press, 1960; Collier Books, 1961, pp. 57–67.

Brodbeck, May, "Mental and Physical," in *Mind, Matter, and Method: Essays in Philosophy and Science in Honor of Herbert Feigl*, ed. by Paul K. Feyerabend and Grover Maxwell. Minneapolis: University of Minnesota Press, 1966, pp. 40–59.

Carnap, Rudolf, "Herbert Feigl on Physicalism," in *The Philosophy of Rudolf Carnap*, ed. by P. A. Schlipp. New York: Tudor, 1963, pp. 882–86.

Coburn, Robert, "Shaffer on the Identity of Mental States and Brain Processes," *JP*, LX (February, 1963), 89–92.

Cornman, James W., "The Identity of Mind and Body," *JP*, LIX (August, 1962), 486–92.

———, "Mental Terms, Theoretical Terms, and Materialism," *POS*, XXXV (March, 1968), 45–63.

Danto, Arthur C., "On Consciousness in Machines," in *Dimensions of Mind*, ed. by Sidney Hook. New York: New York University Press, 1960; Collier Books, 1961, pp. 165–72.

Dechert, Charles R., "Cybernetics and the Human Person," *IPQ*, V (February, 1965), 5–36.

Dreyfus, Herbert L., "Why Computers Must Have Bodies in Order to Be Intelligent," *RM*, XXI (September, 1967), 13–32.

Farrell, B. A., "Experience," *M*, LIX (April, 1950), 170–98. Reprinted in *The Philosophy of Mind*, ed. by V. C. Chappell. Englewood Cliffs, N.J.: Prentice-Hall, 1962, pp. 23–48.

Feigl, Herbert, "The Mind-Body Problem in the Development of Logical Empiricism," *Revue Internationale de Philosophie*, IV (January, 1950), 64–83. Reprinted in *Readings in the Philosophy of Science*, ed. by Herbert Feigl and May Brodbeck. New York: Appleton-Century-Crofts, 1953, pp. 612–26.

———, "The 'Mental' and the 'Physical,'" in *Minnesota Studies in the Philosophy of Science*, II, ed. by Herbert Feigl, Grover Maxwell, and Michael Scriven. Minneapolis: University of Minnesota Press, 1956 and 1958, pp. 370–497.

———, "Mind-Body, Not a Pseudoproblem," in *Dimensions of Mind*, ed. by Sidney Hook. New York: New York University Press, 1960; Collier Books, 1961, pp. 24–36.

———, "Physicalism, Unity of Science and the Foundations of Psychology," in *The Philosophy of Rudolf Carnap*, ed. by P. A. Schlipp. New York: Tudor, 1963, pp. 227–69.

Feyerabend, Paul K., "Mental Events and the Brain," *JP*, LX (May, 1963), 295–96.

Findlay, J. N., "Linguistic Approach to Psycho-Physics," *ASP* (1949–50), 43–64.

Flew, Anthony, "A Rational Animal," in *Brain and Mind: Modern Concepts of the Nature of Mind*, ed. by J. P. Smythies.

New York: Humanities Press, 1965, pp. 111–28.

Fodor, Jerry A., "Explanations in Psychology," in *Philosophy in America,* ed. by Max Black. London: Allen and Unwin, 1965, pp. 161–80.

Garnett, A. Campbell, "Body and Mind—the Identity Thesis," *AJP,* XLIII (May, 1965), 77–81.

Gauld, Alan, "Could a Machine Perceive?" *BJPS,* XVII (May, 1966), 44–58.

Gustafson, Donald, F., "On the Identity Theory," A, XXIV (December, 1963), 30–32.

Harris, Errol E., "The Neural Identity Theory and the Person," *IPQ,* VI (December, 1966), 515–37.

Hocutt, Max, "In Defense of Materialism," *PPR,* XXVII (March, 1967), 366–85.

Hoffman, Robert, "Malcolm and Smart on Brain-Mind Identity," *P,* XLIII (April, 1967), 128–36.

Jacobs, Norman, "Physicalism and Sensation Sentences," *JP,* XXXIV (October, 1937), 602–11.

Joske, W. D. *See* Pitcher, George.

Kane, R. H., "Turing Machines and Mental Reports," *AJP,* XLIV (1966), 344–52.

Kemeny, J. G., "Man Viewed as a Machine," *Scientific American,* CXCII (April, 1955), 58–67.

Kim, Jaegwon, "Psychophysical Laws and Theories of Mind," *T,* XXXIII, Part III (1967), 198–211.

Kuhlenbeck, Hartwig, "The Concept of Consciousness in Neurological Epistemology," in *Brain and Mind: Modern Concepts of the Nature of Mind,* ed. by J. R. Smythies. New York: Humanities Press, 1965, pp. 137–55.

Lachman, Roy, "Machines, Brains, and Models," in *Dimensions of Mind,* ed. by Sidney Hook. New York: New York University Press, 1960; Collier Books, 1961, pp. 172–74.

Lewis, David K., "An Argument for the Identity Theory," *JP,* LXIII (January, 1966), 17–25.

Lucas, J. R., "Minds, Machines, and Gödel," *P,* XXXVI (April–July, 1961), 112–27.

Luce, David Randall, "Mind-Body Identity and Psycho-Physical Correlation," *PS,* XVII (January–February, 1966), 1–7.

Mackay, D. M., "Mentality in Machines," *ASSV,* XXVI (1952), 61–86.

MacRae, Valerie. *See* Routley, Richard.

Malcolm, Norman, "The Conceivability of Mechanism," *PR,* LXXVII (January, 1968), 45–73.

Margolis, Joseph, "Brain Processes and Sensations," *T,* XXXI (December, 1965), 133–38.

———, "Some Prospects of Synoptic Philosophy," *R,* IX (December, 1967), 105–21.

Martin, R. M., "On Computers and Semantical Rules," in *Dimensions of Mind,* ed. by Sidney Hook. New York: New York University Press, 1960; Collier Books, 1961, pp. 174–77.

Mays, W., "The Hypothesis of Cybernetics," *BJPS,* II (1951), 249–50.

Meehl, Paul E., "The Compleat Autocerebroscopist," in *Mind, Matter, and Method: Essays in Philosophy and Science in Honor of Herbert Feigl*, ed. by Paul K. Feyerabend and Grover Maxwell. Minneapolis: University of Minnesota Press, 1966, pp. 103–81.

Miles, T. R., "The 'Mental-Physical' Dichotomy," *ASP*, LXIV (1963–64), 71–85.

Minsky, Marvin L., "Some Methods of Artificial Intelligence and Heuristic Programming," in National Physical Laboratory Symposium *Mechanization of Thought Processes*, I. London: Her Majesty's Stationery Office, 1959, pp. 5–27.

Nagel, Ernest, "Are Naturalists Materialists?" in Ernest Nagel, *Logic Without Metaphysics*. New York: Free Press, 1957.

Ostwald, Wilhelm, extract from "Lectures on Natural Philosophy," in *The Physicist's Conception of Nature*, ed. by W. Heisenberg. New York: Harcourt, Brace & World, 1958, pp. 14–51.

Pap, Arthur, "Semantic Analysis and Psycho-Physical Dualism," *M*, LXI (April, 1952), 209–21.

Pepper, Stephen C., "A Neural-Identity Theory of Mind," in *Dimensions of Mind*, ed. by Sidney Hook. New York: New York University Press, 1960; Collier Books, 1961, pp. 45–62.

Pitcher, George, and Joske, W. D., "Sensations and Brain Processes: A Reply to Professor Smart," *AJP*, XXXVIII (August, 1960), 150–60.

Place, U. T., "The Concept of Heed," *BJP*, XLV (1954), 243–55.

———, "Materialism as a Scientific Hypothesis," *PR*, LXIX (January, 1960), 101–04.

———, "Consciousness and Perception," *ASSV*, XL (1966), 101–24.

Puccetti, Roland, "On Thinking Machines and Feeling Machines," *BJPS*, XVIII (May, 1967), 39–51.

Putnam, Hilary, "Psychological Concepts, Explication, and Ordinary Language," *JP*, LIV (February, 1957), 94–100.

———, "Minds and Machines," in *Dimensions of Mind*, ed. by Sidney Hook. New York: New York University Press, 1960; Collier Books, 1961, pp. 148–79.

———, "Brains and Behavior," in *Analytical Philosophy*, II, ed. by R. J. Butler. Oxford: Blackwell, 1965, pp. 1–19.

Quinton, Anthony, "Mind and Matter," in *Brain and Mind: Modern Concepts of the Nature of Mind*, ed. by J. P. Smythies. New York: Humanities Press, 1965, pp. 201–33.

Raab, Francis V., "Of Minds and Molecules," *POS*, XXXII (January, 1965), 57–72.

Routley, Richard, and MacRae, Valerie, "On the Identity of Sensations and Physiological Occurrences," *APQ*, III (April, 1966), 87–110.

Scheffler, Israel, "The New Dualism: Psychological and Physical Terms," *JP*, XLVII (December, 1950), 737–52.

Scriven, Michael, "The Mechanical Concept of Mind," *M*, LXII (April, 1963), 230–40.

———, "The Compleat Robot: A Prolegomena to Androidology," in *Dimensions of Mind*, ed. by Sidney Hook. New York: New York University Press, 1960; Collier Books, 1961, pp. 118–42.

———, "The Limitations of the Identity Theory," in *Mind, Matter, and Method: Essays in Philosophy and Science in Honor of Herbert Feigl,* ed. by Paul K. Feyerabend and Grover Maxwell. Minneapolis: University of Minnesota Press, 1966, pp. 191–98.

Sellars, Wilfrid, "Mind, Meaning, and Behavior," *PS,* III (December, 1952), 83–95.

———, "A Semantical Solution of the Mind-Body Problem," *Methodos,* V (1953), 45–82.

———, "Empiricism and the Philosophy of Mind," in *Minnesota Studies in the Philosophy of Science,* I, ed. by Herbert Feigl, Grover Maxwell, and Michael Scriven. Minneapolis: University of Minnesota Press, 1956 and 1958, pp. 253–329.

———, and Paul E. Meehl, "The Concept of Emergence," in *Minnesota Studies in the Philosophy of Science,* I, ed. by Herbert Feigl, Grover Maxwell, and Michael Scriven. Minneapolis: University of Minnesota Press, 1956 and 1958, pp. 239–53.

Shaffer, Jerome, "Could Mental States Be Brain Processes?" *JP,* LVIII (December, 1961), 813–22. Reprinted in *Body and Mind: Readings in Philosophy,* ed. by G. N. A. Vesey. London: Allen & Unwin, 1964.

———, "Mental Events and the Brain," *JP,* LX (March, 1963), 160–66.

———, "Recent Work on the Mind-Body Problem," *APQ,* II (April, 1965), 81–104.

———, "Persons and Their Bodies," *PR,* LXXV (January, 1966), 59–77.

Simon, Herbert A., "Thinking by Computers," in *Mind and Cosmos,* ed. by Robert G. Colodny. Pittsburgh: University of Pittsburgh Press, 1966, pp. 3–22.

Smart, J. J. C., "Professor Ziff on Robots," A, XIX (April, 1959), 117–18.

———, "Ryle on Mechanism and Psychology," *PQ,* IX (October, 1959), 349–55.

———, "Sensations and Brain Processes: A Reply to Dr. Pitcher and Mr. Joske," *AJP,* XXXVIII (December, 1960), 252–54.

———, "Further Remarks on Sensations and Brain Processes," *PR,* LXX (July, 1961), 406–07.

———, "Gödel's Theorem, Church's Theorem, and Mechanism," *Synthese,* XIII (June, 1961), 105–10.

———, "Brain Processes and Incorrigibility: A Reply to Professor Baier," *AJP,* XL (May, 1962), 68–70.

———, "Consciousness," in J. J. C. Smart, *Philosophy and Scientific Realism.* London: Routledge & Kegan Paul, 1963, pp. 88–106.

———, "Materialism," *JP,* LX (October, 1963), 651–62.

———, "Causality and Human Behavior," a Symposium, *ASSV,* XXXVIII (1964), 123–48.

———, "The Identity Thesis: A Reply to Professor Garnett," *AJP,* XLIII (May, 1965), 82–83.

Spilsbury, R. J., "Mentality in Machines," *ASSV,* XXVI (1952), 27–60.

Stevenson, J. T., "Sensations and Brain Processes: A Reply to J. J. C. Smart," *PR,* LXIX (October, 1960), 505–10.

Tannenbaum, Jerrold, "In Defense of the Brain Process Theory," *PPR* (forthcoming).

Taylor, Charles, "Mind-Body Identity, a Side Issue?" *PR*, LXXVI (April, 1967), 201–13.

Teichmann, Jenny, "The Contingent Identity of Minds and Brains," *M*, LXXIV (July, 1967), 404–15.

Thompson, Dennis, "Can a Machine Be Conscious?" *BJPS*, XVI (May, 1965), 33–43.

Tomberlin, James E., "About the Identity Theory," *AJP*, XLIII (1965), 295–99.

Turing, A. M., "Computing Machinery and Intelligence," in *Minds and Machines*, ed. by A. R. Anderson. Englewood Cliffs, N.J.: Prentice-Hall, 1964, pp. 4–31.

Weissman, David, "A Note on the Identity Thesis," *M*, LXXIV (October, 1965), 571–77.

Wiener, Norbert, "The Brain and the Machine," in *Dimensions of Mind*, ed. by Sidney Hook. New York: New York University Press, 1960; Collier Books, 1961, pp. 109–13.

Wisdom, J. O., "Mentality in Machines," *ASSV*, XXVI (1952), 1–26.

Zemach, E. M., "Sensation, Raw Feels, and Other Minds," *RM*, XX (December, 1966), 317–40.

Ziff, Paul, "The Feelings of Robots," *A*, XIX (January, 1958), 64–68.

Books

Adrian, E. D., Bremer, F., Jasper, H. H., consulting eds., and Delafresnage, J. F., ed. for the council, *Brain Mechanisms and Consciousness: A Symposium-Council for International Organizations of Medical Sciences*. Springfield, Ill.: Thomas, 1964.

Anderson, A. R., ed., *Minds and Machines*. Englewood Cliffs, N.J.: Prentice-Hall, 1964.

Armstrong, David M., *A Materialist Theory of the Mind* (forthcoming).

Chappell, V. C., ed., *The Philosophy of Mind*. Englewood Cliffs, N.J.: Prentice-Hall, 1962.

Cornman, J. W., *Metaphysics, Reference, and Language*. New Haven: Yale University Press, 1966.

Culbertson, J. T., *The Minds of Robots*. Urbana: University of Illinois Press, 1963.

Feigl, Herbert, Scriven, Michael, and Maxwell, Grover, eds., *Minnesota Studies in the Philosophy of Science*, Vol. I, *The Foundations of Science and the Concepts of Psychology and Psychoanalysis*; Vol. II, *Concepts, Theories, and the Mind-Body Problem*. Minneapolis: University of Minnesota Press, 1956 and 1958.

Feyerabend, Paul K., and Maxwell, Grover, eds., *Mind, Matter, and Method: Essays in Philosophy and Science in Honor of Herbert Feigl*. Minneapolis: University of Minnesota Press, 1966.

George, F. H., *The Brain as a Computer*. London: Pergamon Press, 1961.

———, *Cognition*. London: Methuen, 1962.

Hess, W. R., *The Biology of Mind*, trans. by Gerhardt von Bonin. Chicago: University of Chicago Press, 1964.

Hook, Sidney, ed., *Dimensions of Mind*. New York: New York University Press, 1960; Collier Books, 1961.

Laslett, P., ed., *The Physical Basis of Mind*. Oxford: Blackwell, 1951.

McCulloch, W. S., *Embodiments of Mind*. Cambridge, Mass.: MIT Press, 1965.

Presley, C. F., *The Identity Theory of Mind*. Queensland, Australia: University of Queensland Press, 1968.

Quine, W. V. O., *Word and Object*. Cambridge, Mass.: MIT Press, 1960.

Sayre, K. M., *Recognition: A Study in the Philosophy of Artificial Intelligence*. Notre Dame: University of Notre Dame Press, 1965.

———, and Crosson, Frederick J., eds., *Philosophy and Cybernetics*. Notre Dame: University of Notre Dame Press, 1967.

Sellars, Wilfrid, *Science, Perception, and Reality*. London: Routledge & Kegan Paul, 1963.

Smart, J. J. C., *Philosophy and Scientific Realism*. London: Routledge & Kegan Paul, 1963.

Smythies, J. R., ed., *Brain and Mind: Modern Concepts of the Nature of Mind*. New York: Humanities Press, 1965.

Vesey, G. N. A., ed., *Body and Mind: Readings in Philosophy*. London: Allen & Unwin, 1964.

Ziff, Paul, ed., *Philosophic Turnings: Essays in Conceptual Appreciation*. Ithaca: Cornell University Press, 1966.

A 9
B 0
C 1
D 2
E 3
F 4
G 5
H 6
I 7
J 8